I0764060

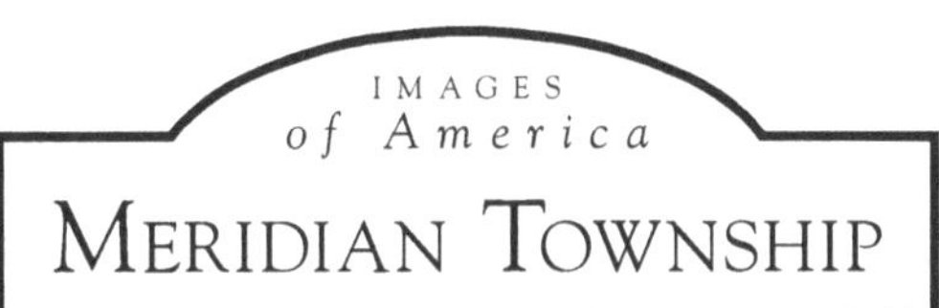
IMAGES
of America
MERIDIAN TOWNSHIP

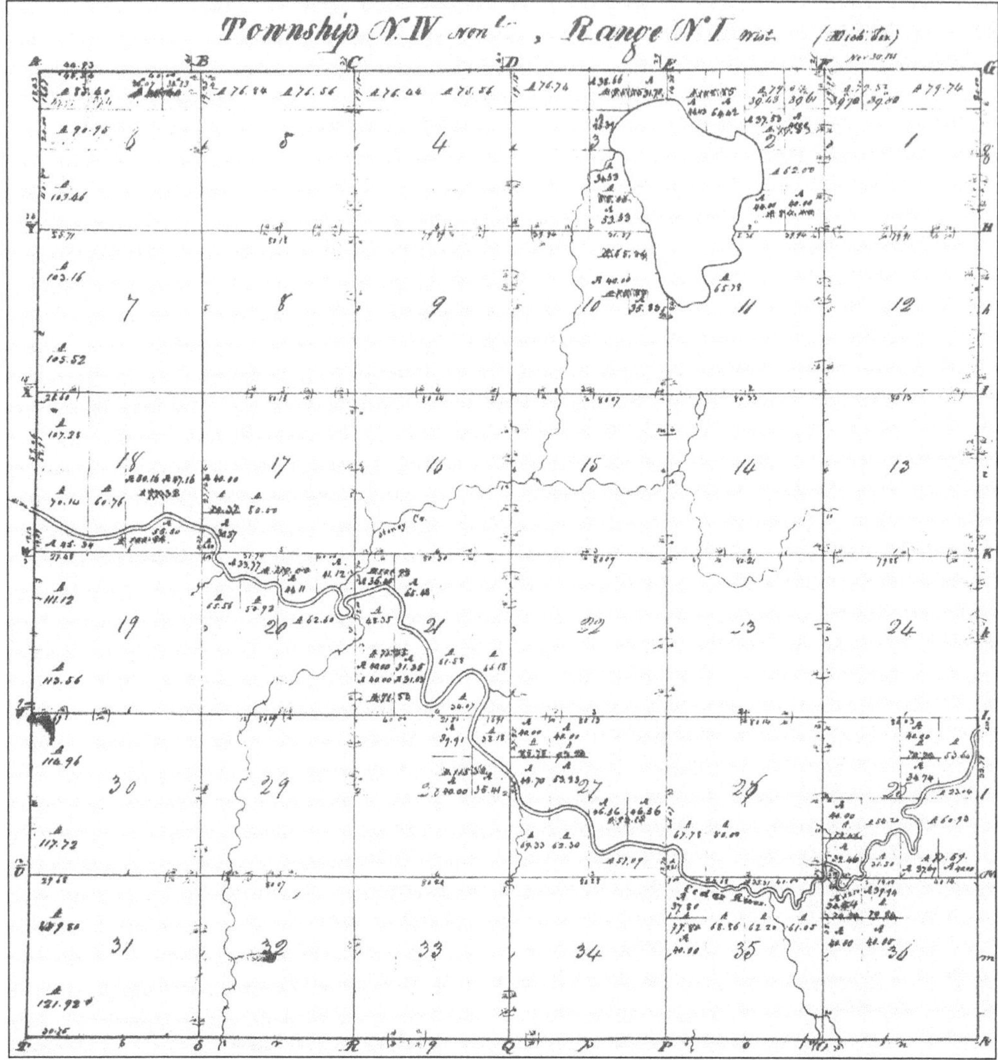

This section map shows Meridian Township as surveyed in 1827 by Musgrove Evans. (Courtesy of the Friends of Historic Meridian.)

On the Cover: This photograph was originally donated by the Elliotts, a pioneer family and longtime members of the Haslett community. It was taken in 1911 of the fledgling Haslett Woman's Literary Club, which still exists today as the Haslett Woman's Club. (Courtesy of the Friends of Historic Meridian Archives.)

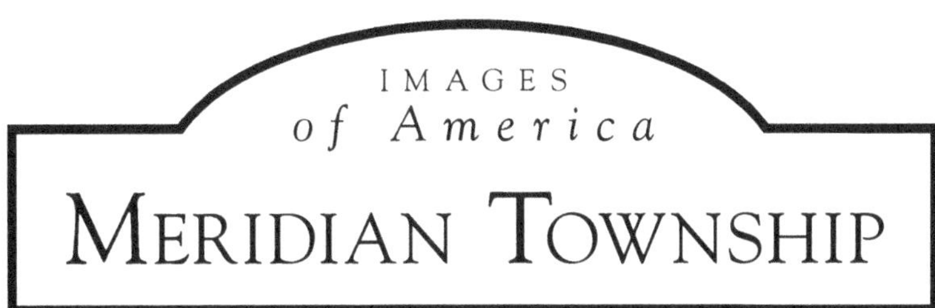

Jane M. Rose

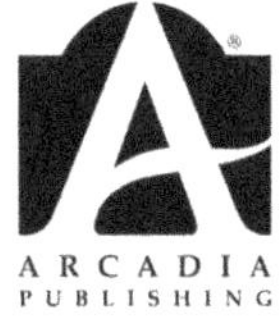

ISBN 978-1-4671-1439-4

Published by Arcadia Publishing
Charleston, South Carolina

Library of Congress Control Number: 2015931615

For all general information, please contact Arcadia Publishing:
Telephone 843-853-2070
Fax 843-853-0044
E-mail sales@arcadiapublishing.com
For customer service and orders:
Toll-Free 1-888-313-2665

Visit us on the Internet at www.arcadiapublishing.com

To my children, Robin and Laurence, for your love, support, and encouragement

Contents

Acknowledgments

I would like to thank the Friends of Historic Meridian (FHM) for lending photographs from their archival collection. Photographs not identified are from the FHM archives.

Thanks also to Rebecca Blair, Frances Coryell, and John Grettenberger Sr., who contributed by lending photographs, expertise, and support, and to Anna Gillette for her photograph of Santa and child.

Thanks and appreciation also to Karen Fraser, Ingham County Parks, for lending images of Lake Lansing Parks South and North.

This book would not be possible without the efforts of Evelyn Huber Raphael, Hope Borbas, and Ruth Stillman. The archives for the Friends of Historic Meridian were developed by Paula Gangopadhyay and include photographs diligently collected by local historian Elaine Davis from descendants of pioneer families.

We all stand on the shoulders of those who have gone before us. I am humbled by the amount of effort and commitment of all who shared their memories and history in order to keep the past alive.

INTRODUCTION

The area that would become Meridian Township began as a crossroads of Native American trails with campsites in multiple locations. Members of the Chippewa and Ottawa tribes travelled through the area during their annual seasonal migrations for hunting and gathering. The natives wore paths through the area that would eventually become modern roads. Today's Grand River Avenue, as well as Meridian, Marsh, and Hulett Roads, follows the paths of Native travelers. Several burial mounds have been discovered in areas near native encampments, with one site showing evidence of a large battle.

Early settlement in Michigan was limited to the areas immediately adjacent to the Great Lakes. The land in the interior was settled much later, as the dense forests and thick underbrush made travel difficult. The Federal Land Act of 1820 reduced the price of land per acre from $1.65 to $1.25, thereby creating a surge of purchases called "Michigan Fever."

It was not until 1836 that the white pioneers began settling the area. The first, Obed Marshal, purchased 160 acres located around the south and west sides of the largest body of water in the county. It was named Pine Lake for the large stand of yellow pines on the east side of the lake. By 1837, an additional 16 families purchased property around or nearby the lake.

What the early pioneers found was a dense wilderness with only native paths to ease the travel. Wild game was plentiful, and settlers had to protect their livestock from both bears and wolves. Diary entries from the time tell of travelers leaving an inn in the early morning hours only to plunge back into the "darkness of the forests." Others complained, "Bears carried off, first and last, more than fifty hogs in the neighborhood."

The first white settler along the main tributary south of the lake was Sanford Marsh, who purchased property in 1839 south of the Red Cedar River at the corner of present-day Okemos and Mount Hope Roads. Freeman Bray followed in 1840 and platted the southeast corner of his property for sale. He named the area "Hamilton" after Alexander Hamilton; the same year, a post office was established and named Sanford Post Office in honor of the first settler.

The first road to connect the township with other communities was built in 1839. State Road ran along modern-day Marsh Road and connected the community at Pine Lake with the Hamilton community on the river. From there, the road continued south to Mason, the county seat.

In 1847, the state capital was moved from Detroit in southeast Michigan to the new city of Lansing, six miles west of the township. The move resulted in considerable increase in traffic along the old Grand River Trail, and improvements were made to the dirt trail to accommodate traffic. The Lansing-Howell Plank Road was chartered in 1850. The portion from Lansing to the river community of Hamilton was completed in June 1851 and extended to Howell in Livingston County by 1853. Both mail and passenger coaches used the route. The coaches were pulled by four horses and could carry up to 20 passengers. Sections of the old plank road can still be found under portions of Grand River Avenue and Hamilton Road in Okemos.

The increased traffic along the plank road encouraged the establishment of hotels and inns within the village of Okemos. In 1849, Melzor Turner erected the first frame house in the village just two buildings south of the plank road. After the plank road was built, Russell Blakeslee purchased the property in 1853 and converted the structure to an inn and tavern that continued to serve visitors into the 20th century.

The little village of Hamilton along the Red Cedar River saw many members of native groups visit throughout the year. Freeman Bray traded with the natives and plowed land for their crops. Even so, Bray added iron bars to his cellar windows to keep hungry travelers from helping themselves to stored food. The leader of this group was Chief Okemos, who travelled frequently from the village of Hamilton to the present-day Portland area to the northwest. He became well known and respected by community residents. After Okemos died in 1858, the local residents petitioned the Michigan Legislature to rename the village in honor of this popular and respected chief. On February 12, 1859, the legislature officially renamed the village "Okemos" in honor of Chief Okemos of the Chippewa.

By 1887, the area around the lake had grown and attracted James Haslett, a Port Huron haberdasher, to purchase property on the southwest side of Pine Lake to use as the site of a summer camp for people interested in the practice of Spiritualism. Haslett Park became the location for Michigan Spiritualists for their annual meetings. Later, in about 1888, Haslett also purchased a hotel, the Pine Lake House, and property along the north shore to house the growing number of summer visitors.

James Haslett died in 1891, and the use of the property by the Spiritualist community declined. Haslett's widow, Sarah, sold the property in 1898 to the Haslett Park Association. The area was converted to an entertainment park and continued to attract summer visitors. Ransom Eli Olds, founder of Oldsmobile, built his summer home along the north shore so his family could leave the heat of city living and enjoy the cool breezes along the bluffs of the lake.

More wealthy businessmen purchased property along the lake and, in the late 1890s, built a men's social club in the middle of the lake. The clubhouse was a two-story, square building with a covered porch on all four sides. The structure no longer remains, although there are still remnants of the pilings in the center of the lake.

Population continued to grow throughout the 20th century as Haslett and Okemos expanded. The 1920s saw farmland divided into neighborhoods. The 1950s saw a surge of development when Michigan State University professors moved their families into the community. The complexion of the area changed when pipe-smoking professors in tweed jackets found themselves in opposition to the old farming families who disagreed with the need to improve schools and public services.

Development continued in the 1970s with the construction of the Meridian Mall, a large enclosed shopping mall, and Meijer, a major food and department store. The introduction of urban renewal destroyed many beautiful examples of architecture throughout the area. In 1972, the Charter Township of Meridian established a study committee to identify buildings and structures throughout the township that were of historical significance. The first part of this inventory was submitted in December 1972 and focused on the village of Okemos. Studies of the village of Haslett and Rural Meridian Township soon followed.

As a result of these studies, a group of township residents formed the Friends of Historic Meridian in 1974. The organization is responsible for rescuing, relocating, and restoring eight local buildings to their original beauty. These buildings reside in Central Park, Okemos, and form the Meridian Historical Village.

Ongoing support by the Charter Township of Meridian and the Parks and Recreation Department have allowed the Friends of Historic Meridian to continue preservation efforts and promote the history of the area and the story of those who braved the wilderness to carve out a thriving community.

One

First Settlement

Before the white pioneers from eastern states and Canada arrived in the area, the natives who lived here were members of the Chippewa (also known as Ojibwa) and Ottawa (also known as Odawa) tribes. Waterways were important to the natives to speed travel from one campsite to the next. Travel was an important part of survival, allowing access to seasonal camps and the ability to trade goods. Before trading centers were opened by white pioneers, the natives traded with other tribes and clans.

The largest body of water in the area was located in the northeast section of the future township and drew people to fish and camp along its shores during the summer. The lake covered 485 acres and was 1.2 miles long. The Shiawassee-Moccasin trail led around the west side of the lake and curved to the northeast. It also connected to another trail leading to the planting grounds near present-day Meridian Road. According to Dr. F.N. Turner, as quoted in the *Pioneer History of Ingham County, Michigan*, "This trail had been used so long that no bushes grew in the tract, but it was overgrown with grass." Another trail forked off from the Shiawassee-Moccasin trail to the northwest and connected the natives to another lake campsite, now called Park Lake.

These trails were used by the earliest white pioneers coming to the area, and it is no surprise that the first land purchase was around the lake. Obed Marshall and his brother arrived in the area in 1836 and found the lake had clear water with a large number of fish. Surrounding the lake were large stands of yellow pine along the north and east shores and hickory and oak along the north and west shores.

Marshall purchased property along the southwest and west sides of the lake on November 1, 1836. The purchase gave him 248 acres for $318.08, and Marshall went to work harvesting the yellow pine stands and transporting them on barges across the lake to build his home. Thus began the first development of the area.

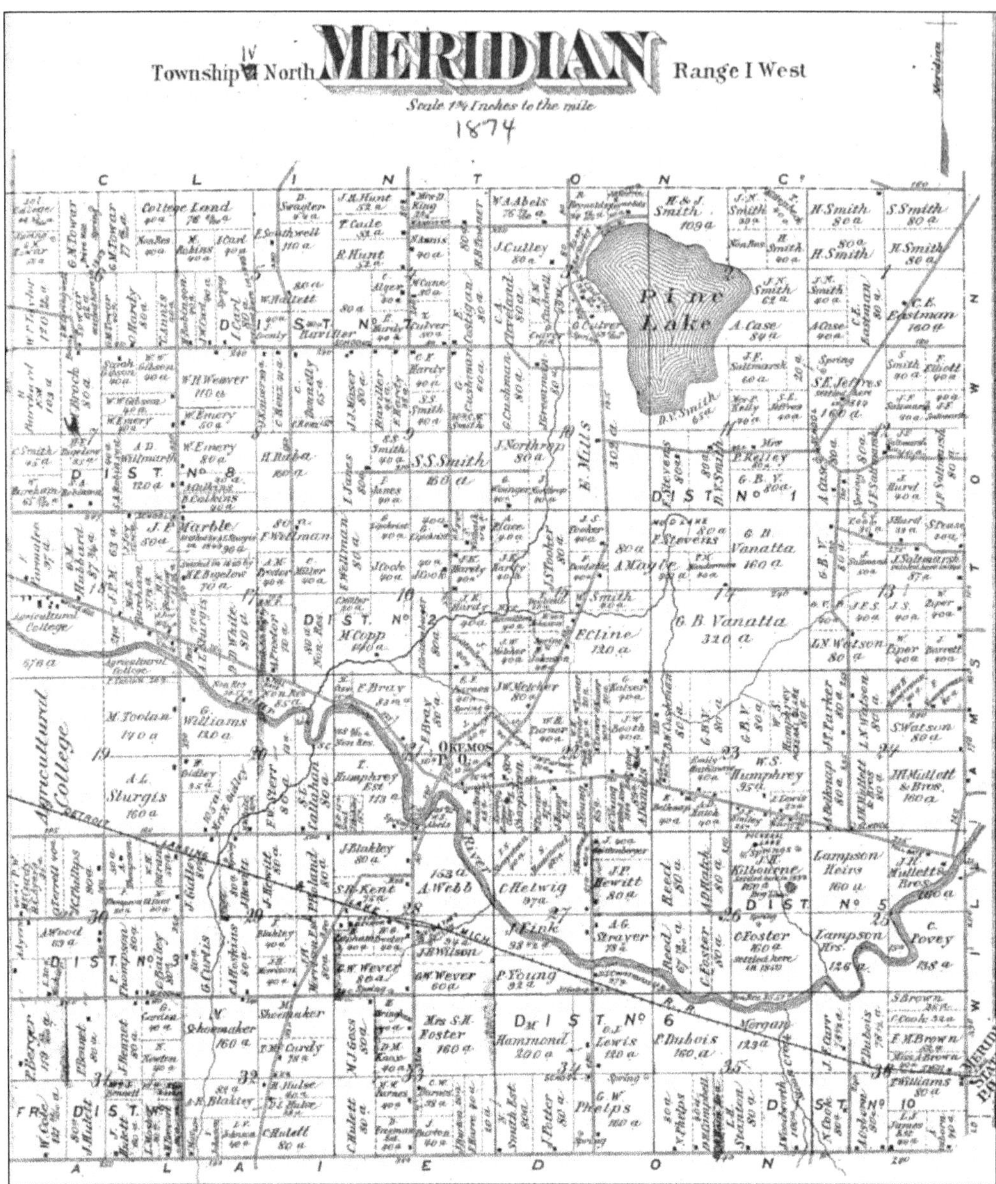

Obed Marshal purchased 248 acres of land on the south and southwest sides of the lake in November 1836. The lake became known by local settlers as "Pine Lake." By 1842, the area had 50 residents. The first post office was established in 1852 in Section 1 and continued at "Smith's Crossing" at Barry and Shoeman Roads until 1896.

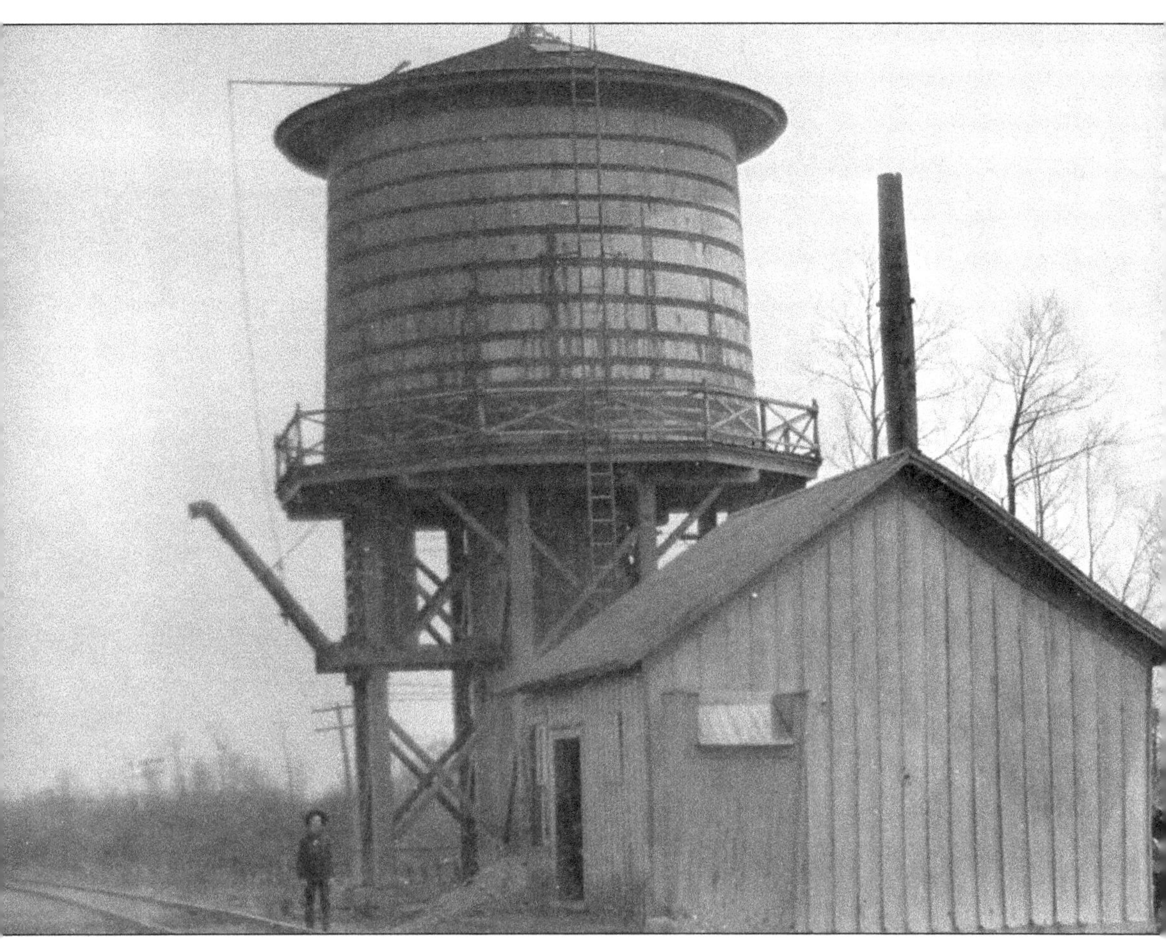

A railroad line was built by the Chicago & Grand Trunk Railway Company to connect the capital city, Lansing, to the southwest and the city of Flint to the northeast. The line passed through later-day Haslett and was completed in 1879. A water tower was built, and the Pine Lake Post Office was opened.

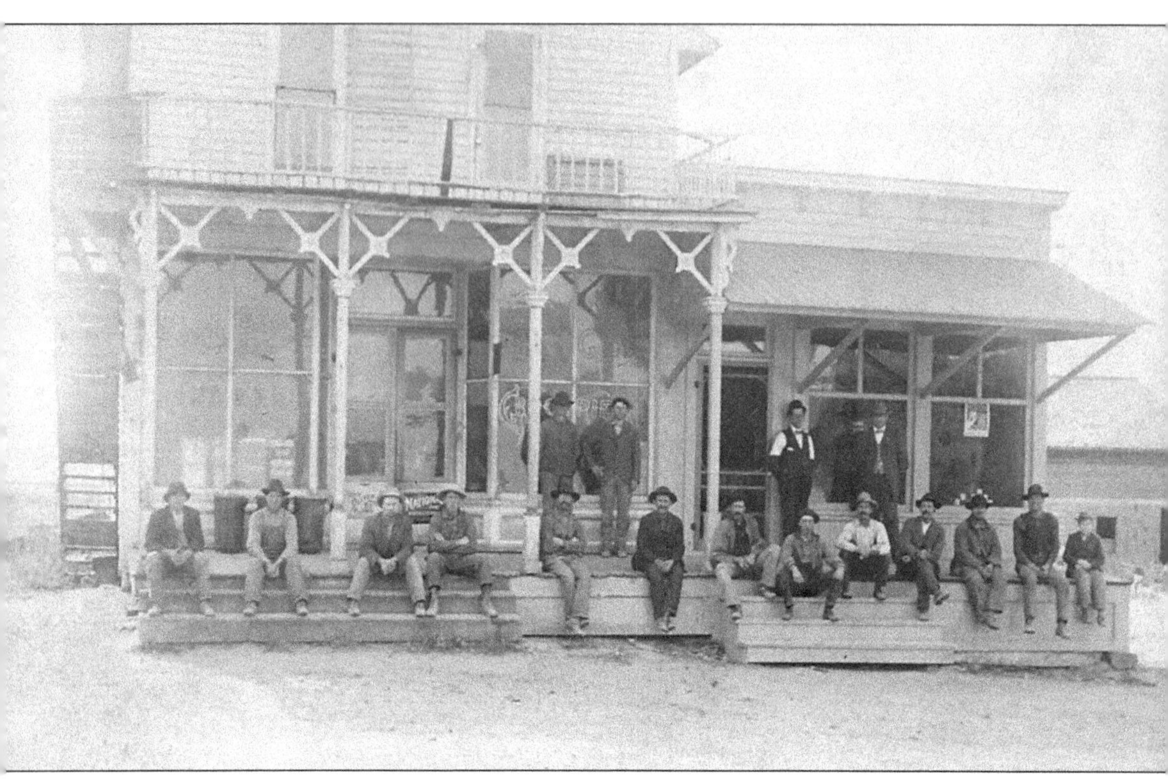

With the completion of the Chicago & Grand Trunk Railway in 1879, entrepreneurs began establishing businesses at the crossing. By 1887, two general stores, a post office, a mill, and blacksmith shop joined the area where the office of the railway agent had been located. In 1891, Emroy "Roy" M. Babbit purchased one of the general stores from his uncle A.E. Andrews, and he continued the business for years to come.

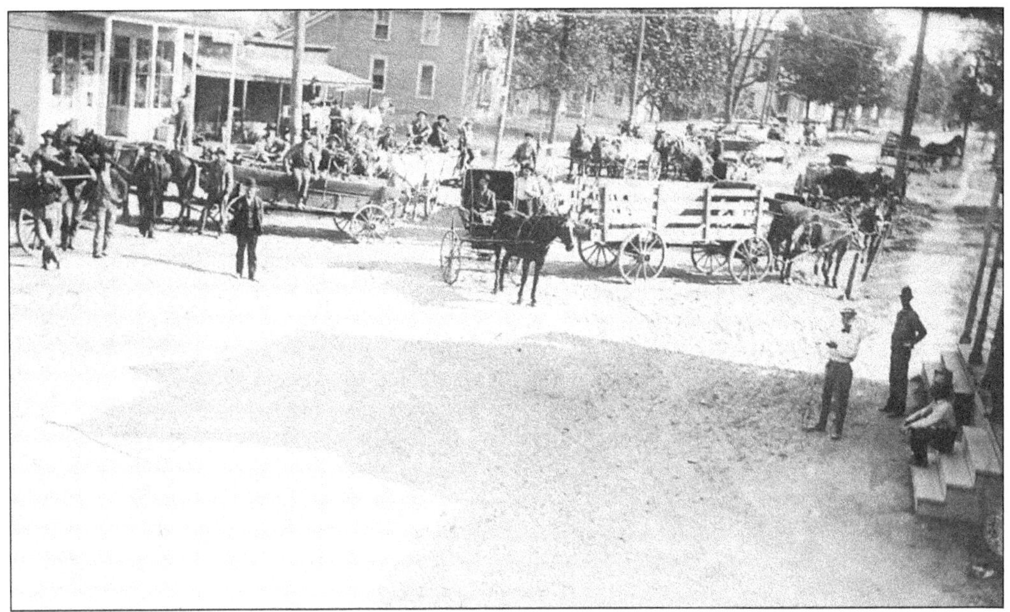

Farmers gather in front of the Babbit Store to pick up supplies. In addition to groceries, customers could purchase hardware, dry goods, and medicines. Babbit went on to build an icehouse, a building in which to dry apples, and a beanery to dry harvested beans.

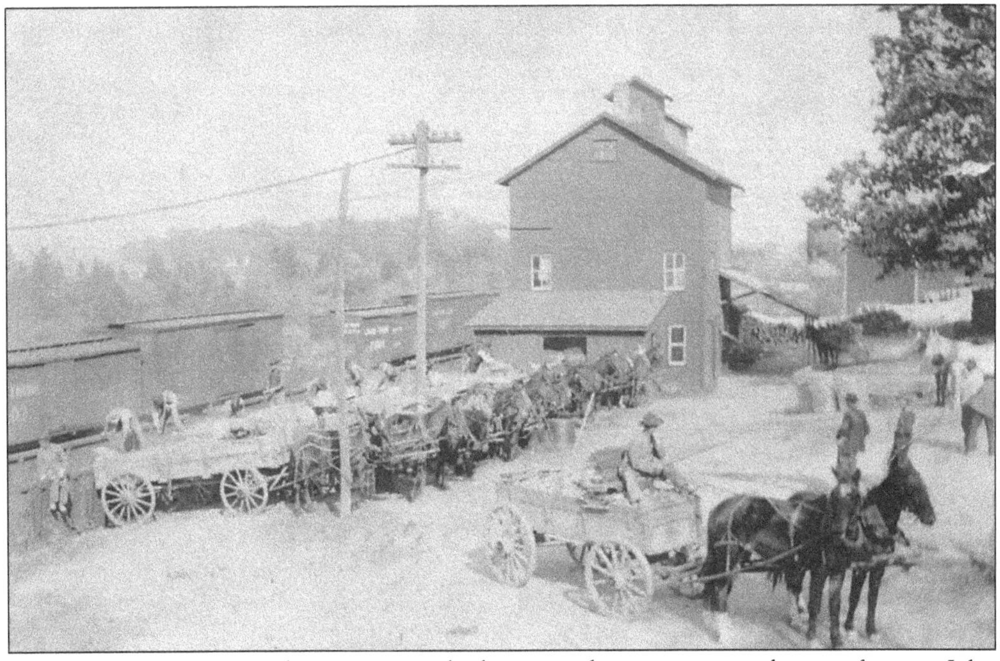

By the 1890s, the Pine Lake community had a grain elevator to serve the area farmers. John Lockwood began an elevator at the track site and bought grain and beans from the farmers to be stored for future delivery when the prices were most desirable. Lockwood served as the local agent for the railroad and also bought lumber and other local products to be shipped out to markets.

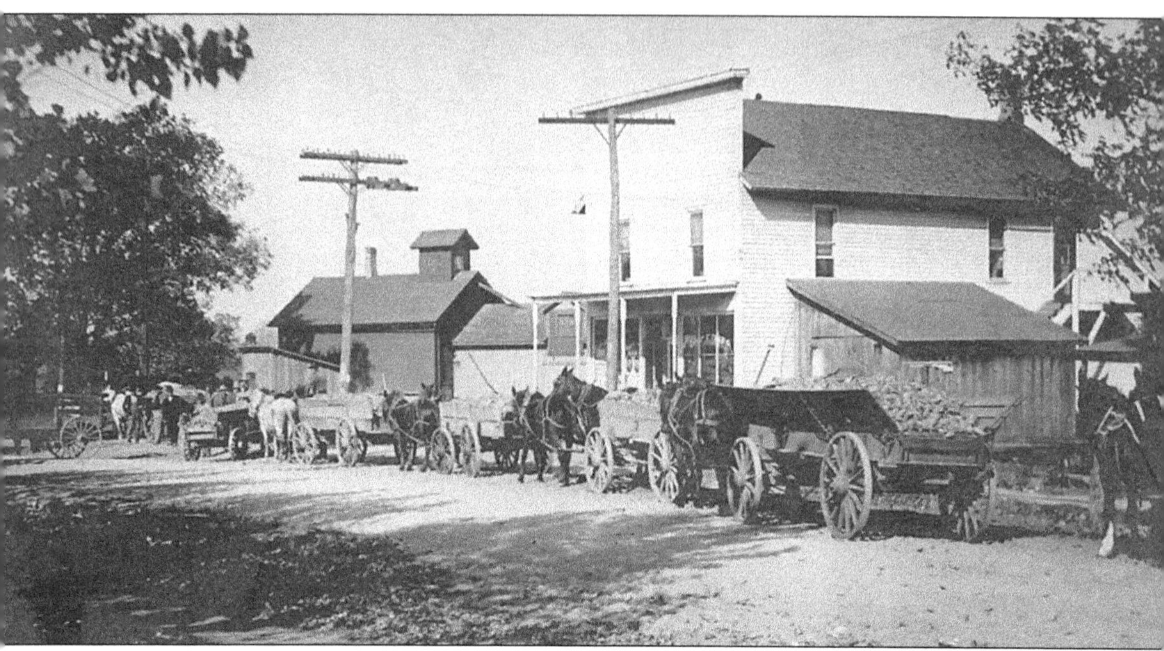

Farmers depended on the rail system to get their produce to market. Produce was delivered to the elevator for transfer to railroad cars. Farmers would bring wagons full of produce, especially beets, to be weighed and shipped out via the rail. The community was a shipping center for farm produce, wool, and livestock.

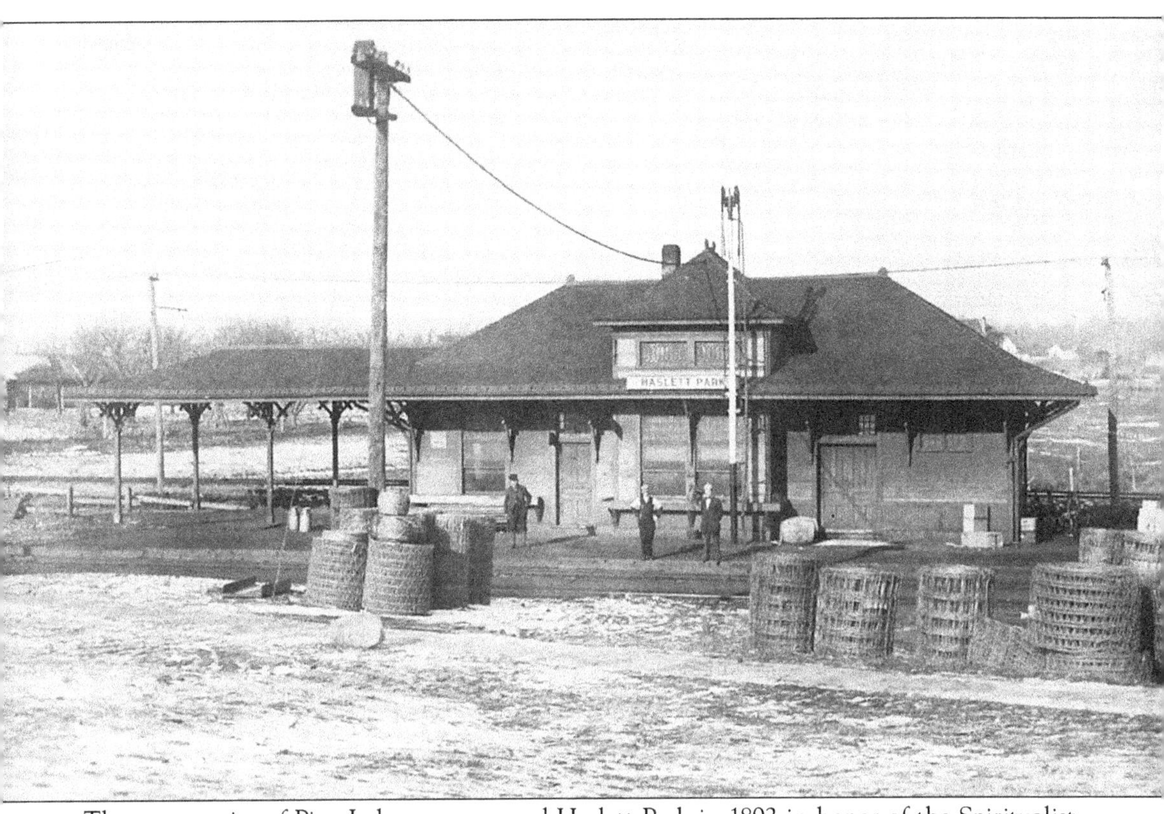

The community of Pine Lake was renamed Haslett Park in 1892 in honor of the Spiritualist James Haslett. A new station, named the Haslett Park Station, was built on the west side of the tracks around 1900. A double-track system was needed to respond to an ever-increasing need for transport to and from the area.

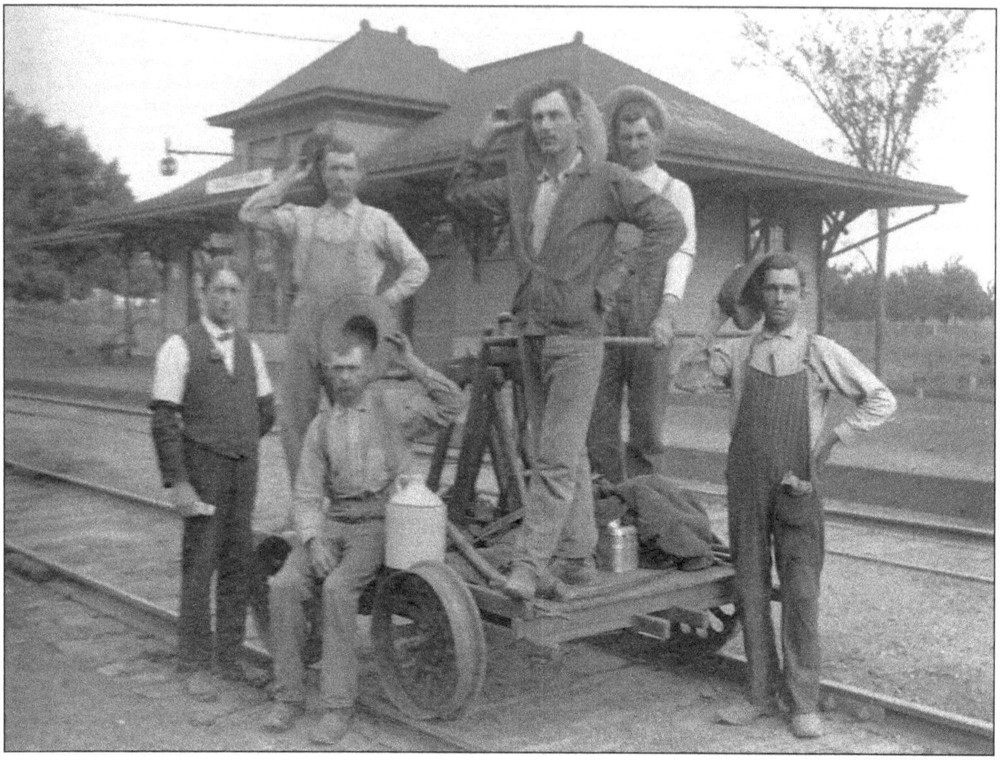

The railroad hired maintenance workers, known as gandy dancers, to travel up and down the railroad line to make necessary repairs. They travelled via hand-operated flatbeds, pumping the handles up and down to move the flat bed along. This up-and-down movement is where the phrase "gandy dancers" comes from. This photograph shows railroad agent J.G. Marsh on the left.

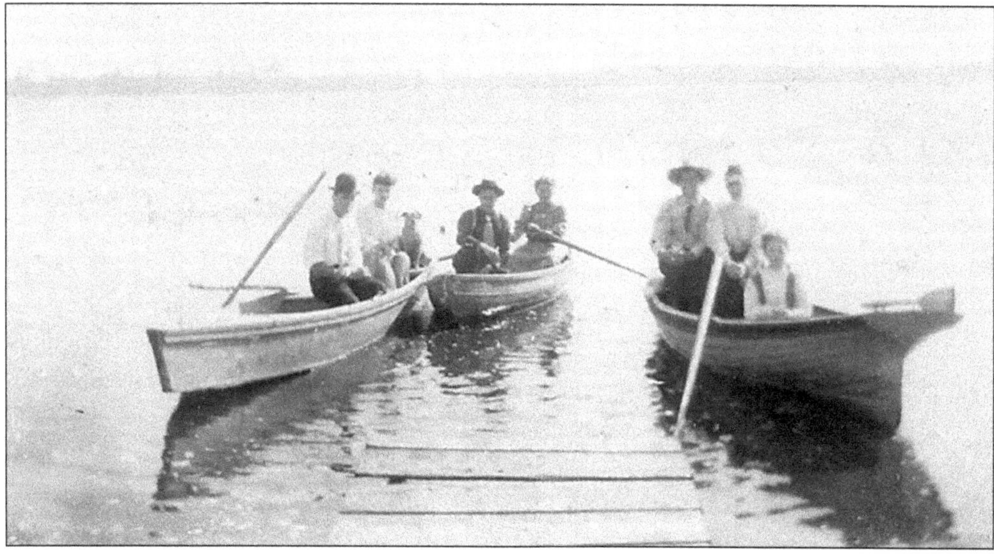

The lake itself drew summer residents and weekend guests who sought relief from the heat. Boating became a popular pastime, and docks were built and rowboats were plentiful on the lake. The popularity of the lake resulted in investments to develop the property next to the sandy north shore.

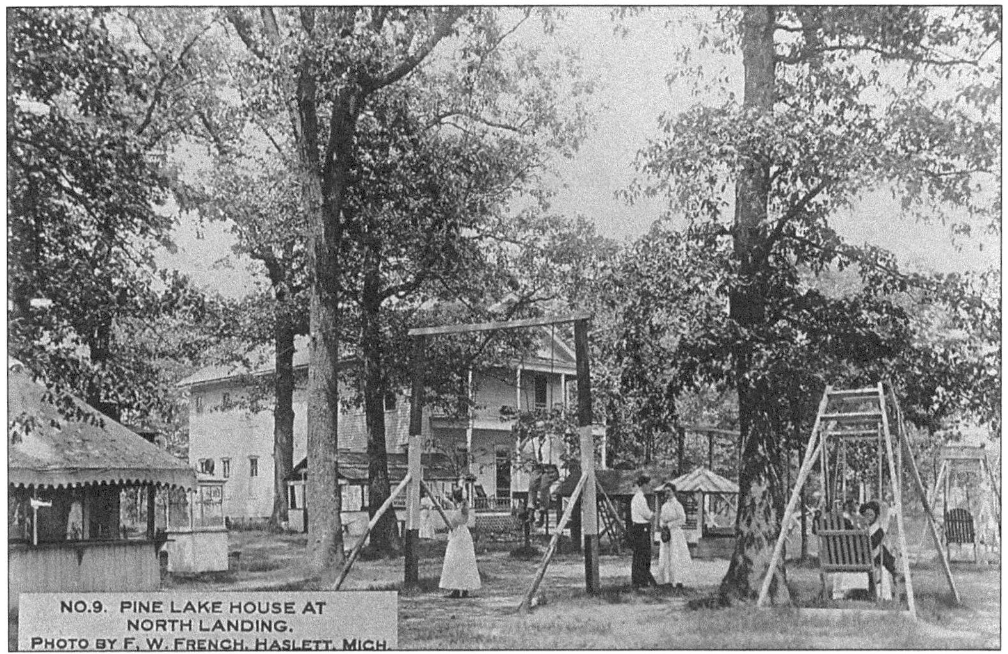

The north shore of Pine Lake, with its natural sand beach and groves along the shore, attracted summer visitors who sought relief from cities such as the state capital, Lansing, located six miles to the west. In 1874, partners George W. Northrup and Origin Hardy completed the construction of the Pine Lake House to serve as a hotel for area visitors.

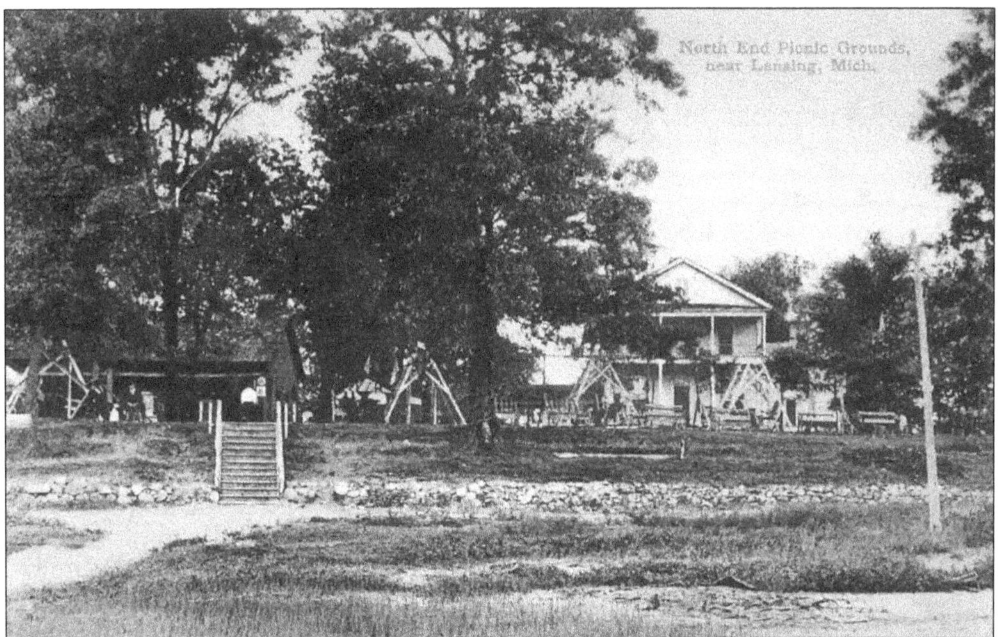

Pine Lake House offered playgrounds and picnic areas for guests. The property also included a dance hall, bathhouse, boathouses, an icehouse, and two barns to house carriage horses. The hotel hosted visitors until it burned down in 1929.

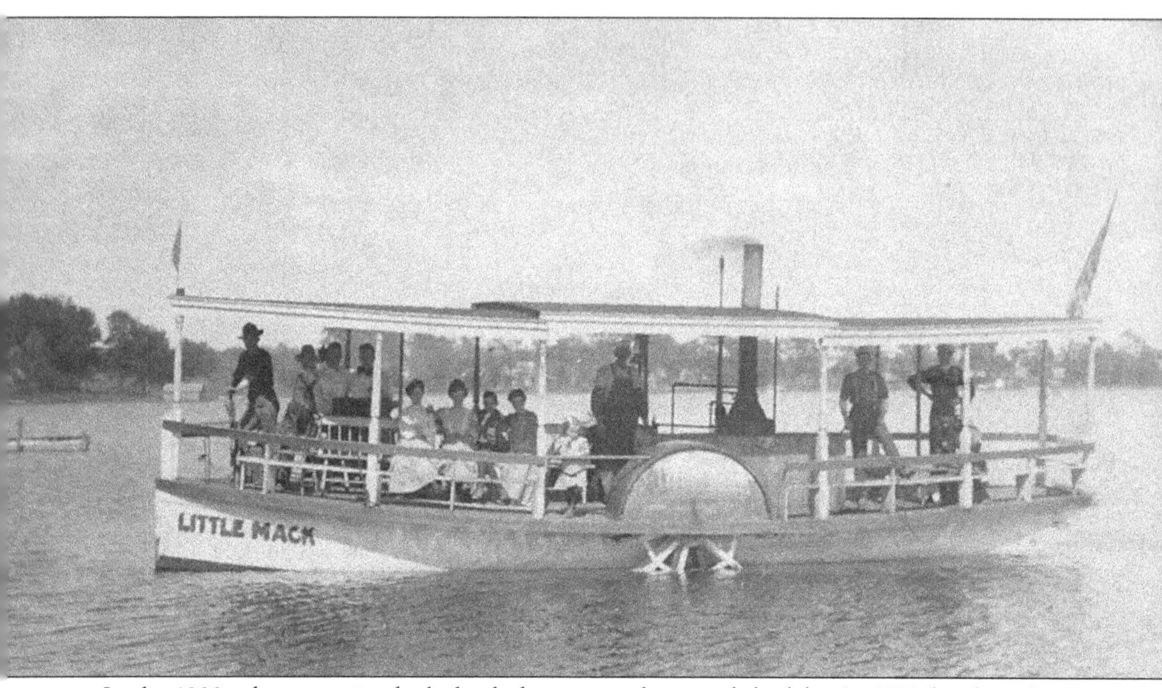

In the 1880s, there remained a lack of adequate roads around the lake. In 1881, brothers Origin and Anson Hardy responded by adding a steamer to transport guests from the town dock to their resort on the north side of the lake. By 1880, the Hardy brothers had more than 25 boats—both row and sail—available for use by their guests.

Two

The Spiritualists Arrive

Life expectancy in the 19th century was much lower than it is today. People then had access neither to immunizations nor antibiotics. Children were the most vulnerable to diseases such as measles, mumps, rubella, smallpox, strep throat, and scarlet fever. Germs were not discovered by the medical community until after the American Civil War. Until that time, people shared drinking cups and did not cover their mouths when they coughed or use a handkerchief when they sneezed. Baths were taken only once a week, and when water was not available in large quantities, it was shared with all family members. Cholera was introduced into the Detroit area in 1832, sickening more than 700 people and causing the deaths of at least 50 of those sickened.

It was with this backdrop that people began to search for solace when their loved ones died. The Civil War saw a surge of people who clung to the thought they could still communicate with their deceased loved ones. This practice became known as Spiritualism, a belief that the spirit lives on and can stay in touch with the living.

James Haslett, a wealthy businessman from Port Huron, Michigan, used his wealth and enthusiasm for Spiritualism to purchase property to serve fellow believers. Haslett purchased property at the southwest corner of Pine Lake in April 1887 to offer a resort for those interested in Spiritualism "philosophically and religiously." The goal was to teach Spiritualism in a beautiful spot in order to counter "error and superstition."

The site, named Haslett Park, attracted believers from around Michigan, New York State, and beyond. The camp met from late July through the end of August each year. Attendance was so large that a trolley had to be built to bring people in from the city of Lansing, and Haslett purchased a hotel and property on the north shore to house visitors. Support for the camp waned after Haslett's death in 1891, and his widow, Sarah, sold the property in 1898 to the Haslett Park Association.

HASLETT PARK

CAMP-MEETING BULLETIN.

(DEVOTED TO THE INTERESTS OF SPIRITUALISM.)

VOL. 2. JULY 26, 1888. No. 2.

The Sixth Annual Camp-meeting of the Michigan Spiritualists will be held at "Haslett Park," commencing Thursday, July 26, and closing Monday, August 27, including five Sundays.

PROGRAMME.

Sunday, July 29.

10:00 A. M.—Welcome address by the presiding officer, G. H. Brooks, of Wisconsin.
10:30 A. M.—Dedication of new Auditorium, by Mrs. R. S. Lillie, of Boston.
2:00 P. M.—Speech by the Hon. Wm. L. Bancroft, of Port Huron. Subject: "The Enterprise."
3:00 P. M.—Address by Mrs. Lillie.

Saturday, August 4.

MEMORIAL DAY.

Sunday, August 5.

10:30 A. M.—Address by Mrs. R. S. Lillie.
2:00 P. M.—Address by Mrs. R. S. Lillie.

Sunday, August 12.

10:30 A. M.—Address by Mrs. Nellie Baade, Capac.
2:00 P. M.—Address by Hon. A. B. French, of Clyde, Ohio.

Sunday, August 19.

10:30 A. M.—Address by Hon. Giles B. Stebbins, Detroit.
2:00 P. M.—Address by Mrs. E. C. Woodruff, South Haven.

Sunday, August 26.

10:30 A. M.—Address by Mrs. Carrie Firth, Coldwater.
2:00 P. M.—Address by Hon. F. M. Fogg, of Lansing. Subject: "Ancient and Modern Religions."

REGULAR DANCE FRIDAY EVENING OF EACH WEEK.

COMMITTEES.

Entertainments.

Mrs. S. S. Marcy, Lyons. Mrs. Tracy Merrill, Lansing. Mrs. W. O. Knowles, G. Rapids.

Decorations.

Mrs. M. J. Mead, Mason. Mrs. P. Payne, Maple Rapids. Mr. Guy Weter, Belding. Mrs. A. E. Weter, Belding.

Music.

Mrs. Jas. H. Haslett, Port Huron. Miss Leta Buck, Lansing. Mrs. A. E. Sheets, G. Ledge.

Police.

O. H. Soules, Ionia. S. P. Buck, Lansing. E. Curtiss, Charlotte.

Reception.

Mrs. A. B. Spinney, Detroit. Hon. Jas. H. White, Pt. Huron. Mrs. A. W. Anthoney, Marengo.

Tents and Privileges.

C. B. Ketchum, Belding. Giles G. Tucker, Fowlerville.

In 1887, James Haslett, a haberdasher from Port Huron, purchased property at the southwest side of Pine Lake for a Spiritualist camp. The park became very popular with the Spiritualist community and attracted a large number of visitors in the summer to attend programs and lectures. Bulletins were distributed listing the speakers and mediums scheduled for the summer camp. These bulletins included advertisements for housing and transportation for guests and highlighted yearly improvements made to the camp.

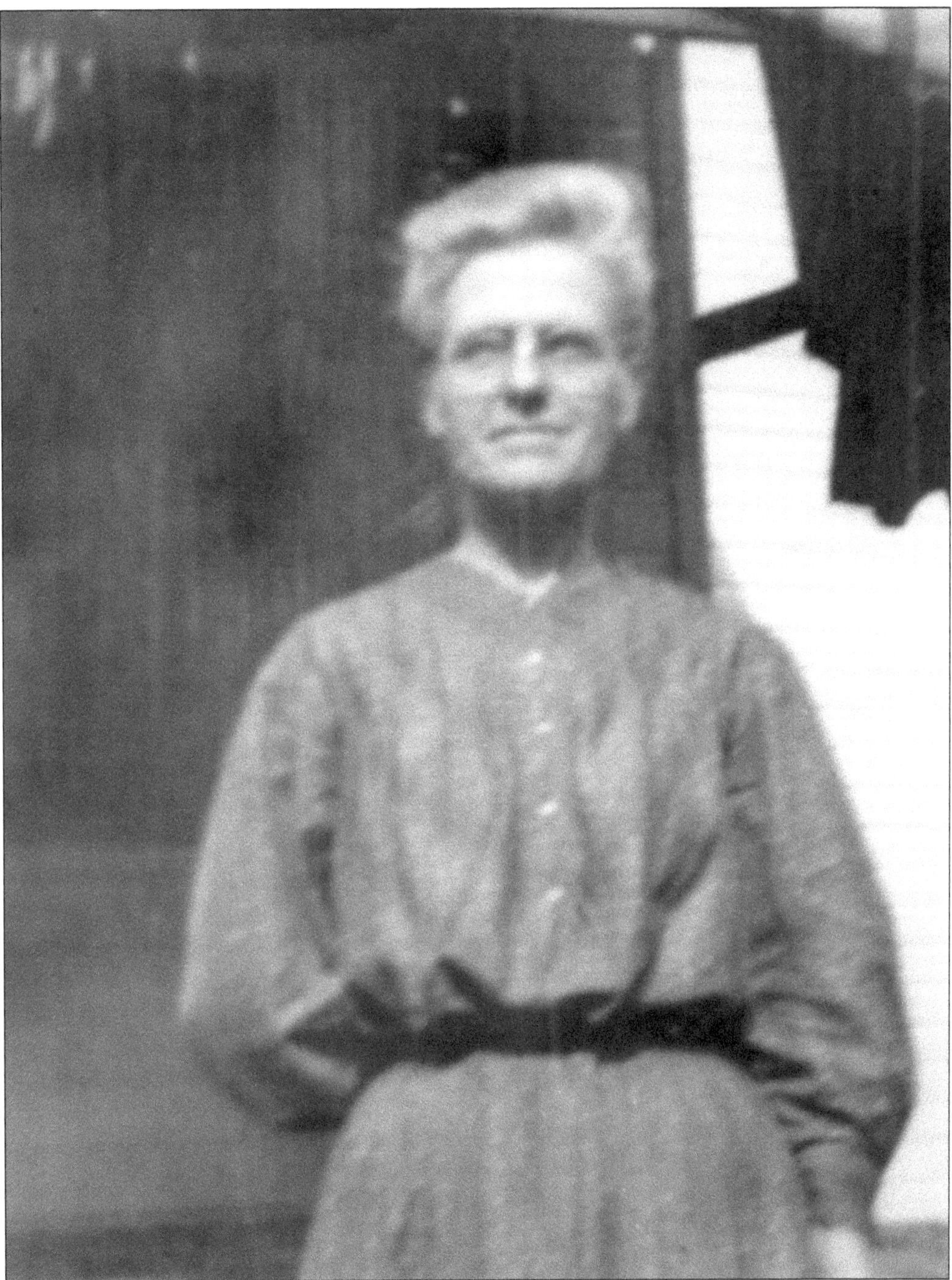

May Ayers was a member of a local pioneer family who became a member of the Spiritualist camp and participated in the summer camp meeting. Ayers is listed in the July 1888 bulletin as a "magnetic healer and writing medium." She had her own tent on the campgrounds and was available for "treatments and sittings." (Courtesy of Ayers descendant and Haslett resident Fran Coryell.)

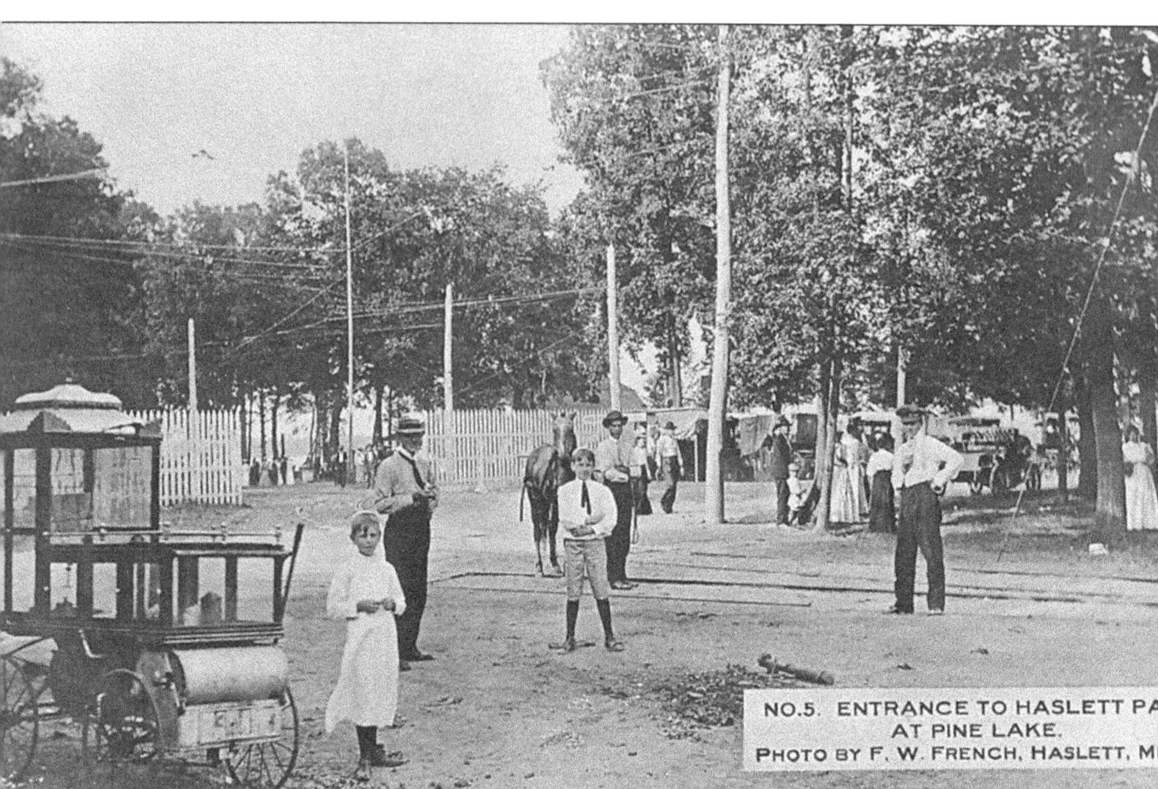

James Haslett's efforts and sponsorship of Spiritualism earned him recognition as a champion to the cause. The camp was named Haslett Park in his honor. The entrance was at Potter Street close to the corner of current-day Lake Lansing and Marsh Roads.

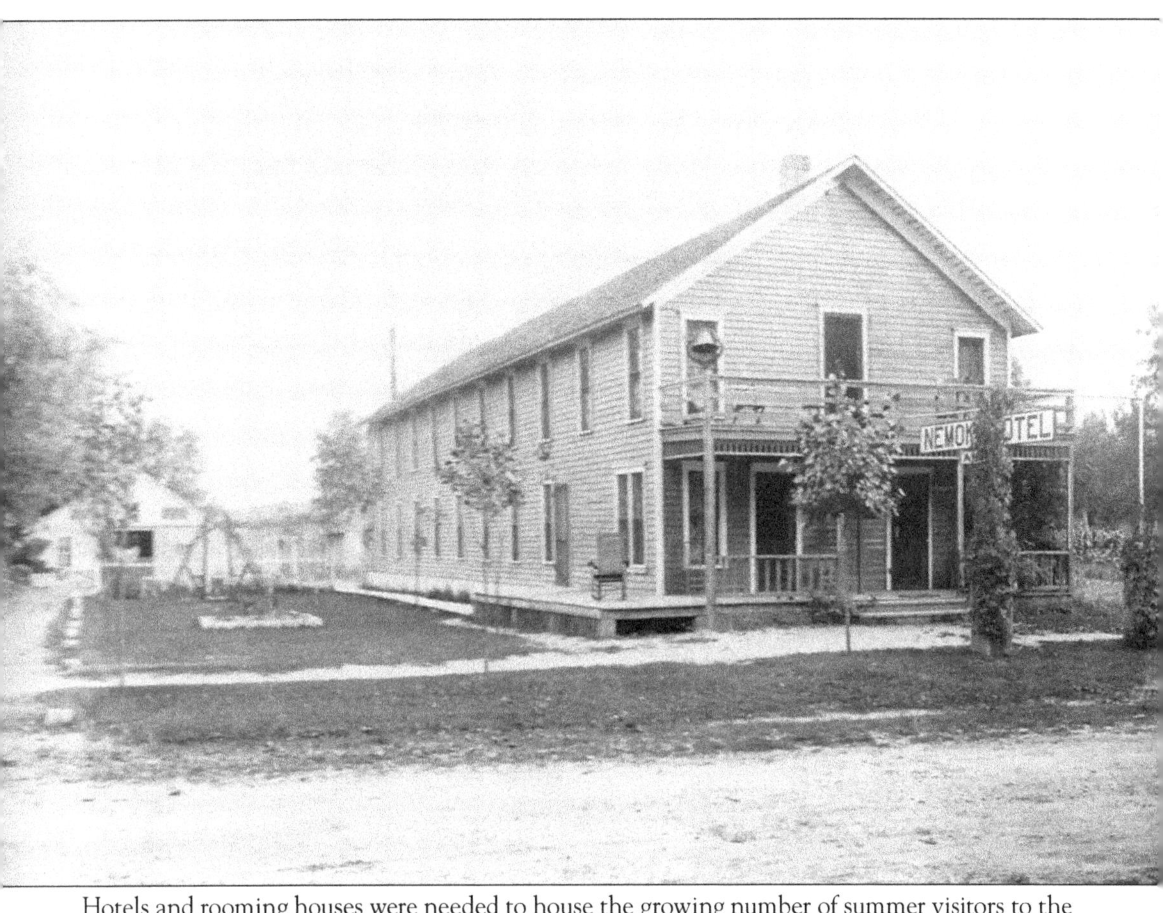

Hotels and rooming houses were needed to house the growing number of summer visitors to the Spiritualist camp. As many as 2,000 to 4,000 came to the park on summer weekends. The Nemoke Hotel (originally the Titus House) served as one of the many rooming houses.

HASLETT PARK

CAMP MEETING BULLETIN.

(DEVOTED TO THE INTERESTS OF SPIRITUALISM.)

VOL. 5. JULY 29, 1891 NO. 5.

The Ninth Annual Camp-Meeting of the Haslett Park Association will be held at "Haslett Park," commencing Thursday, July 29, and closing Monday, August 31, including five Sundays.

PROGRAMME.

Sunday, Aug. 2—10:00 A. M.—Address of Welcome, by Presiding Officer, Hon. H. C. Hodges.

Sunday, Aug. 2—10:30 A. M.—Lectures by Jennie B. Hagan, of South Farmington, Mass.

Sunday, Aug. 2—2:00 P. M.—Lectures by Jennie B. Hagan.

Monday, Aug. 3—2:00 P. M.—Lectures by Jennie B. Hagan.

Tuesday, Aug. 4—2:00 P. M.—Lectures by Jennie B. Hagan.

Wednesday, Aug. 5—10:30 A. M.—Reading Circle. 2:00 P. M.—Lecture by Mrs. R. S. Lillie, of Boston.

Thursday, Aug. 6—10:30 A. M.—Reading Circle. 2:00 P. M.—Conference.

Friday, Aug. 7—10:30 A. M.—Reading Circle. 2:00 P. M.—Lecture by Mrs. R. S. Lillie.

Saturday, Aug. 8—10:30 A. M.—Reading Circle. 2:00 P. M.—Lyceum.

Sunday, Aug. 9—10:30 A. M. and 2:00 P. M.—Lectures by Mrs. R. S. Lillie.

Monday, Aug. 10.—

Tuesday, Aug. 11—10:30 A. M.—Reading Circle. 2:00 P. M.—Conference.

Wednesday, Aug. 12—10:30 A. M.—Reading Circle. 2:00 P. M.—

Thursday, Aug. 13—10:30 A. M.—Reading Circle. 2:00 P. M.—Lecture by Lyman C. Howe.

Friday, Aug. 14—10:30 A. M. Reading Circle. 2:00 P. M. —Memorial Day—Address by Lyman C. Howe.

Saturday, Aug. 15—10:30 A. M.—Reading Circle. 2:00 P. M.—Lyceum.

Sunday, Aug. 16—10:30 A. M.—Lecture by Lyman C. Howe, of Fredonia, N. Y.

Sunday, Aug. 16—2:00 P. M.—Lecture by Mrs. Adah Sheehan, of Cincinnati, O.

Psychometric Reading after morning and afternoon lectures by Mrs. Adah Sheehan, who has no equal.

Monday, Aug. 17—

Tuesday, Aug. 18—10:30 A. M.—Reading Circle. 2:00 P. M.—Lecture by Mrs. Sheehan.

Wednesday, Aug. 19—10:30 A. M.—Reading Circle. 2:00 P. M.—Lecture by Mrs. Sheehan.

Thursday, Aug. 20—10:30 A. M.—Reading Circle. 2:00 P. M.—Conference.

Friday, Aug. 21—10:30 A. M.—Reading Circle. 2:00 P. M.—Conference.

Saturday, Aug. 22—10:30 A. M.—Lyceum. 2:00 P. M.—Edgar W. Emerson.

Sunday, Aug. 23—10:30 A. M., and 2:00 P. M.—Lectures and tests by Edgar W. Emerson, of Manchester, N. Y., the noted medium.

Monday, Aug. 24—

Tuesday, Aug. 25—10:30 A. M.—Reading Circle. 2:00 P. M.—Lecture by Giles B. Stebbins, of Detroit.

Wednesday, Aug. 26—10:30 A. M.—Reading Circle. 2:00 P. M.—Mrs. E. C. Woodruff, of South Haven.

Thursday, Aug. 27—10:30 A. M.—Reading Circle. 2:00 P. M.—Lecture by Giles B. Stebbins.

Friday, Aug. 28—10:30 A. M.—Reading Circle. 2:00 P. M.—Mrs. E. C. Woodruff.

Saturday, Aug. 29—10:30 A. M.—Reading Circle. 2:00 P. M.—Lyceum.

Sunday, Aug. 30—10:30 A. M.—Lecture by Hon. L. V. Moulton, of Grand Rapids.

Sunday, Aug. 30—2:00 P. M.—Lecture by Dr. A. B. Spinney, of Detroit.

COMMITTEES.

Entertainments—Mrs. Horton, Lowell; Mrs. Tracy Merrill, Lansing; Mrs. Kate Cleveland, Detroit.

Decorations—Mrs. H. J. Mead, Mason; Mrs. A. E. Sheets, Grand Ledge; Mrs. Dr. Higbie, Burton; Mrs. E. A. Payne, Grand Rapids.

Music—Mrs. James H. Haslett, Port Huron; Miss Leta Buck, Lansing; H. A. Walker, Lansing.

Police—Ted Cutler, Riley; S. P. Buck, Lansing; Dr. Dryer, Bath.

Reception—Mrs. A. B. Spinney, Detroit; Hon. James H. White, Port Huron; A. G. Leathers, East Saginaw; H. A. Martin, Dimondale.

By 1891, Haslett Park was known nationally and attracted lecturers from Boston and South Farmington, Massachusetts, and Fredonia, New York. The 1891 bulletin shown above boasted, "Many improvements will be noted this year. The walk has been graded to the Auditorium and seeded down, many unsightly stumps removed and trees planted."

Rental housing boomed around the lake to house summer visitors. Small cottages such as the Celeste were in frequent use. Mrs. Owen of Lapeer, Michigan, was one developer who added a number of cottages around the lake. Cottages were available for rent by the week or by the season.

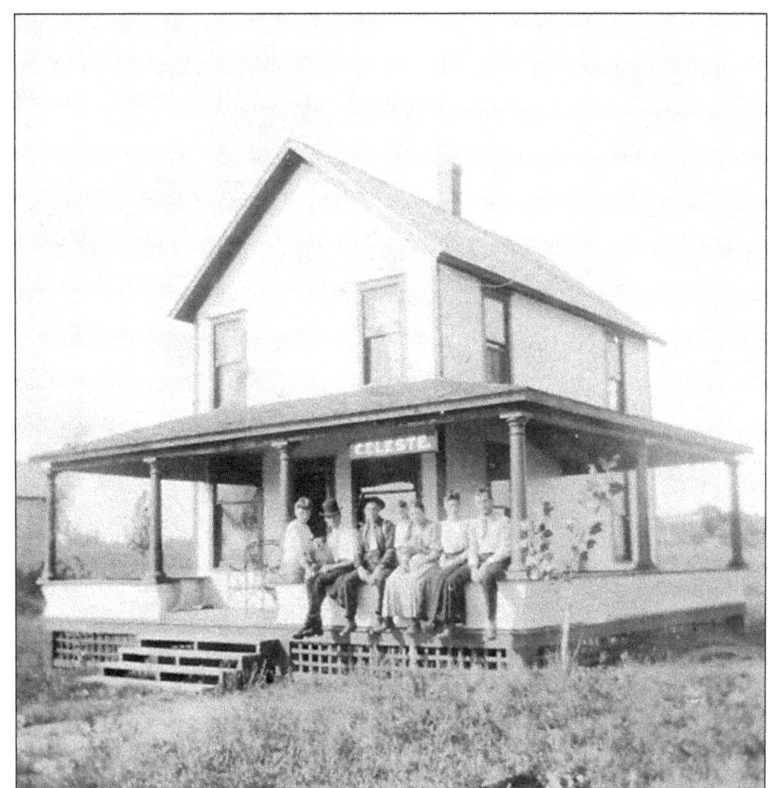

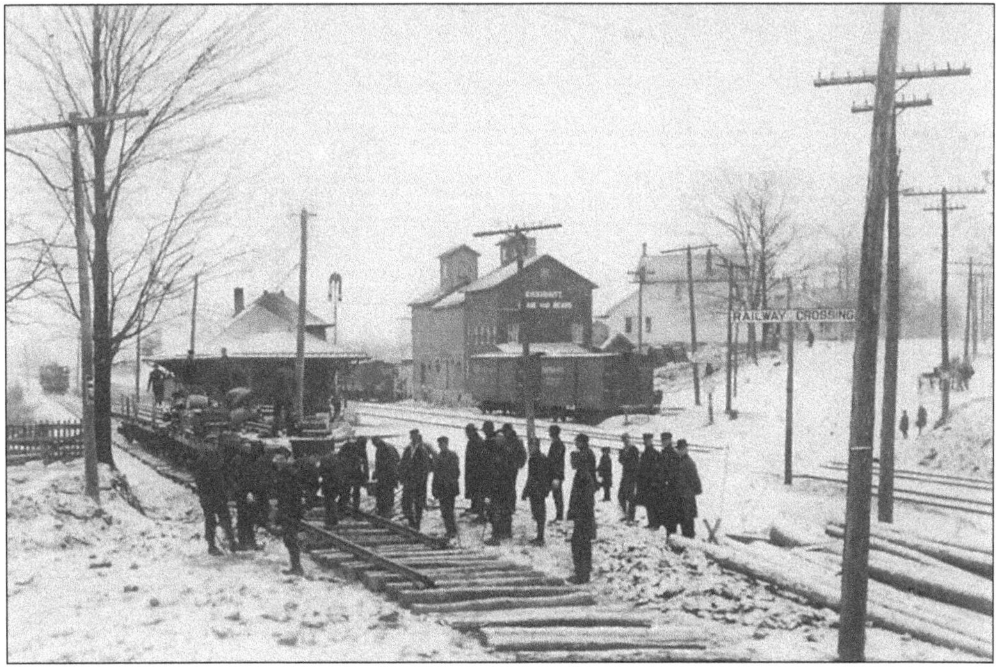

The Michigan Electric Railroad extended a line to Haslett in 1905. The interurban railway included an electric trolley, which improved transportation from Lansing to Haslett Park. The line included a third, electrified, line in between the two outer rails.

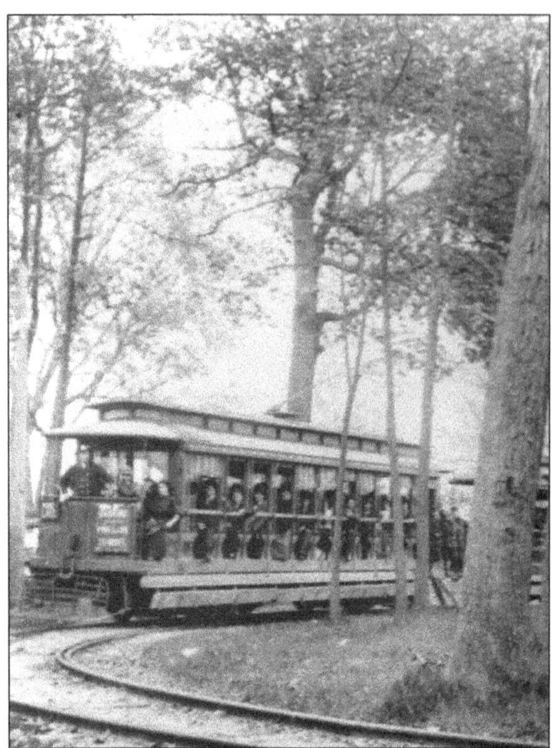

The trolley company used open cars to bring visitors to and from Lansing for swimming in the summer and skating in the winter. These open cars had canvas shades that could be lowered to help protect the passengers from the wind and rain.

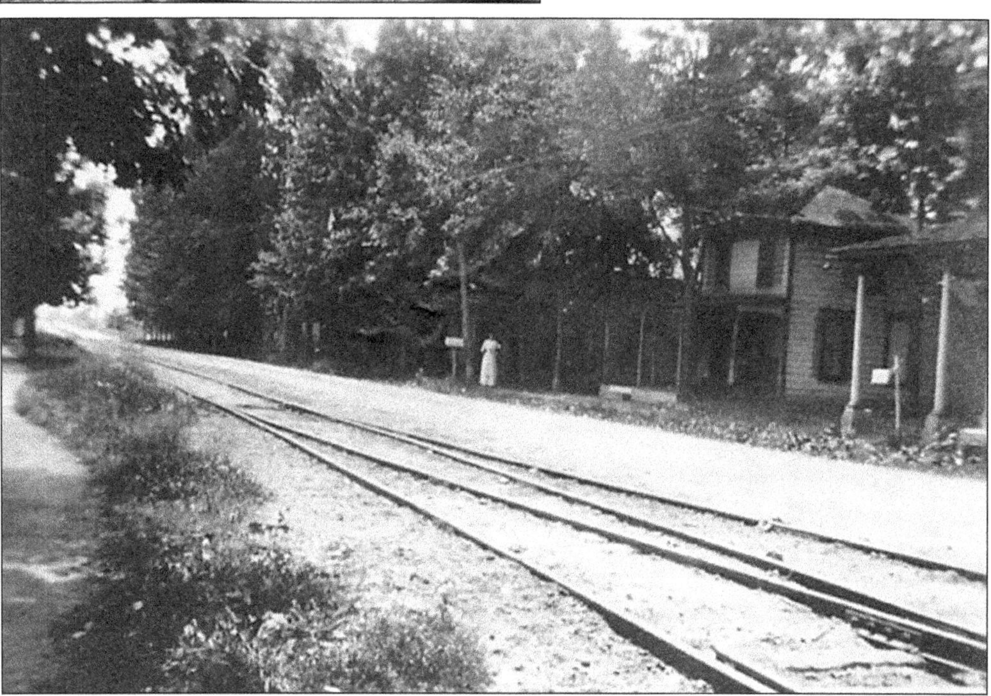

The trolley line was built adjacent to the Grand Trunk Railroad tracks until it reached the south foot of Potter Street. There, the tracks turned north along Potter Street to Haslett Park. This photograph shows the line looking south from the intersection of Potter Street and Lake Lansing Road.

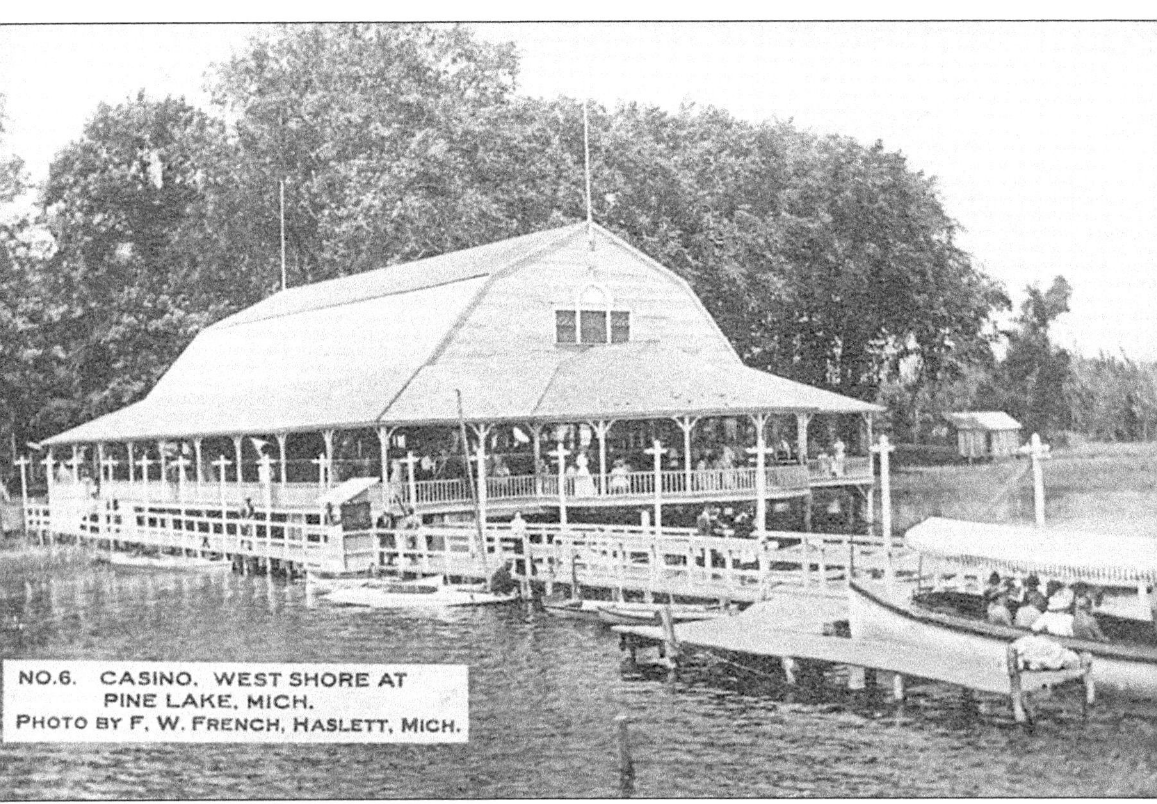

Attendance at the Spiritualists' Haslett Park Camp dwindled after the death of James Haslett in 1891. His widow sold the property to the Haslett Park Association, who repurposed the buildings to serve the summer entertainment interests of visitors. The trolley company added a large pavilion consisting of a covered porch that extended over the water. Named the Casino, it sold ice cream for visitors to enjoy while overlooking the lake.

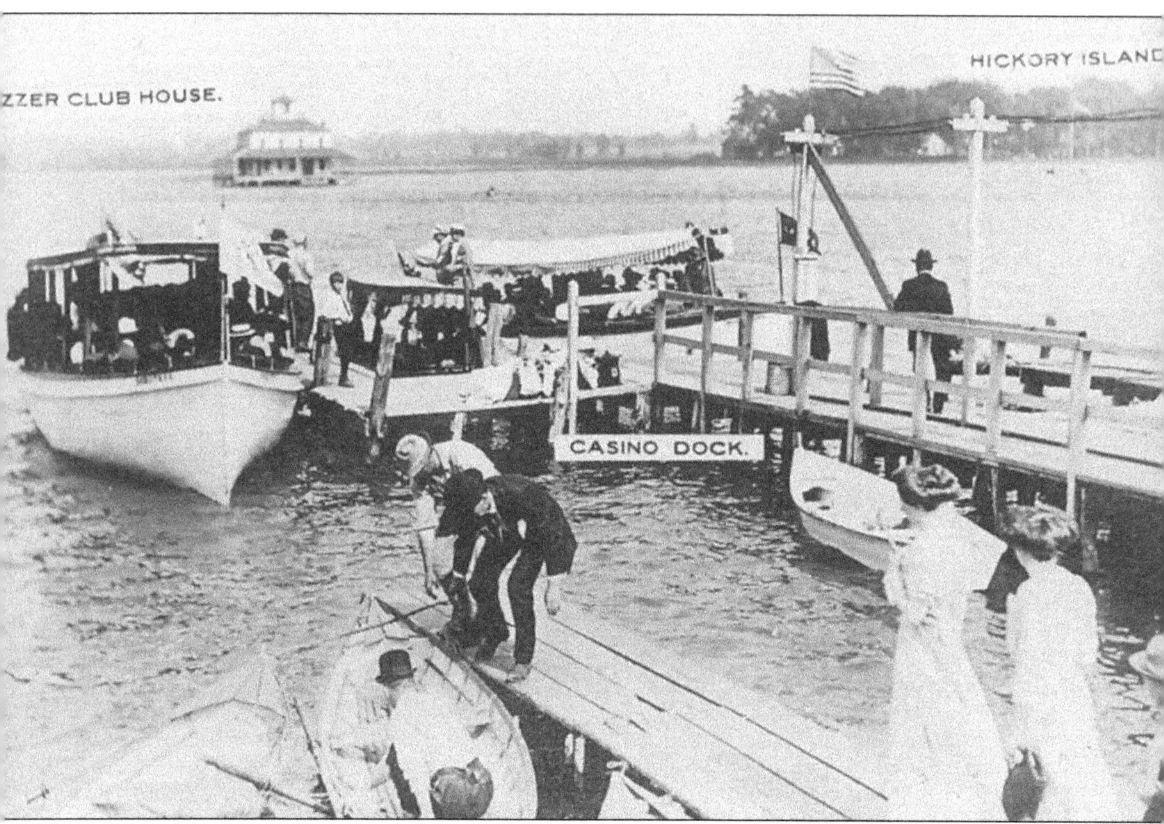

The trolley company also extended the line into the former Spiritualist camp and built a turnaround to bring visitors closer to the Casino area. The Casino dock was located at the southwest corner of the lake and allowed for water transportation to and from the private clubhouse in the center of the lake and also to Hickory Island.

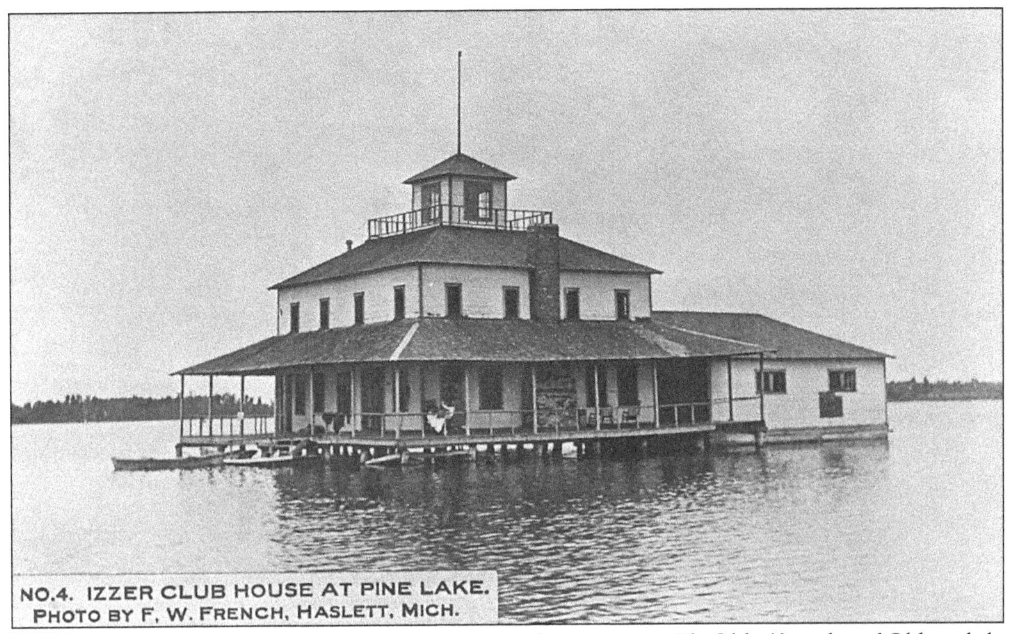

By the 1890s, wealthy Lansing businessmen, including Ransom Eli Olds (founder of Oldsmobile and the Diamond REO Company) built summer homes along the sandy north shore. These men also built a gentlemen's club in the center of Pine Lake. The two-story building had a porch around all sides. A trapdoor in the floor is rumored to have been used to drop unsuspecting guests into the lake. The club was also used as a blind pig during the Depression to provide the members with a place to enjoy outlawed alcohol.

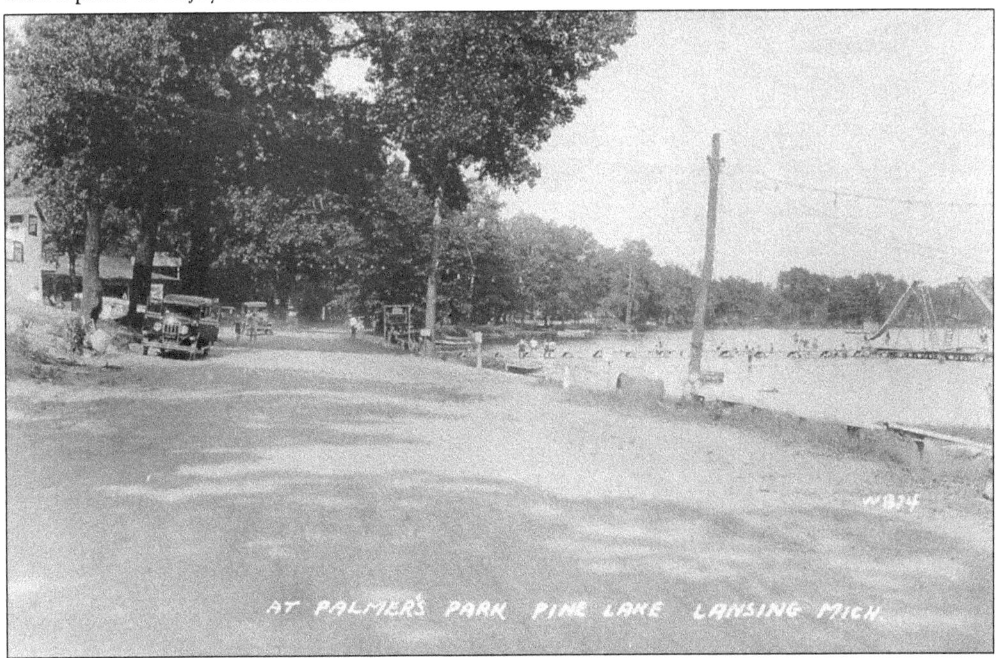

The Pine Lake House property was purchased from James Haslett's son Frank in 1895 by H.H. Hammond and Cliff Foster. The partners developed the 40 acres to include numerous entertainments, including horse races. Buildings were added to serve and feed guests.

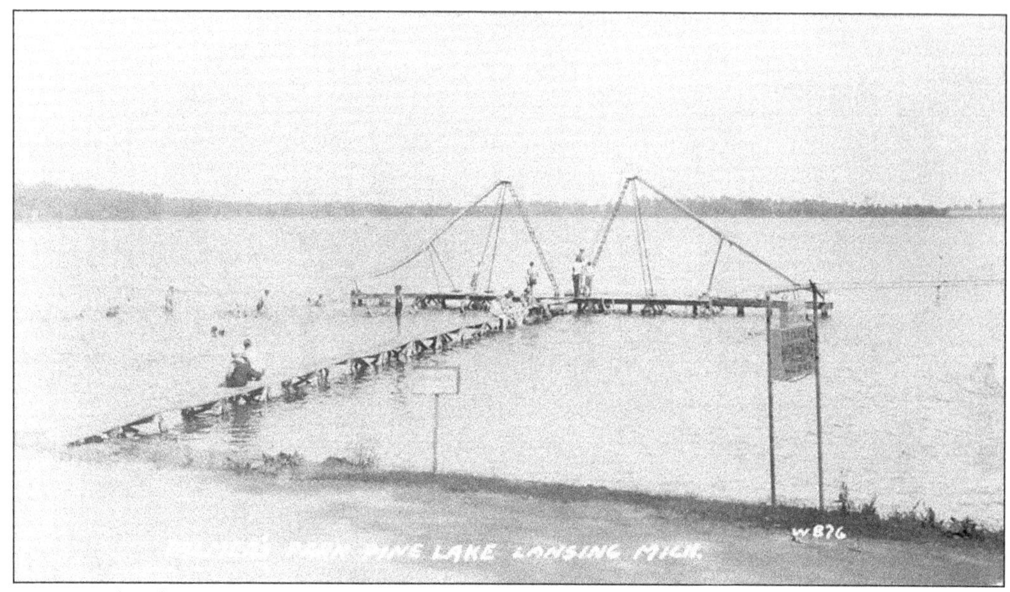

Hammond and Foster continued to expand the attractions at the Pine Lake House site and beaches, a process that included the addition of waterslides (called water toboggans) and steamer rides around the lake. The site attracted swimmers looking for relief from the summer heat.

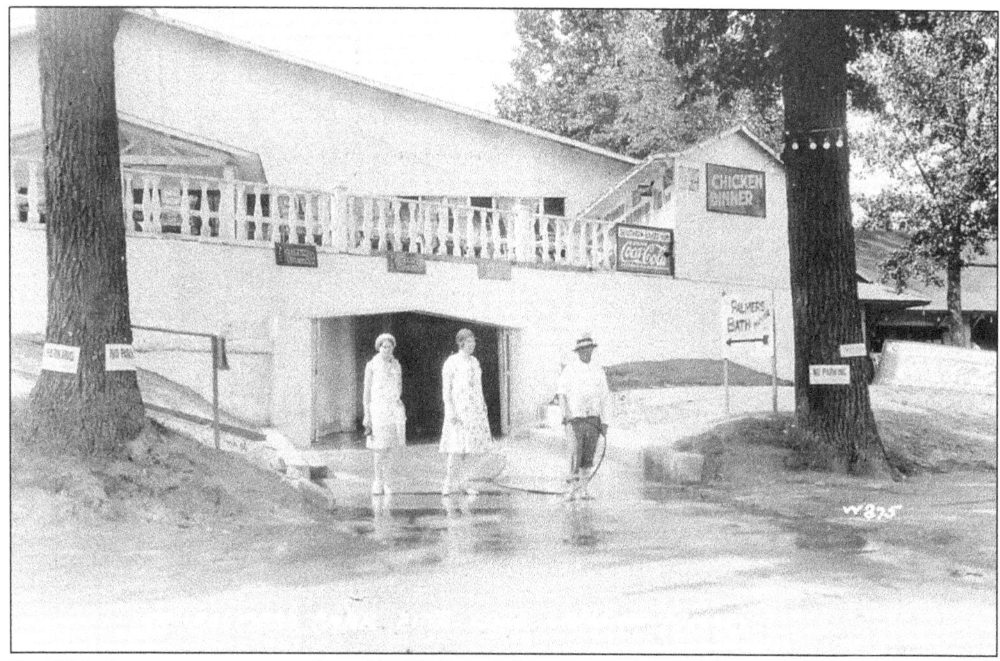

By 1900, the property was purchased by William Megiveron, who had formerly owned the Namoka Hotel on the west shore of the lake during the time of the Spiritualist camp. The bathhouse was one of the improvements made by Megiveron to accommodate locals visiting for the day. Guests could change into their bathing suits to enjoy the beach and later change back to street dress for a meal on the top floor of the building.

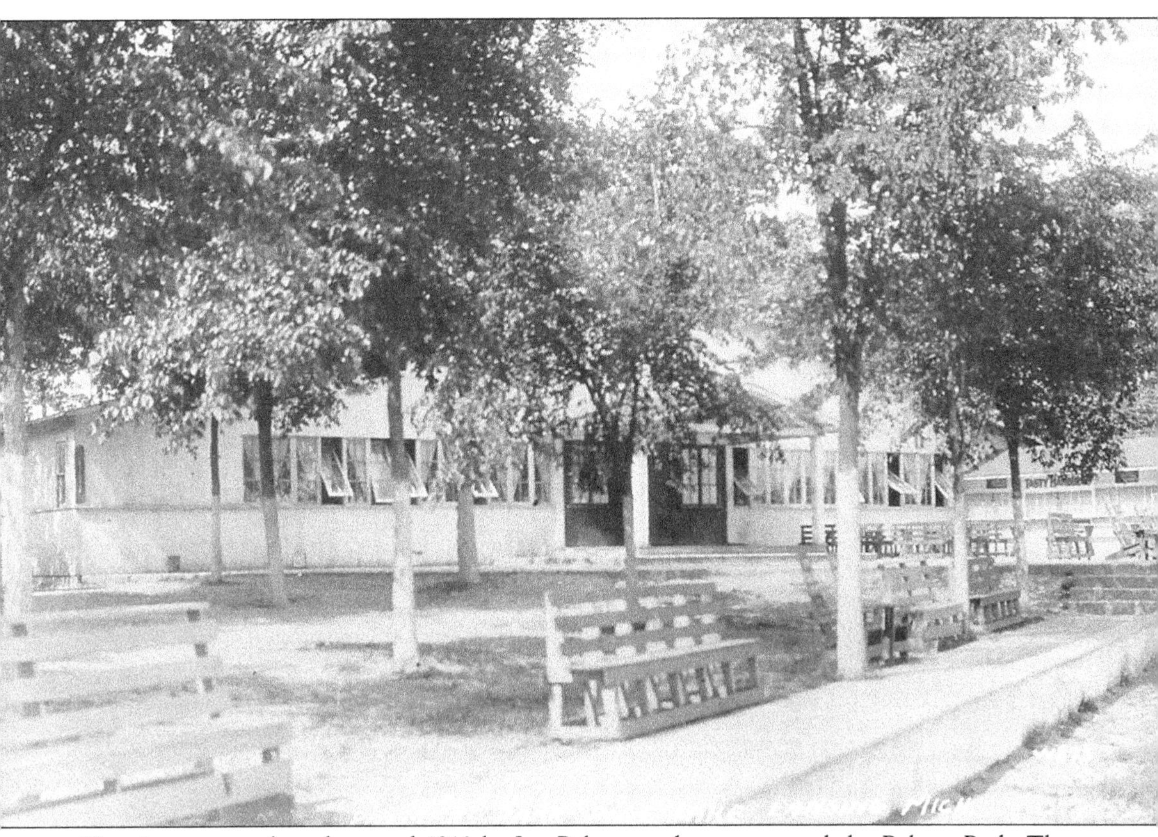

The site was purchased around 1910 by Joe Palmer and was renamed the Palmer Park. The buildings at the site were destroyed by fire in 1929. After the fire destroyed the late-19th-century buildings, Palmer built a large, modern dance hall. The building, known as the Dells Ballroom, attracted numerous big bands from around the country.

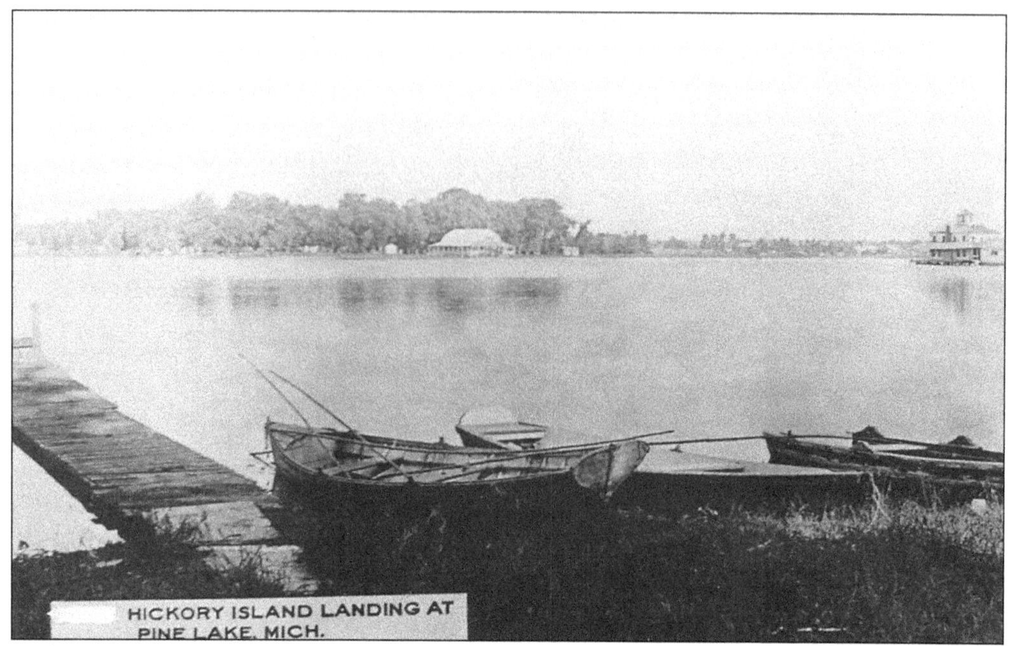

Hickory Island was a popular picnic spot for local families. As it was situated on the marshy east side of the lake, the island could only be accessed by boat during the 19th century. Eventually, a small plank bridge named Devil's Lane was built over the marsh to connect the island with the mainland area. As automobile use increased, the roads around the lake were improved. Carlton Street was built in 1907 and provided a road connection to Hickory Island on the east side of the lake. Ray Whitehead took the opportunity to plat the island and sell property to year-round lake tenants. The buildings were destroyed by fire in 1920.

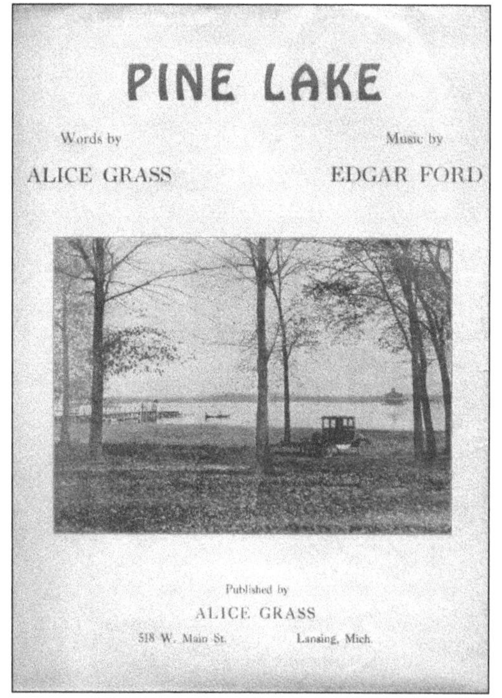

Published in 1924 by Alice Grass, the song "Pine Lake" extolled the joys of spending a Saturday at the park and boating on the lake. The second verse celebrated the "merry merry-go-round, [t]he roller coasters, weeny roasters, everything was there!"

Three

The Haslett Community Grows

As the area became known as a beautiful summer retreat, the little community around Pine Lake grew. Farming was the primary business, with a small cluster of supporting businesses suited to the needs of the farmers. A railroad track was built from the capital city of Lansing to the northeast and ran through Haslett to the counties of Shiawassee, Genesee, and Saginaw. The track was the logical gathering point for farmers to ship their harvest and animals to markets. A small railroad station was soon joined by a post office and general stores. The Babbit family constructed a store at the location, and farmers gathered there for discussion of crops, weather, and politics.

As the community grew, schools were needed for the children. The original school property was located just to the south of the main trail and now is the site of Ralya Elementary. A literary club was formed by local women to encourage the ongoing education of adults. The club also supported organizations for local children, including one of the first Boy Scout groups in the country and sports for the students.

One local family, the Fosters, had enough sons to create their own baseball team. Mr. C.S. Foster challenged any other family to compete with them. The Foster family descendants have held annual reunions at the park on the lake since 1900.

Education has always been a priority for the Haslett community, and families have donated land and resources for the betterment and success of their children.

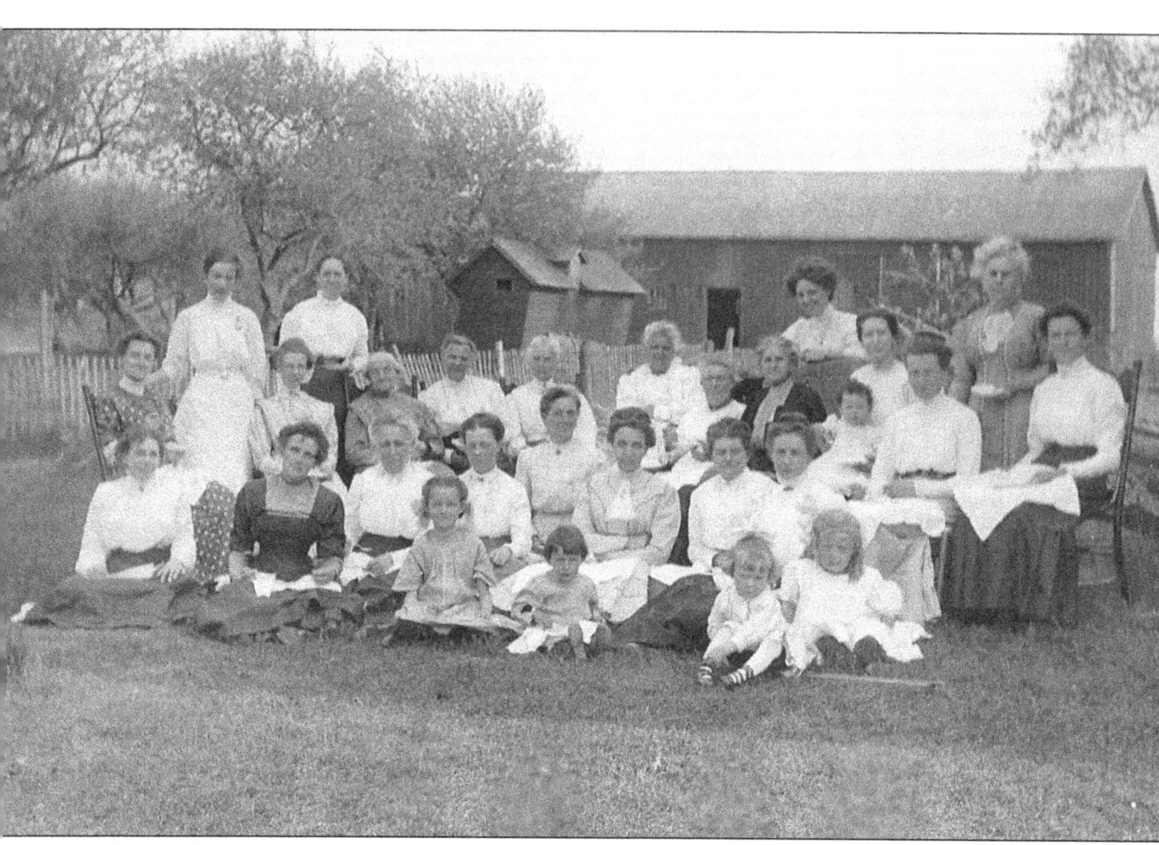

The Haslett community continued to grow in the early 20th century, and social organizations were formed. The Woman's Literary Club was formed in 1906. Members pictured in 1911 include, from left to right, (first row) Cora Brusselbach, Olive Foster, Cynthia Elliott, Ella Cochrane, Kate Smith (with Clinton Mumby in front), Mae Mercer, Belle Hammond, and Beatrice Dunn (with Irene Kaiser front right); (second row) Emma Smith, Ada Douglas, Sarah Cade, Mary Douglas, Alice Hardy, Mamie Foster, Augusta Donley, Lucy Baldwin, Anna Foster (holding Dorothy Foster), Lottie Wellman, and Myrtie Smith; (third row, standing) Dora Kaiser, Kate Carr, Lou Mumby, and Nettie Ferguson. The club continues today as the Haslett Woman's Club.

The club met twice a month to encourage individual and community betterment. Fundraisers were held to provide finances for projects. One project was the construction of a retirement home for senior women located in north Lansing.

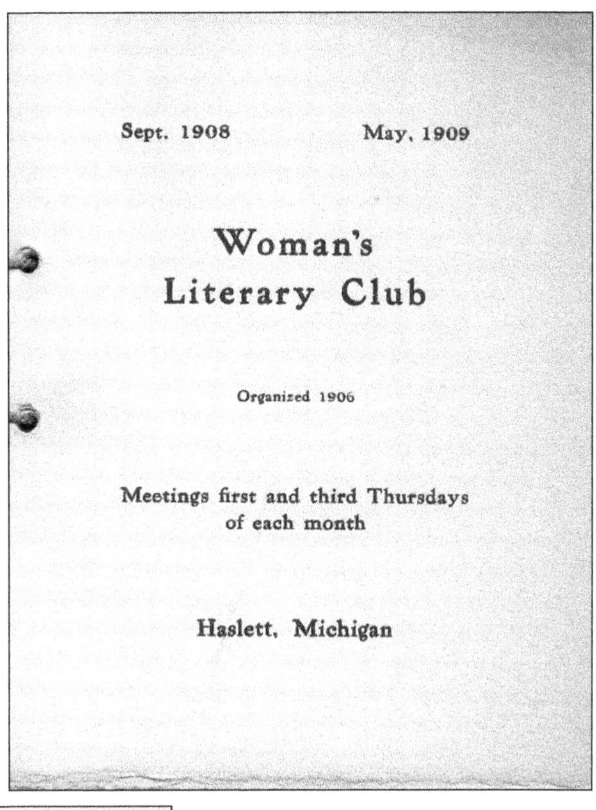

Sept. 1908 May, 1909

Woman's Literary Club

Organized 1906

Meetings first and third Thursdays of each month

Haslett, Michigan

Officers

President - - Mrs. Belle Hammond
Vice President Mrs. Sadie Codrington
Secretary - - Mrs. Emma Smith
Assistant Secretary Mrs. Emma Foster
Treasurer - - Mrs. Edna Brundige
Librarian - - Mrs. Ethel Marsh

Committees

Program

Mrs. Ollie Foster
Mrs. Nettie Ferguson
Mrs. Mae Maser
Mrs. Sara Smith

Flower

Mrs. Cora Brusselbach
Mrs. Nettie Ferguson

Parliamentarian—Mrs. Sara Smith

Prominent women in the community organized and led the direction of the club by planning the annual meeting topics and programs. The leaders were from long-standing pioneer families such as the Hammonds, Fosters, and Marshes.

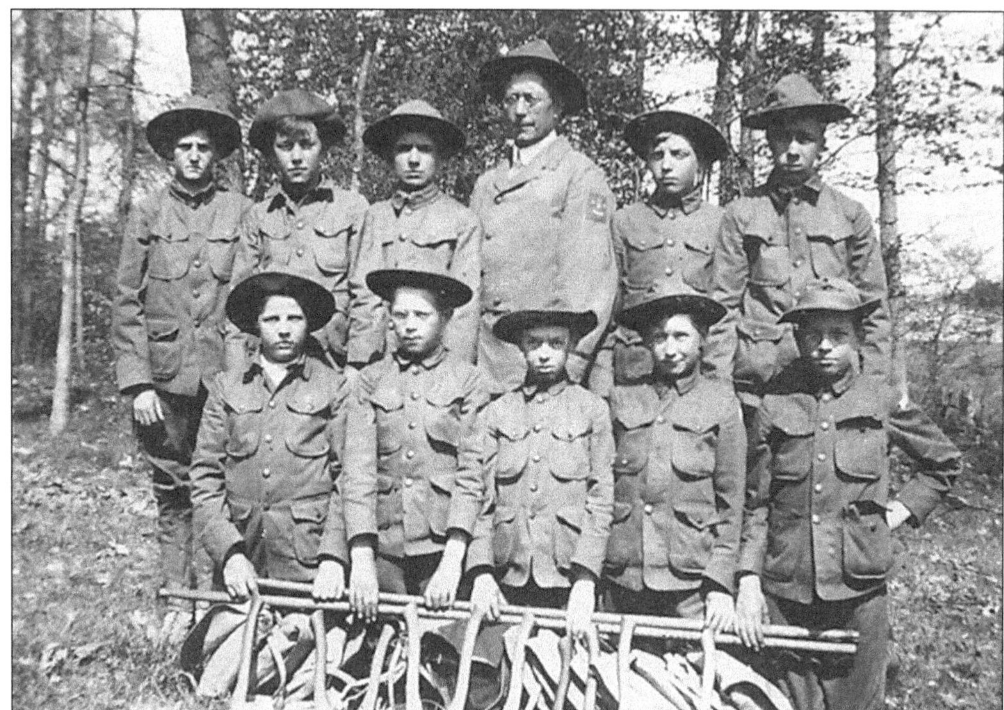

The Haslett Boy Scouts were one of the first troops to be organized after the establishment of the Boy Scouts in America in 1910. The Haslett Scouts were formed in 1911 by railroad agent J.G. Marsh. Pictured above, from left to right, are (first row) Russell Ferris, Lester Smith, John Joy, Kenneth Marsh, and Arthur Heimerdinger; (second row) Ray Wagner, Leslie Buxton, Harold Knickerbocker, J.G. Marsh, Reuben Everett, and Ford Elliot.

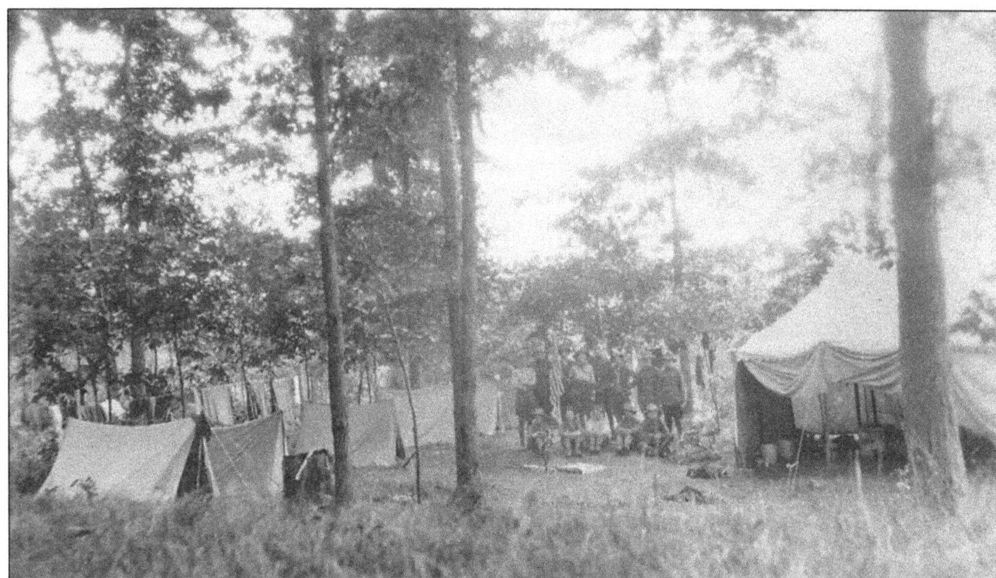

The troop spent a year raising money, with support from the Women's Literary Club, to provide equipment for the Scouts. The troop was able to participate in a camp in June 1913, fully uniformed and with all the necessary gear, including pup tents.

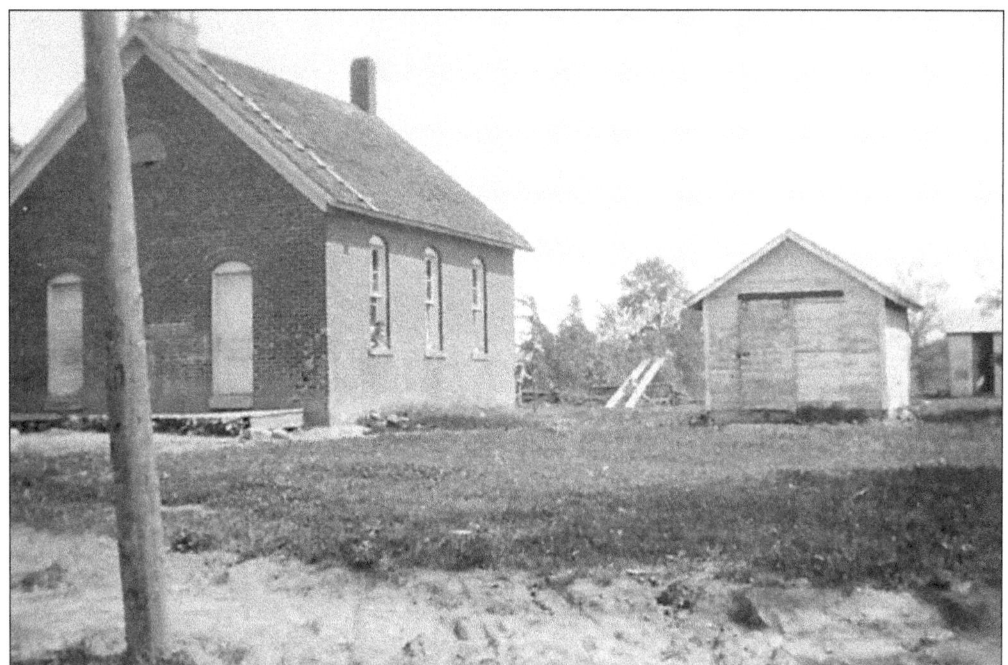

The Hart School was one of the rural one-room schools used in the area for students in grades one through eight. Girls entered through one door and boys through the other. Most schools required the girls and boys to sit on opposite sides of the room. The youngest children sat in the front, with the older students in the back. These small, one-room schools remained in use until 1923, when the older students were housed in a single, consolidated building.

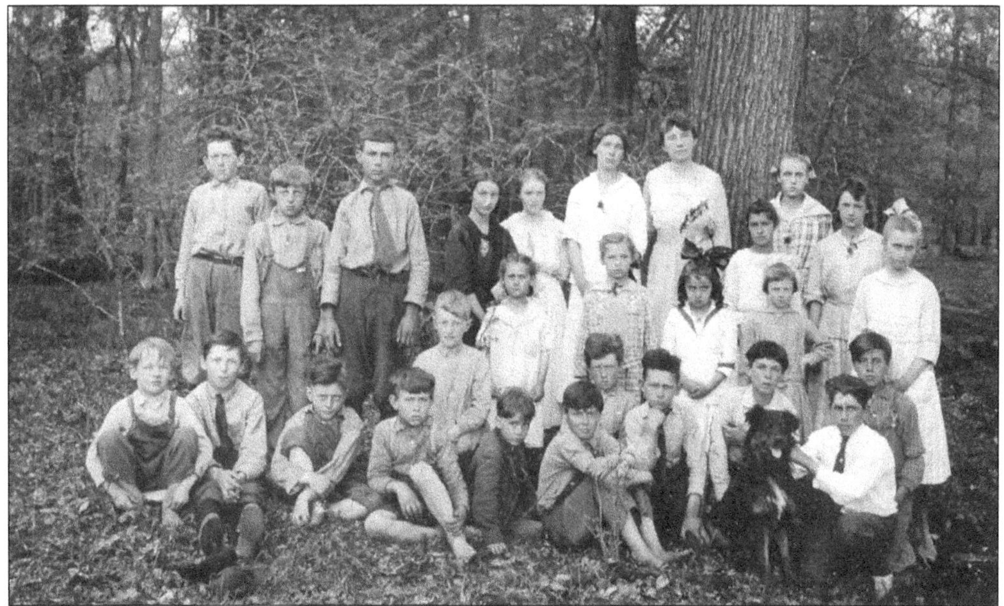

Students from the Hart School pose for their class picture. Ruth Foster served as teacher for this class. One teacher was responsible for instructing all subjects to all grades. Women were allowed to teach as long as they remained single. Male teachers were preferred during the winter season, when the older boys were able to attend to keep potentially unruly teenagers in order.

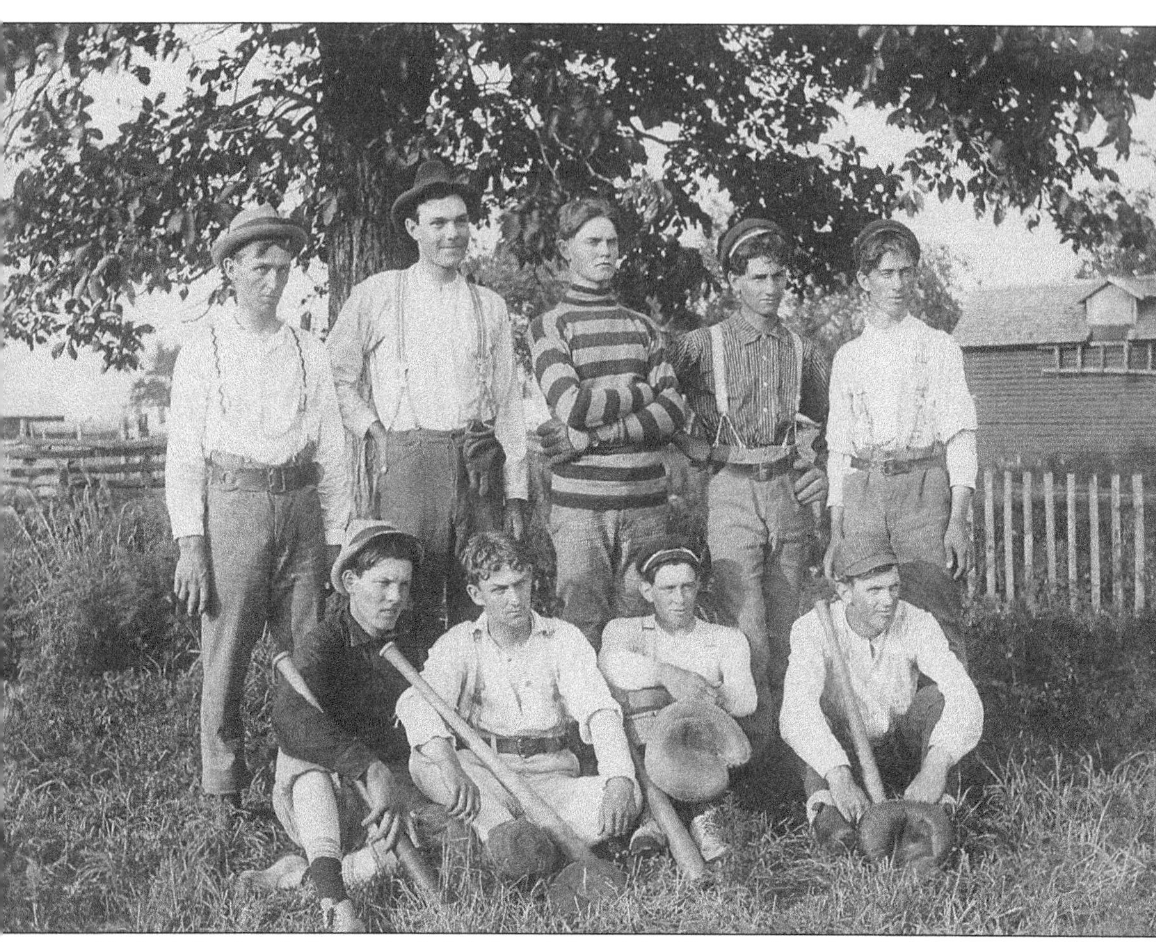

Haslett's first baseball team included, from left to right, (first row) unidentified, Burr Foster, Ed Douglas, and Gary Peterson; (second row) Roy Douglas, ? Kaiser, Bert Allshouse, Fred Karber, and Hugh Megiveron. Burr Foster was a member of a family large enough to have its own team. By 1913, the nine sons of C.S. Foster formed the Foster Brothers Team, whose slogan was "World's Championship Family Nine, or Nothing."

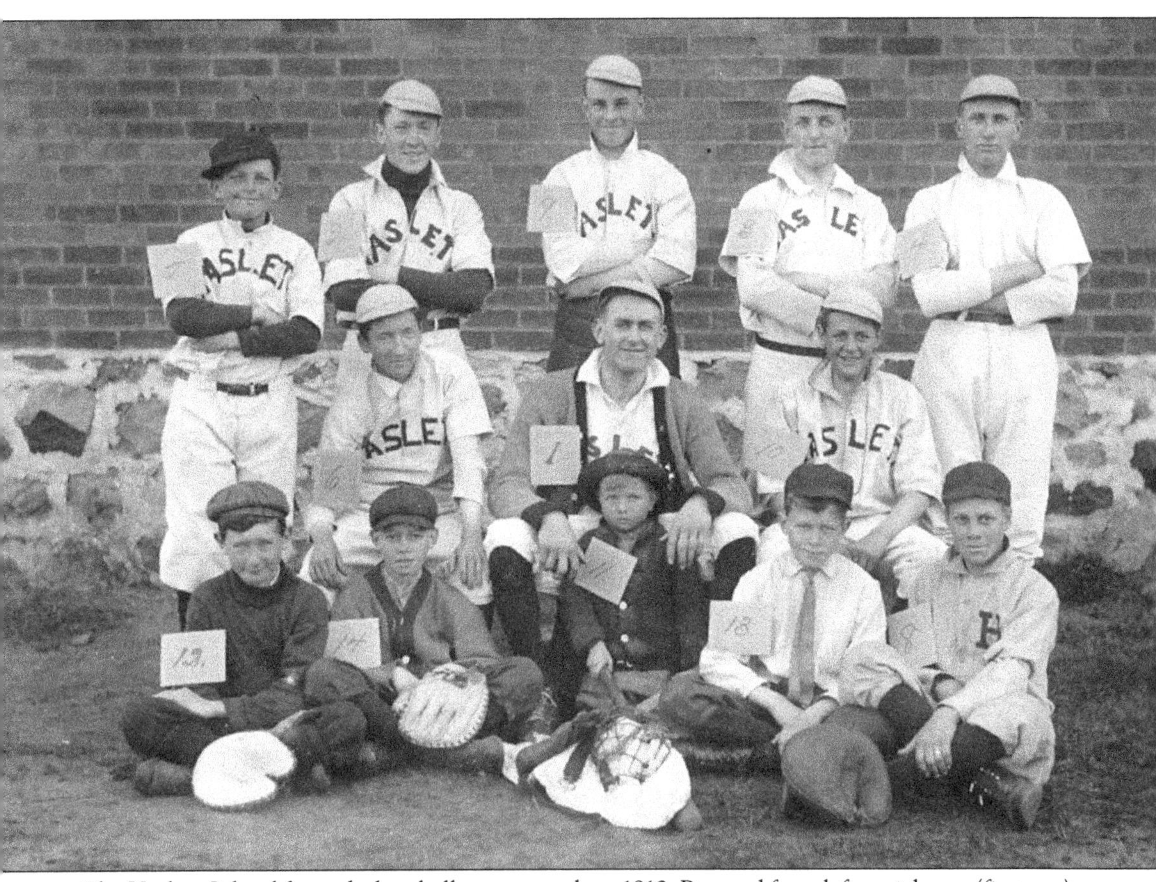

The Haslett School formed a baseball team as early as 1912. Pictured from left to right are (first row) Marsh, Joy, unidentified mascot, Smith, and Scott; (second row) Beebe, Capt. P. Brusselbach, and Seely; (third row) Heimerdinger, team manager Greene, Cochrane, P. Brusselbach, and Brook.

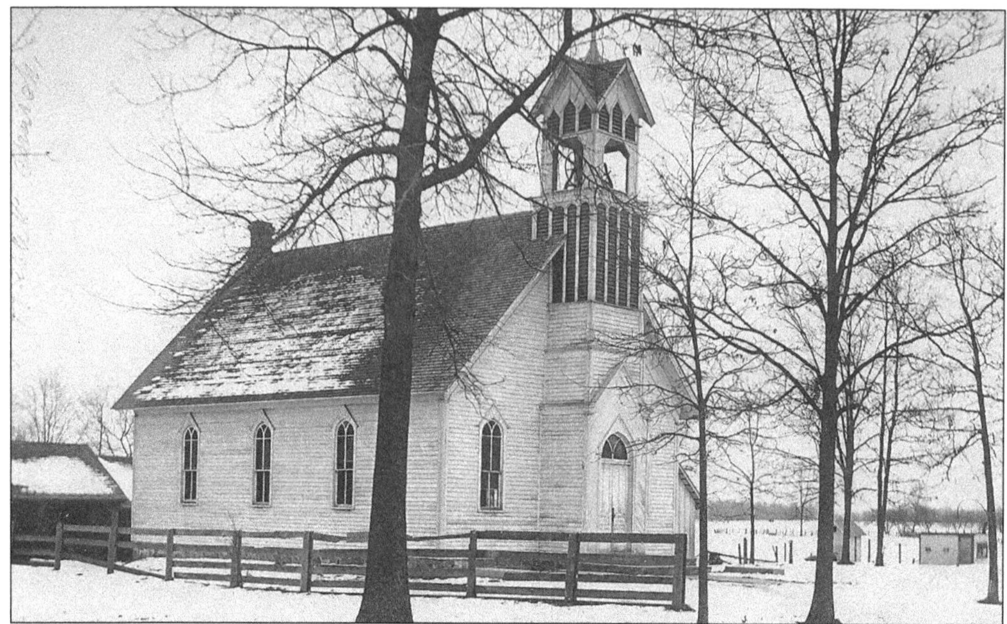

The Pine Lake community organized the Free Will Baptist Church in March 1892 and held services in the Carl School House on the north side of Haslett until the following autumn. The school was located in District No. 7 of Meridian Township. The original church building was completed by September 1892 and was located along Haslett Road in the Haslett Park community. It was moved to a new foundation in 1923 just east of the original location.

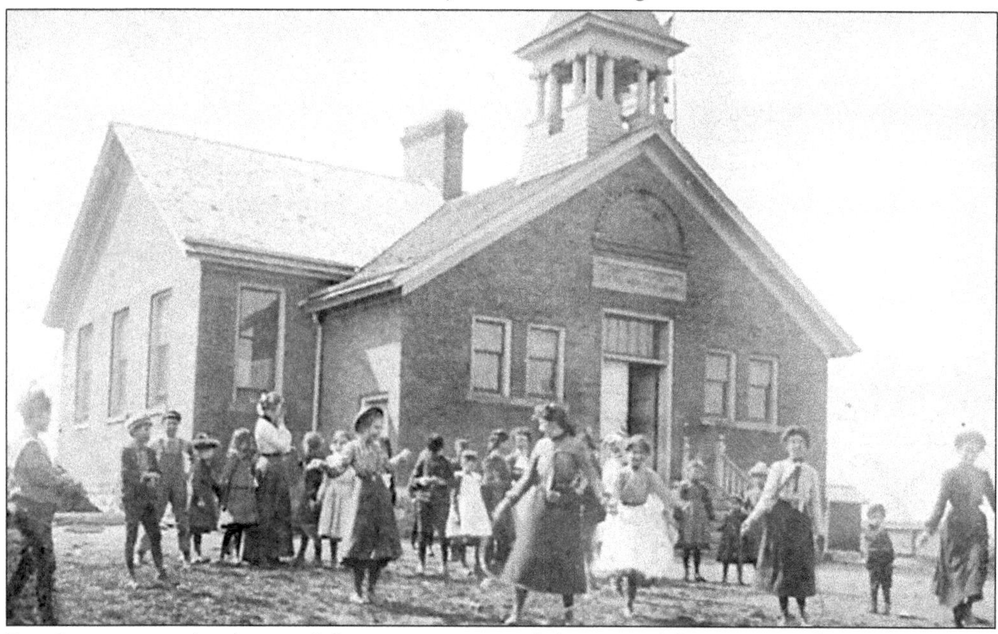

Rural one-room schools served the community until the turn of the century, when a single-story brick building was built on donated property along present-day School Street. The condition and resources of the one-room schools were minimal, and a movement was forwarded in the early 20th century to consolidate community resources for the benefit of all area students. The consolidation resulted in a centralized building within the town limits of Haslett.

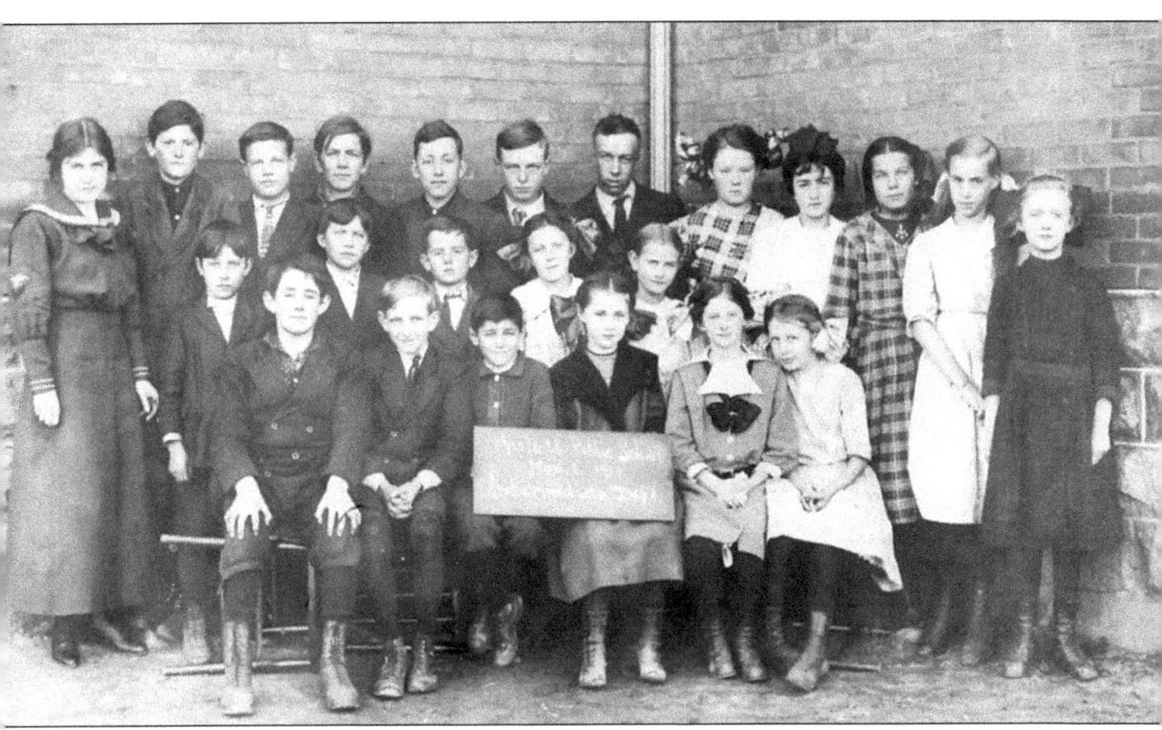

The youngest students continued to be schooled at the small rural schools; however, a centralized school allowed for the older students to be housed in one building. The younger students were grouped together as the intermediate-level class. This transitional level would be considered a middle school according to today's standards.

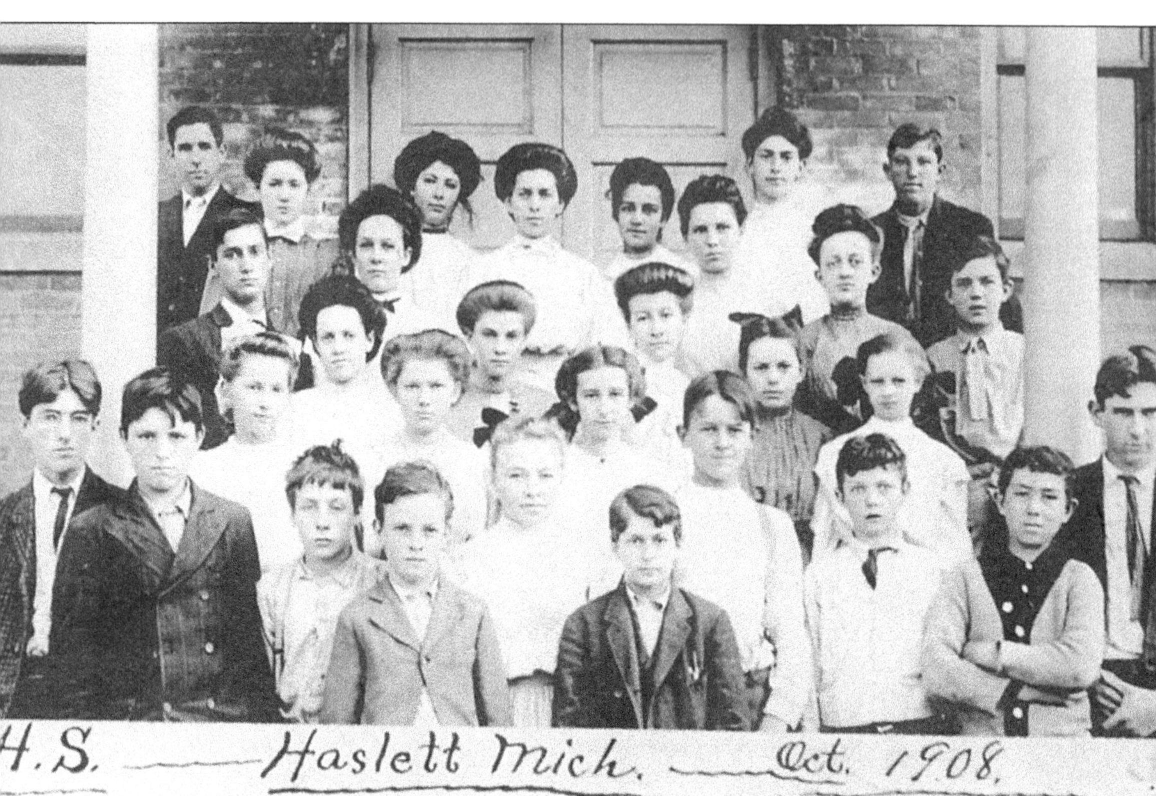

The central school site also allowed for grades at the highest level of the area. The oldest students could continue their education at the high school level through the 10th grade. In rural communities, completing 10th-grade education was considered advanced.

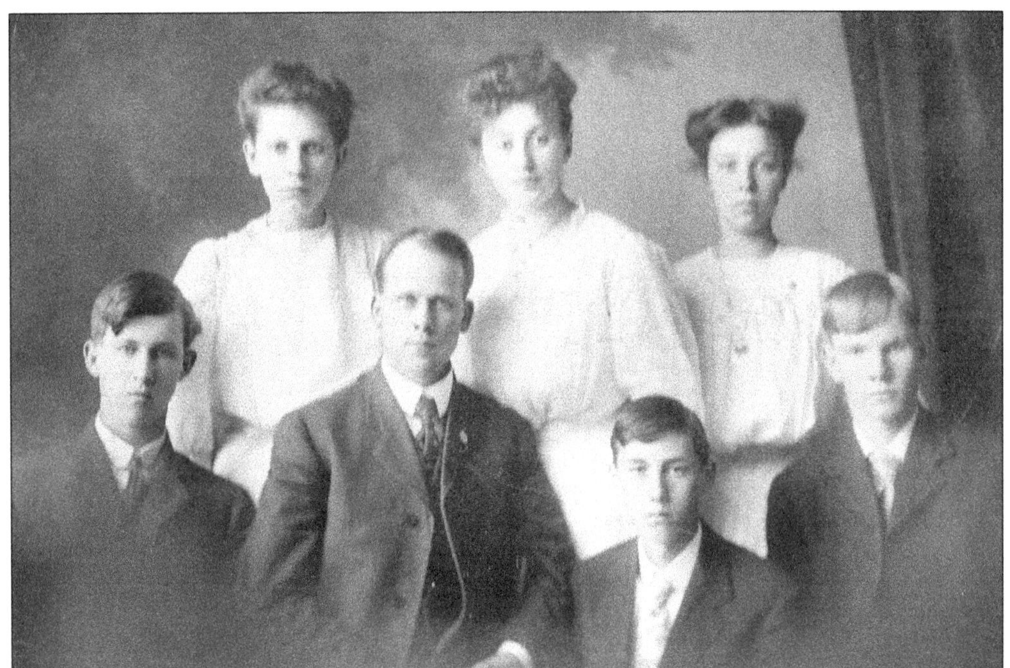

Considered the first graduating class from Haslett, these students in 10th grade (the highest grade at the time) are pictured in June 1907. Students who wanted to continue their education beyond 10th grade had to travel to larger cities in the surrounding area. Pictured from left to right are (first row) Milo Clark, superintendent Louis Mixter, J. Russell Ferguson, and Walter Moore; (second row) Pearl Smith, Lyla Smith, and Mary Elliott.

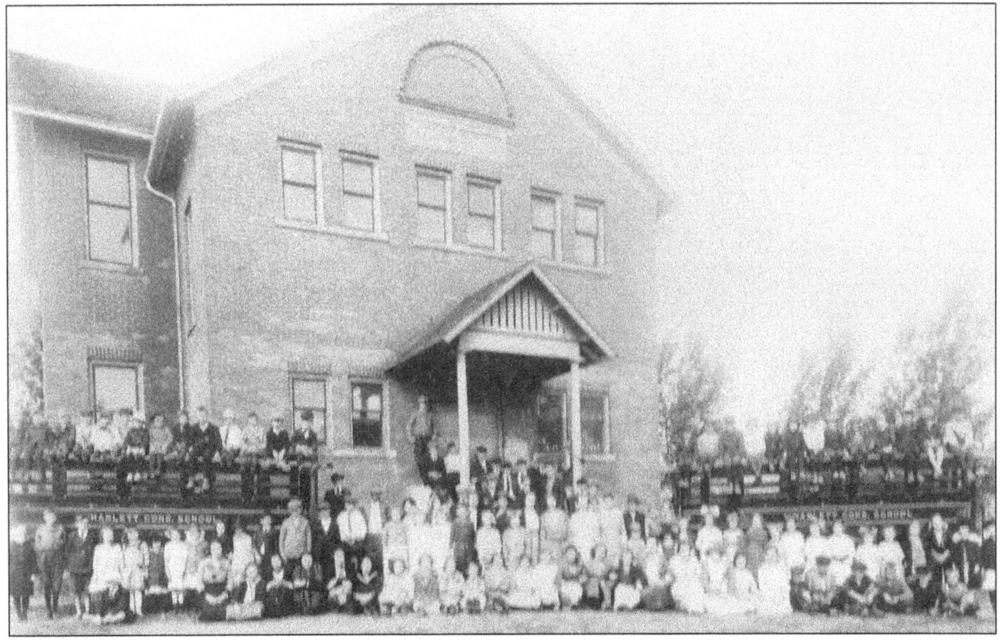

The growing number of pupils enrolled in the consolidated Haslett School required the addition of a second floor to accommodate older students. The floor was added around 1921, and bus transportation was introduced to allow children from the entire district to attend the central site.

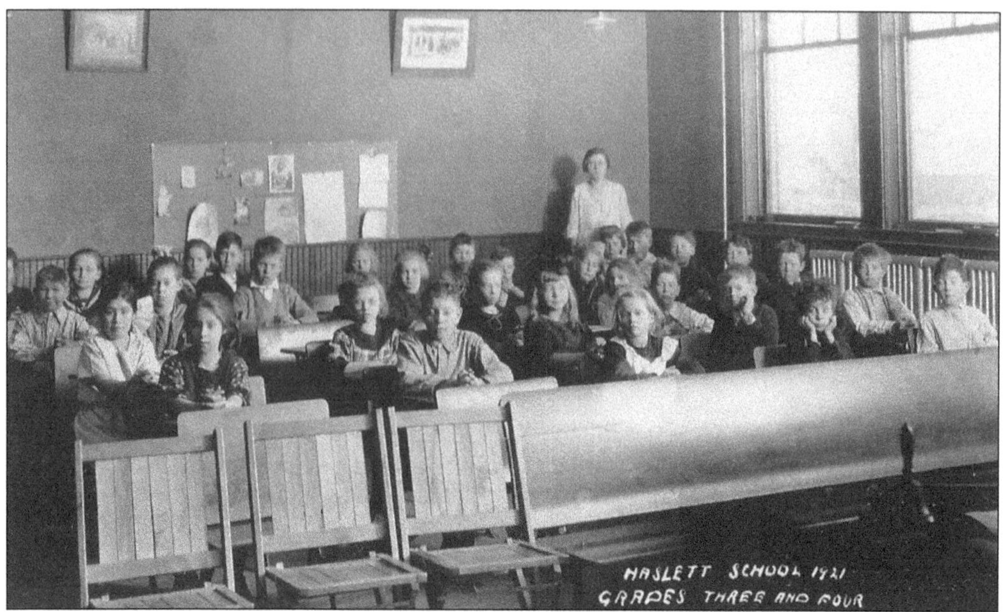

Once the individual schools were consolidated into a central facility, class sizes increased, and classrooms were organized by age group, with one teacher for the single classroom. This image shows the combined third and fourth grades of 1921.

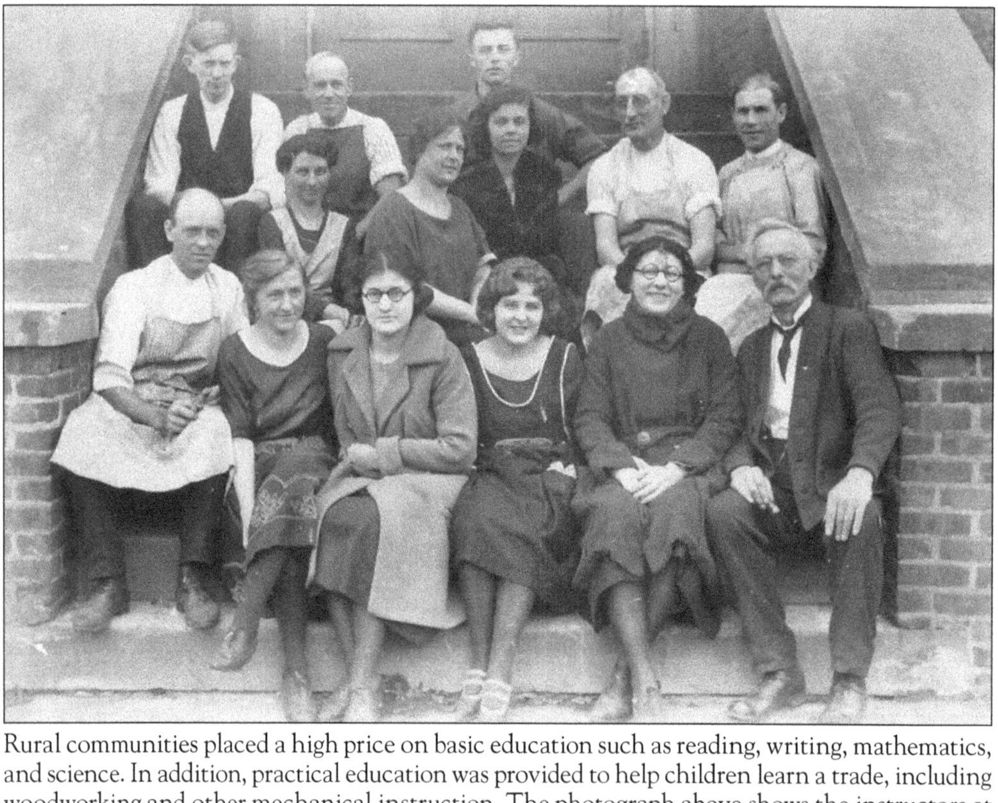

Rural communities placed a high price on basic education such as reading, writing, mathematics, and science. In addition, practical education was provided to help children learn a trade, including woodworking and other mechanical instruction. The photograph above shows the instructors at the consolidated school who taught numerous subjects to prepare the students for a livelihood.

Four

From Pine Lake to Lake Lansing

Prior to the introduction of the automobile, pleasure travel was limited to the local area via horse and buggy or, perhaps, trolley. The proximity of Pine Lake to the capital city of Lansing encouraged weekend outings by couples and families seeking relief from the heat of the city.

When the Haslett Park Association purchased the property on the southwest corner of the lake from James Haslett's widow, Sarah, there were buildings already available for a new use. The association built the Casino on the waterfront with its own dock to accommodate the steamer boats ferrying visitors around the lake. Dances were also very popular on the weekends and attracted many residents who travelled the trolley to enjoy the cool summer breezes.

The sandy beach on the north shore drew visitors for many years and attracted wealthy businessmen to build summer homes, such as Ransom Eli Olds (founder of Oldsmobile and the R.E. Olds Company). The former Pine Lake House property on the north shore became Palmer's Park, and waterslides and bathhouses were added.

The popularity of Pine Lake at the time has been compared to the modern-day popularity of "up north" communities such as Traverse City and Charlevoix. Frank Johnson came to the area in 1917 and rented a cottage on the east side of Pine Lake. He saw the potential for development of year-round lakefront homes and set about to market the property. In 1927, he gave the lake a new name, Lake Lansing. His explanation was that "there are dozens of Pine Lakes" in Michigan, but only one capital, so "Lake Lansing" would stand out and attract more investors.

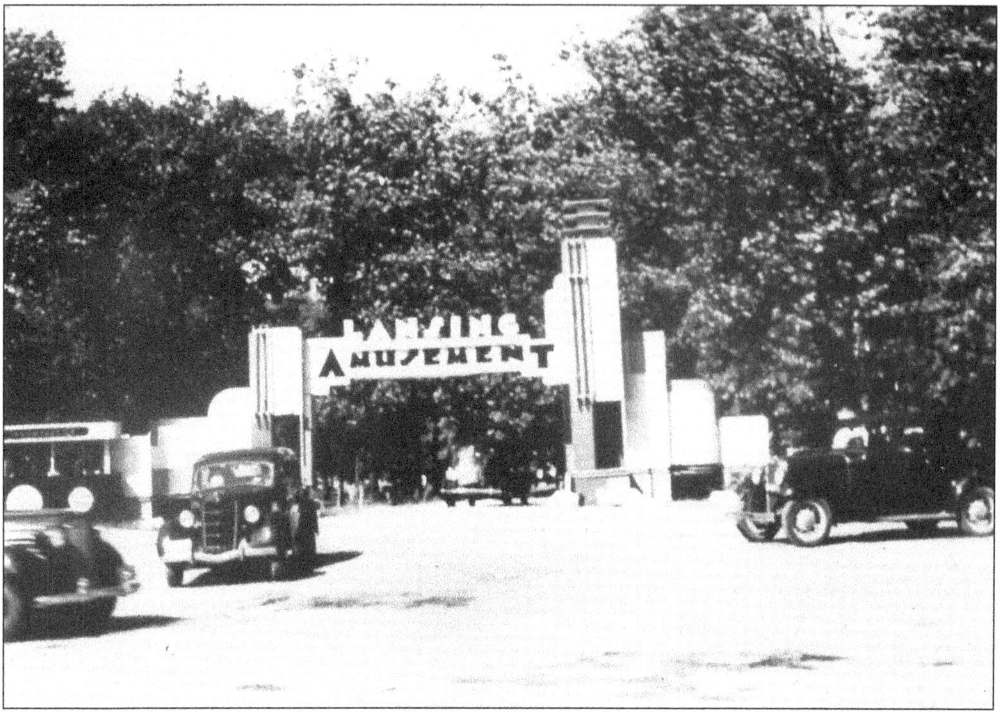

The lake had been known as Pine Lake for decades; however, Frank Johnson began developing the east side of the lake and renamed it Lake Lansing in 1927. The former recreation area of Haslett Park at Pine Lake was renamed Lansing Amusement Park. (Courtesy of the Ingham County Parks Department.)

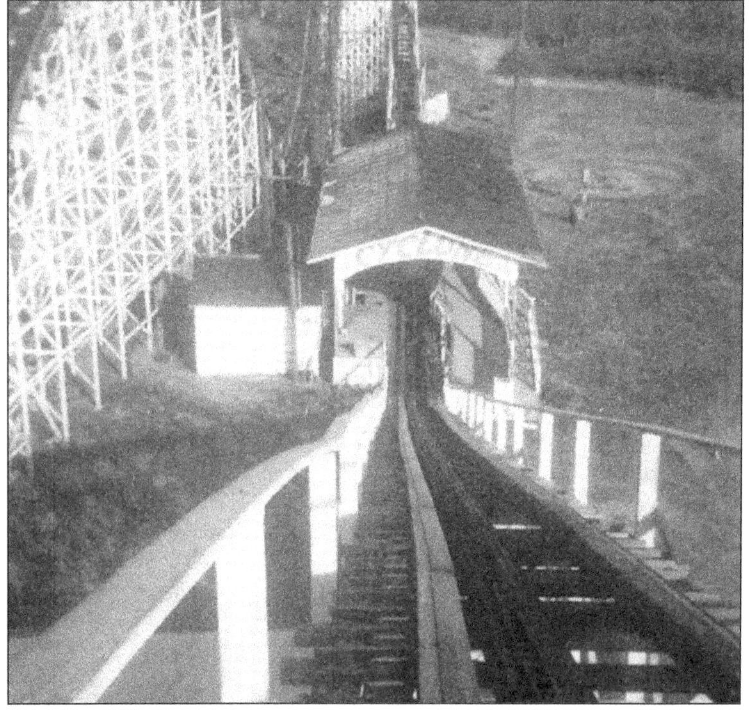

The amusement rides began to be added in the early 20th century when the Michigan Catering Company constructed a roller coaster on a site nearby the Casino building. By the early 1930s, more rides were added by subsequent owners. (Courtesy of Ingham County Parks Department.)

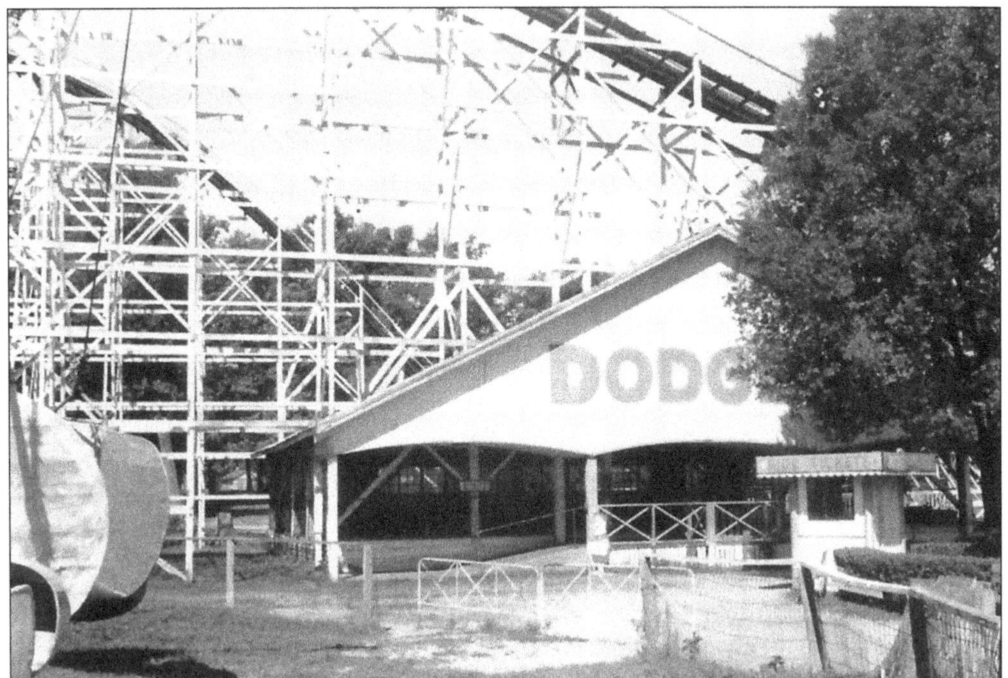

Al Sprague served as the park's superintendent beginning in 1916. He bought the park in 1934 and began a campaign to expand the number of rides. The Dodgem Car ride was added in the 1930s in the former lecture hall at the Spiritualist camp. It joined the existing roller coaster and, with a carousel, remained one of the three most popular rides throughout the years. (Courtesy of the Ingham County Parks Department.)

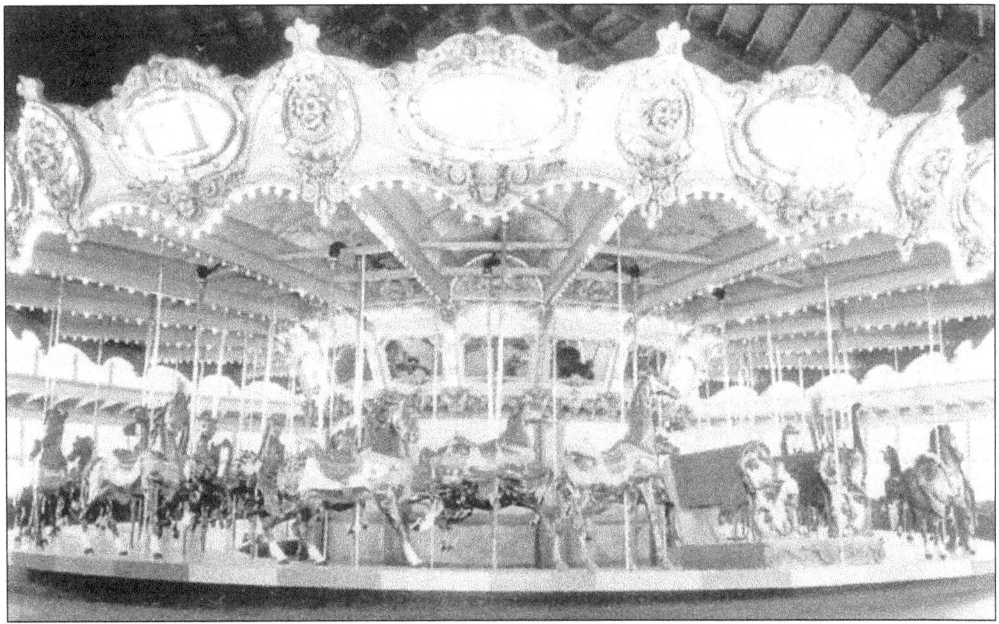

The carousel ride was built in 1921 and included sculpted wooden animals. The ride was moved to the park and was contained in its own building starting in 1942. (Courtesy of Ingham County Parks Department.)

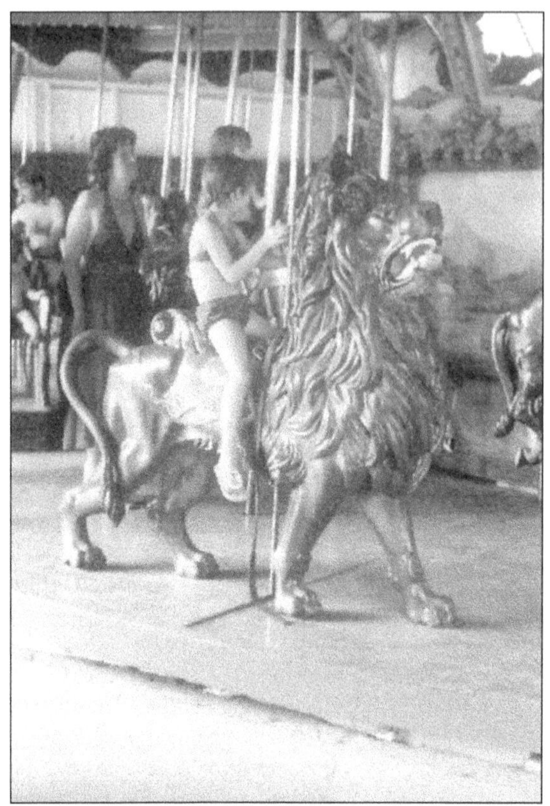

The carousel ride was a major attraction for decades. The ride was restored and moved to the Frontiertown section of Cedar Point when the amusement park closed. (Courtesy of the Ingham County Parks Department.)

The park was a major attraction from the 1920s through 1960s. Local children often drove their first "car" at the park. Every spring, more than 3,000 local safety patrols received a free outing courtesy of the Greater Lansing Safety Patrol organization. (Courtesy of Ingham County Parks Department.)

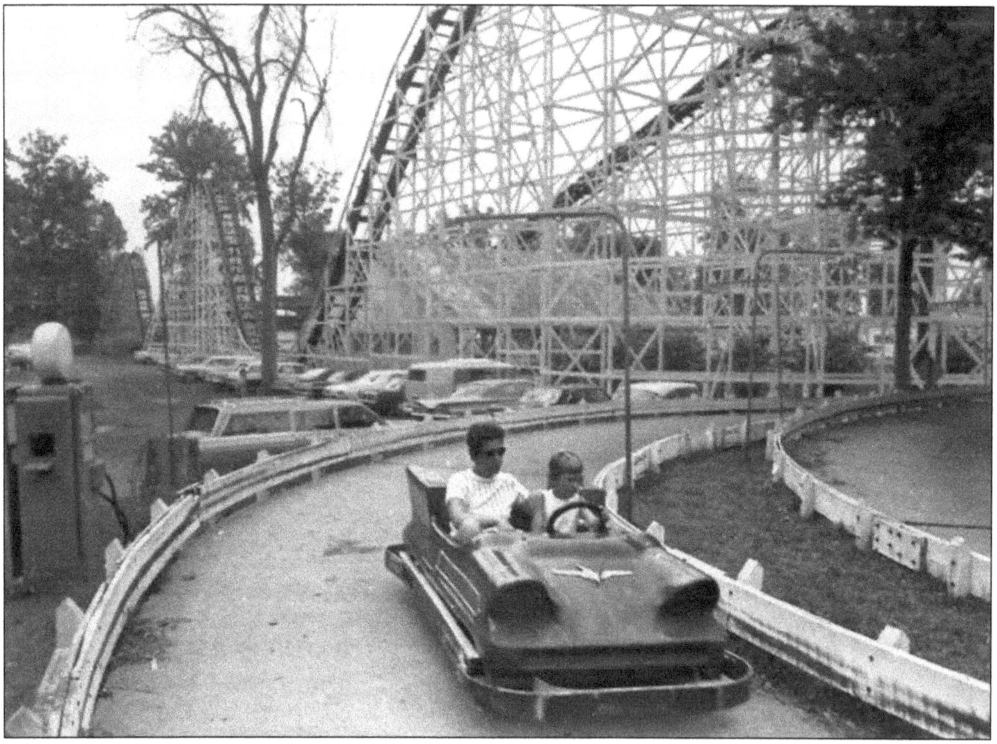

The roller coaster, the Cyclone, was built from wood and required ongoing maintenance. The ride was deemed unsafe in the 1960s. (Courtesy of the Ingham County Parks Department.)

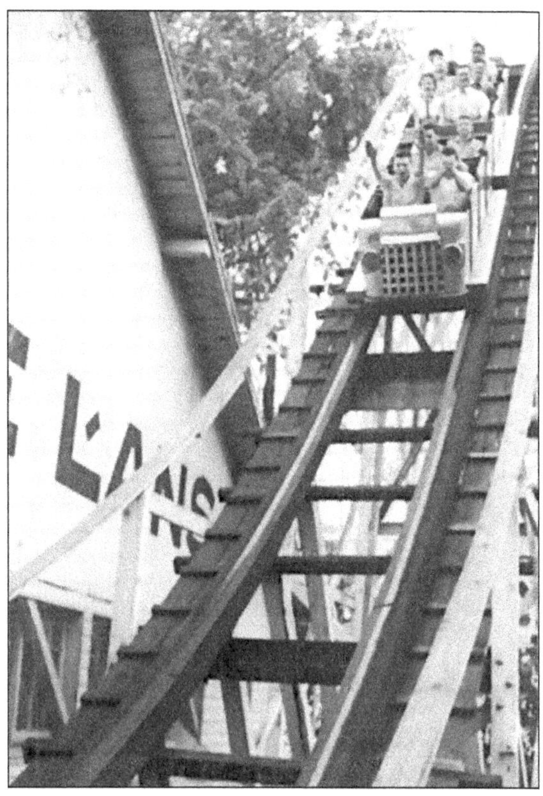

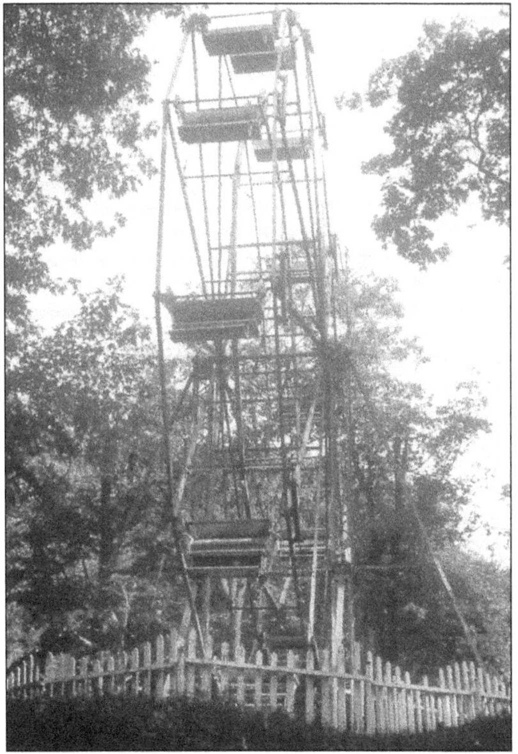

A subsequent ride added to the park was the open-seat-style Ferris wheel. The bench-style seat could fit two to three riders held in place with a bar snapped along the front of the seat. Many local residents recalled riding the wheel and having the operator stop their car at the top. Lansing resident George Petroff confessed that when he was a boy, he was stuck at the top and "upchucked" onto the riders below. Then he "pointed to [his] sister to make them think she did it." (Courtesy of the Ingham County Parks Department.)

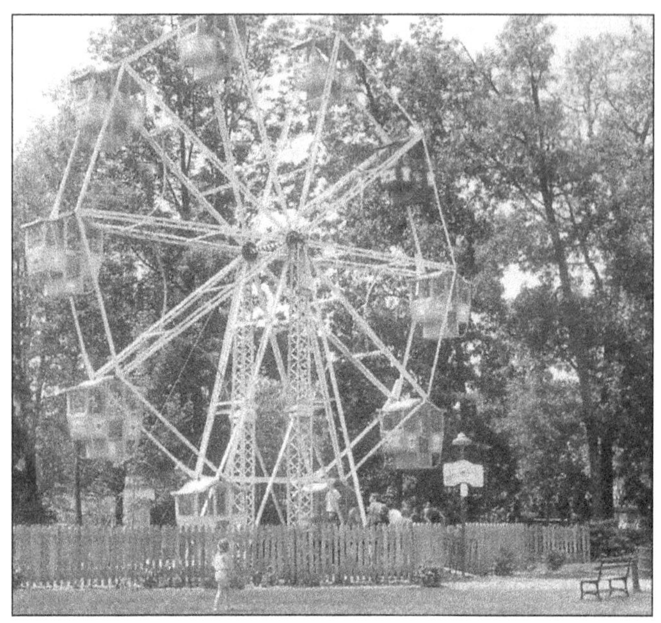

Another ride used in the final years of the park was similar to the Ferris wheel. The Rock-O-Plane–style wheel used enclosed cages, which could rock and roll back and forth as the ride turned. Inside the cage was a control available to the riders, which could lock the cage so it would not rock (for the more timid) or could be manipulated to lock the control when the cage was upside down at the top of the ride. The ride at Lake Lansing was brought to the park in 1963 by Tom and Kimberly Wolf. (Courtesy of the Ingham County Parks Department.)

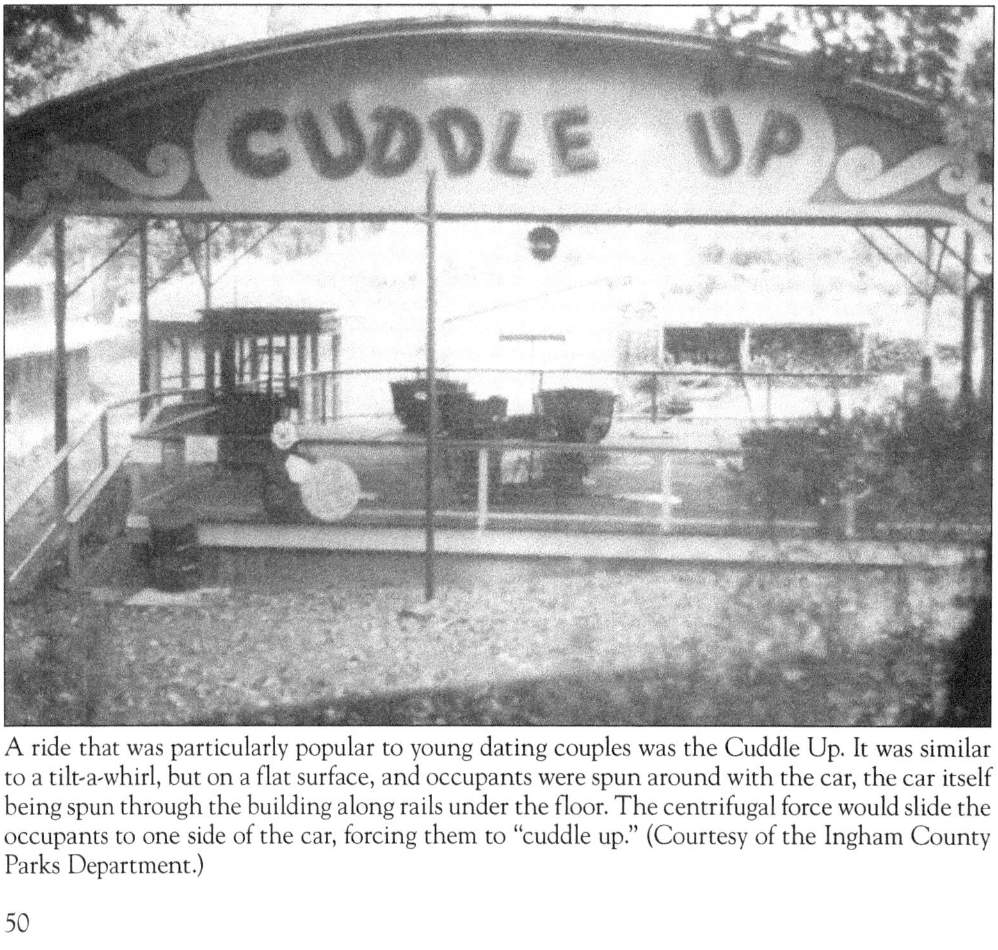

A ride that was particularly popular to young dating couples was the Cuddle Up. It was similar to a tilt-a-whirl, but on a flat surface, and occupants were spun around with the car, the car itself being spun through the building along rails under the floor. The centrifugal force would slide the occupants to one side of the car, forcing them to "cuddle up." (Courtesy of the Ingham County Parks Department.)

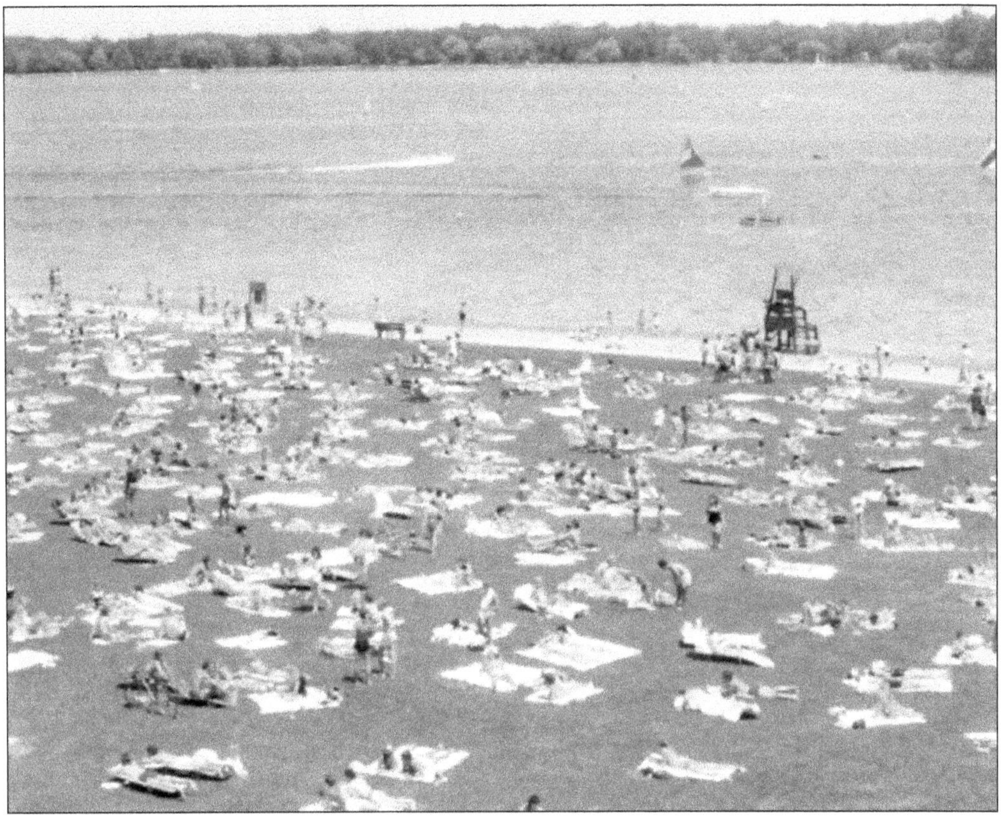

The above photograph was taken from the top of the Ferris wheel in the final days of the amusement park. Even though the condition of the rides was questionable, visitors still flocked to the large, flat beach to take advantage of the sun and water. (Courtesy of the Ingham County Parks Department.)

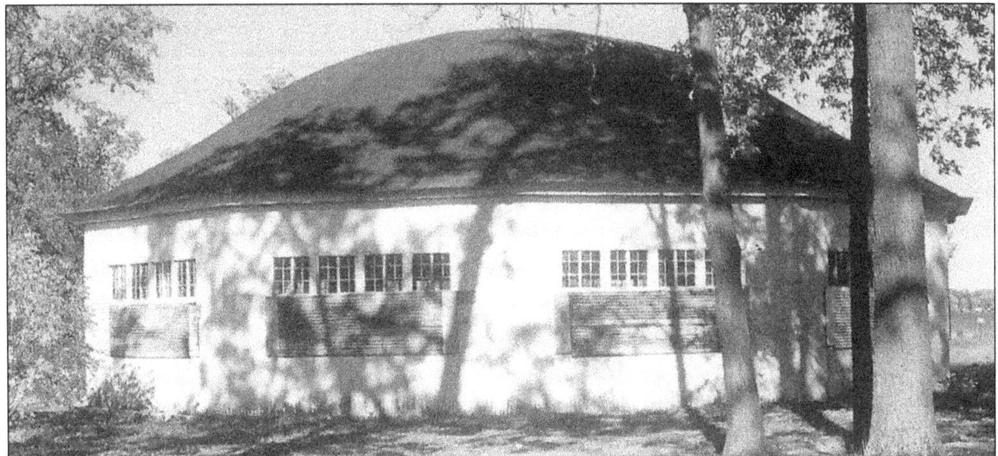

The amusement park finally closed in the 1970s as attendance dropped and the age of the rides discouraged use. The only structure still standing today is the old carousel building, which was erected to house and protect the beautiful carousel. In July 1974, Ingham County purchased the property to develop into a county park that is still in use today as Lake Lansing Park South. (Courtesy of the Ingham County Parks Department.)

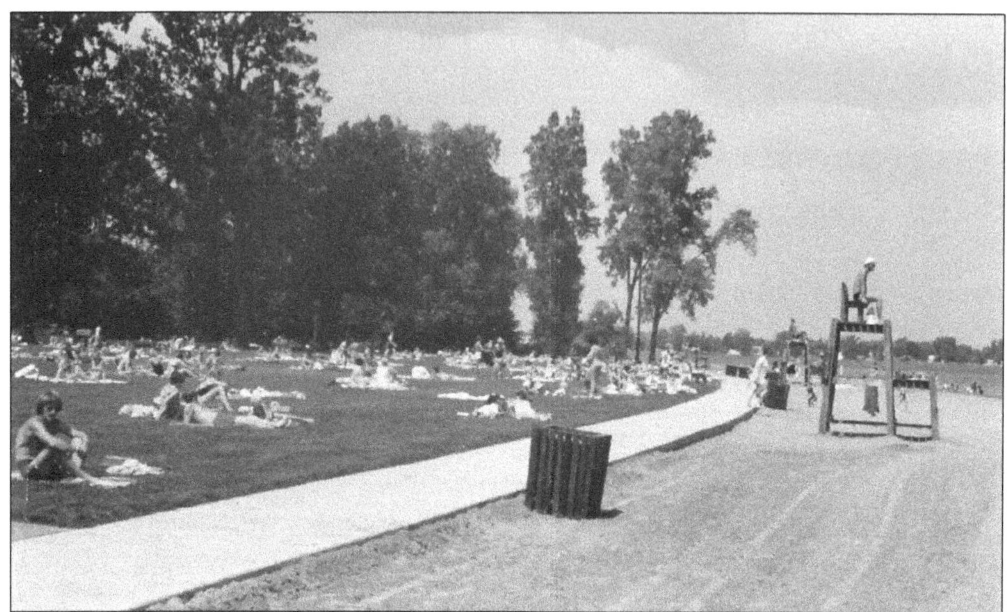

After the park was purchased by Ingham County in 1974, outbuildings and covered picnic areas were constructed to attract visitors. The beach on the southwest corner of the lake was groomed, and lifeguards were employed to ensure safety for swimmers. The park continues to draw visitors during the summer to escape the heat from the city. (Courtesy of Ingham County Parks Department.)

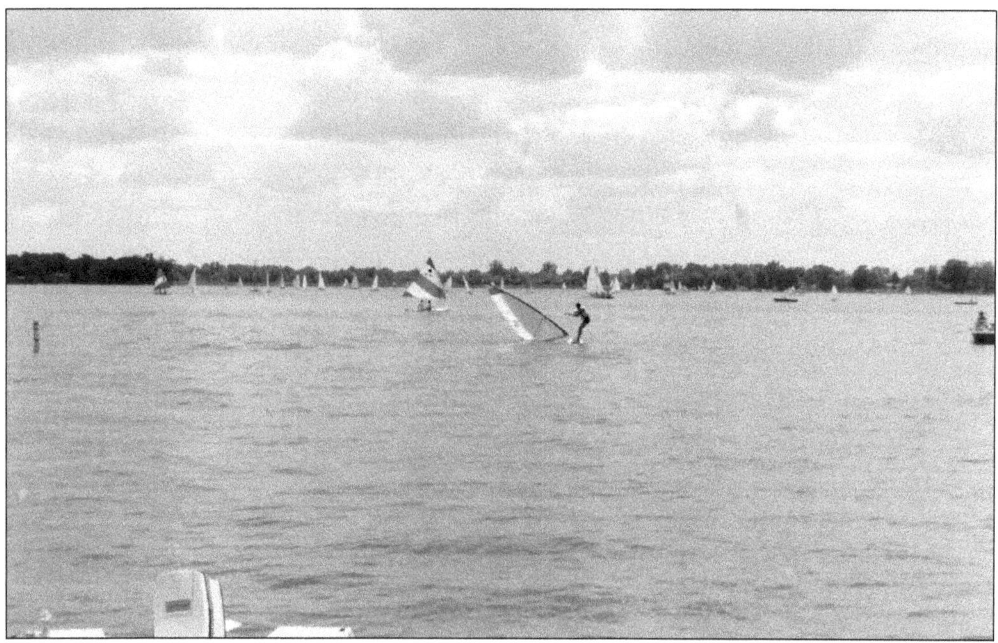

Ingham County also purchased the property on the north side of the lake that had formerly housed the Pine Lake House, then Palmer Park, and finally, the Dell's Ballroom. A long-term development plan begun in 1974 at Lake Lansing Park South continued until Park North was completed in 1986. The park contains a boat launch, picnic grounds, horseshoe pits, a softball diamond, and volleyball and basketball courts. (Courtesy of the Ingham County Parks Department.)

Lansing Lake Park North covers 410 acres of land and contains 5.3 miles of hiking trails. The trails travel mostly through wooded areas. However, much like the old Devil's Lane to the old Hickory Island, a few wooden boardwalks cross marshy areas in the park. (Courtesy of the Ingham County Parks Department.)

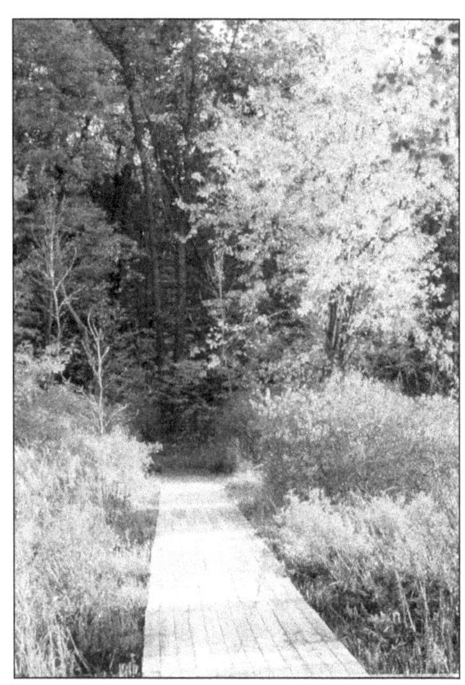

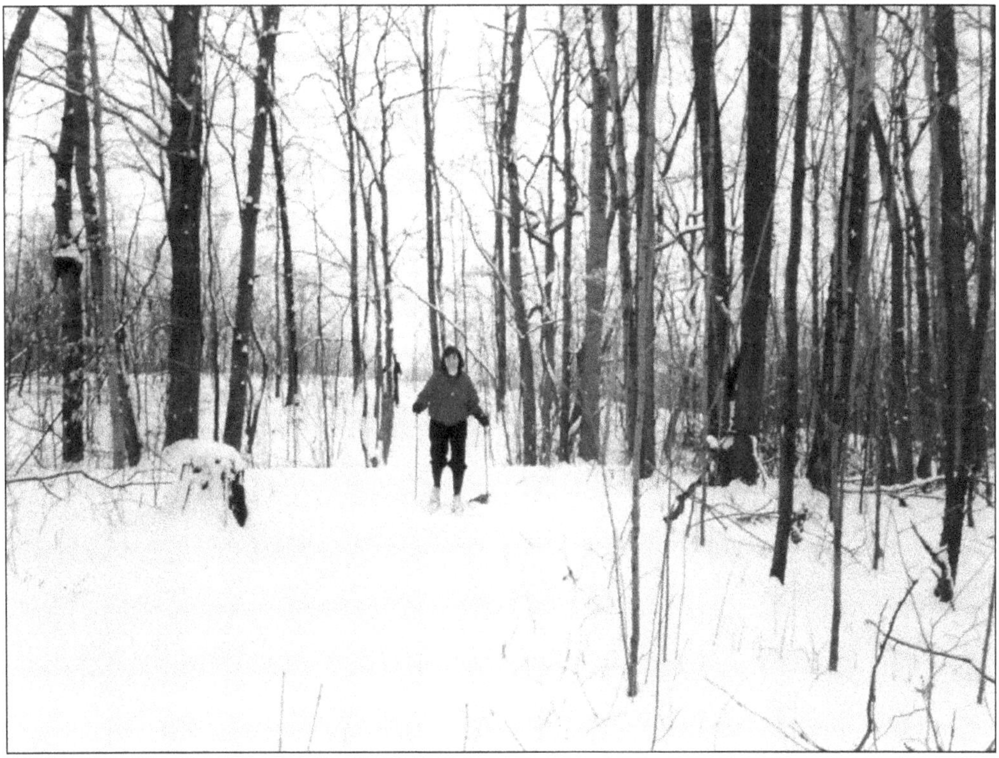

The trails in Lake Lansing Park North are also open for use during the winter for cross-country skiing. In recent years Ingham County has expanded the size of the park with the efforts and support of local residents to include a total of 530 acres. The expansion protects the area from future development. (Courtesy of the Ingham County Parks Department.)

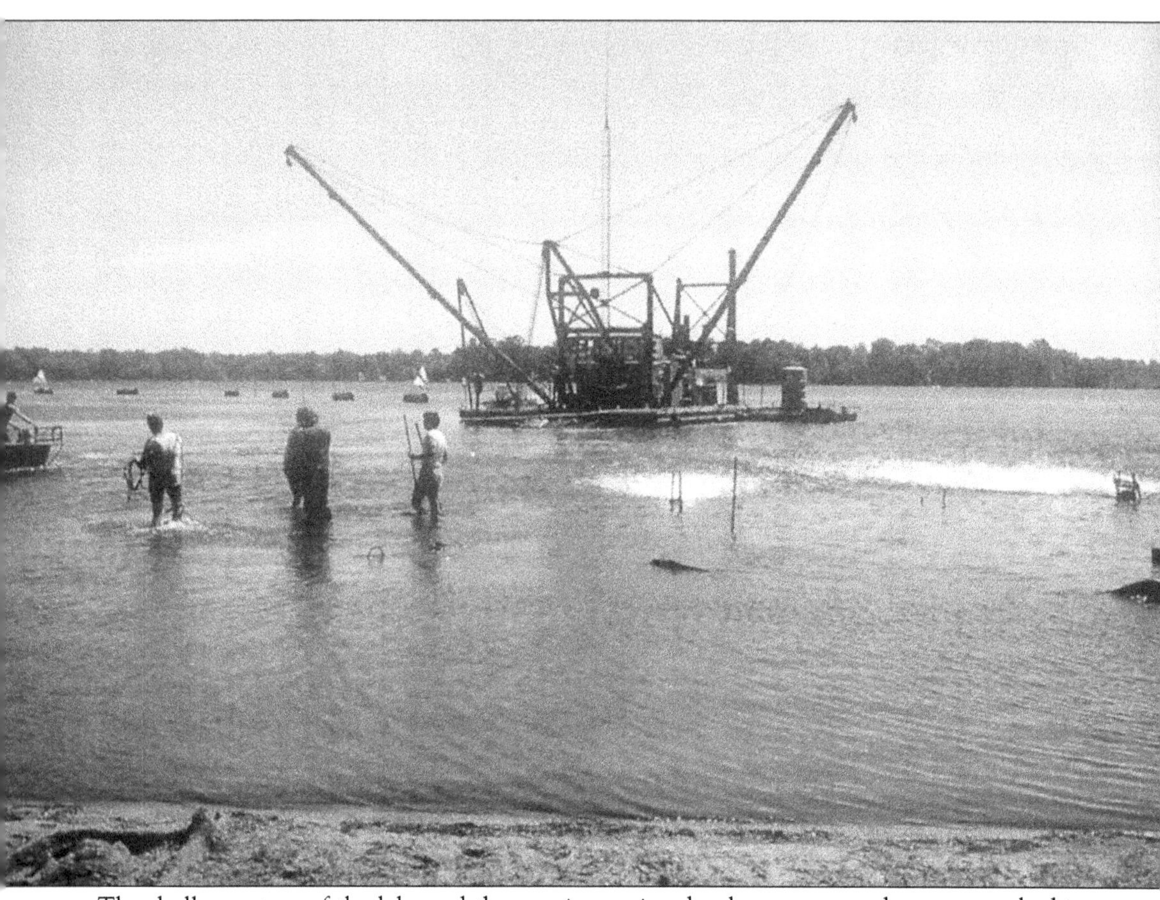

The shallow nature of the lake and the ever-increasing development over the years resulted in periodic health problems as the growth of weeds and algae were accelerated by septic systems. From 1978 to 1983, the Ingham County Board of Commissioners waged a campaign to clean up the lake by dredging the bottom to remove the weeds and algae. Again, in 1994, the commission and the Ingham County Health Department issued a comprehensive report on the quality of the water in the lake and identified potential polluters. The health of the lake continues to be monitored, with special attention during the summer when weed and algae growth coincide with increased use by swimmers and boaters. (Courtesy of the Ingham County Parks Department.)

Five

Early Pioneers on the River

The area along the river to the south of Pine Lake was used by Native Americans to travel to campsites and planting areas throughout the area. A summer campsite was located along the river in current-day Okemos. White settlers did not come to the area until 1839, three years after the Marshall brothers settled on the west side of Pine Lake. Sanford Marsh was the first pioneer to purchase land, followed shortly by Joseph Kilbourne, who purchased property for his brother-in-law Freeman Bray. The Marsh property was on the south side of the river, the Bray property on the north side.

After the Federal Land Act of 1820 reduced the price of land per acre to $1.25, speculation soared, and investors rushed to the territory to purchase the most attractive parcels. Bray and his wife, Carolyn, hoping to benefit from the resulting "Michigan Fever," platted out the southeast corner of their acreage to sell to other settlers interested in the area. The little village was named Hamilton in honor of Alexander Hamilton. Early maps also identify the site as the Sanford Post Office in honor of Sanford Marsh.

The river, named Red Cedar by the settlers, had two natural bends that provided an excellent spot for a millrace. A dam was built at the easternmost bend to funnel some of the water flow through the millrace, and a mill was constructed at the site. Eventually, three sawmills were built along the race: the Davis mill and broom factory, the Bray mill and cabinet shop, and the Walker sawmill and gristmill.

The state capital was moved in 1847 from Detroit to Lansing, and the road through the center of the village of Hamilton became well traveled by people who had business with state government. The east-west route was named Detroit Road, and hotels were built along it to accommodate overnight guests. All the village buildings were made from hewn trees and constructed in the log-cabin style until Melzor Turner erected the first frame building in 1849.

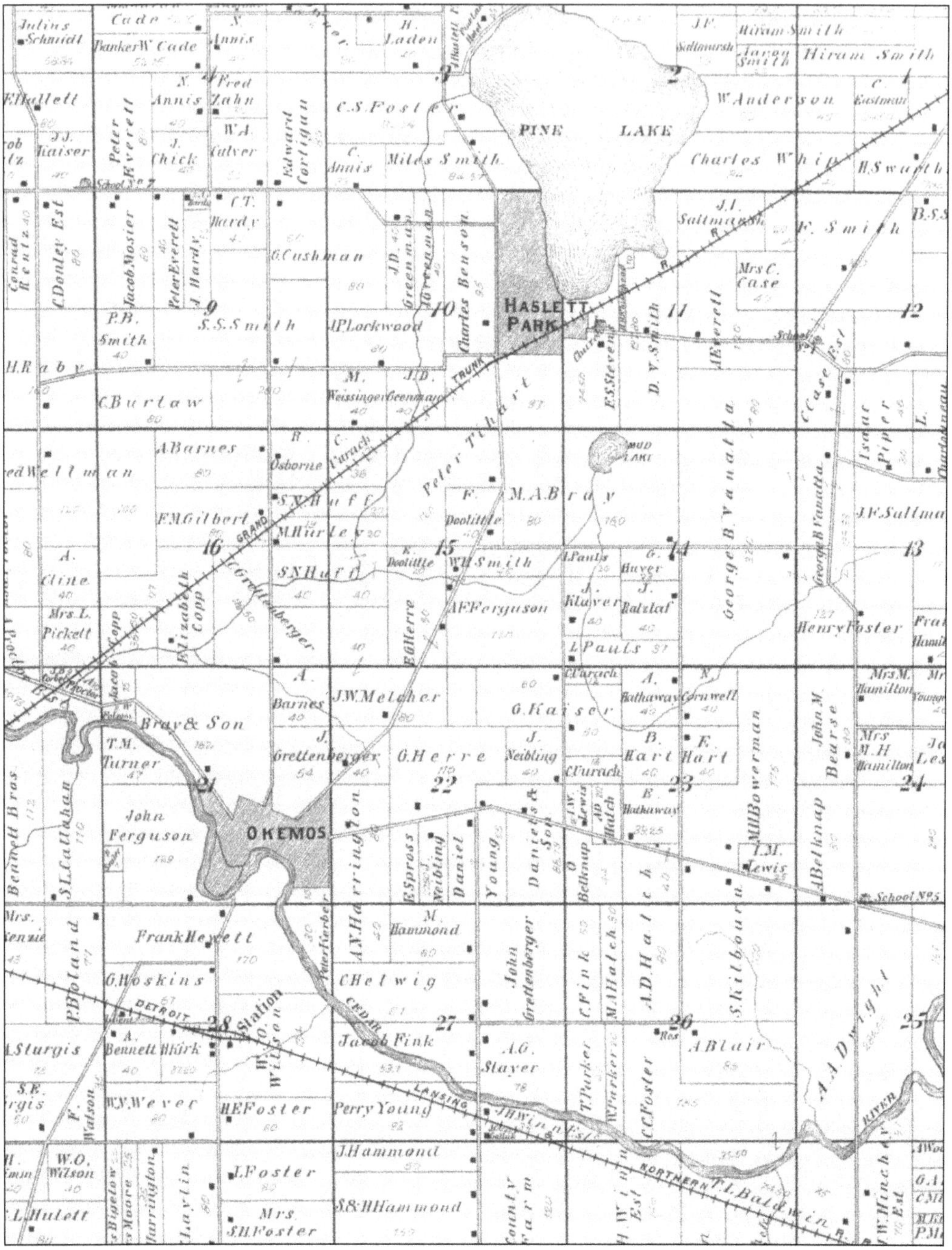

Waterways were the original highways of the wilderness, facilitating travel throughout the area. Settlement in the lower half of Meridian Township first developed along this water highway. The river was used by the Native Americans in the area, including the Ojibwe and Odawa followers of Chief Okemos. The double bend southwest of Pine Lake was used by the chief as a regular summer campsite and was referred to by the chief as "Okemos Town."

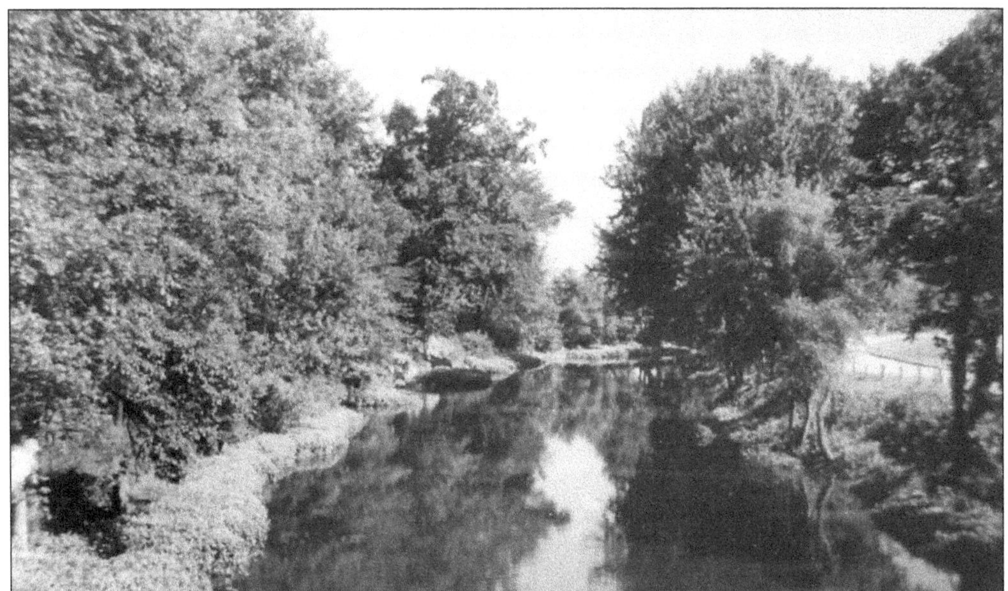

The waterway became known by the early pioneers as the Red Cedar River, reflecting the primary type of tree planted on both banks. It connects to a major east-west river in Michigan's Lower Peninsula, the Grand River. Once on the Grand River, a boater can travel all the way to Lake Michigan.

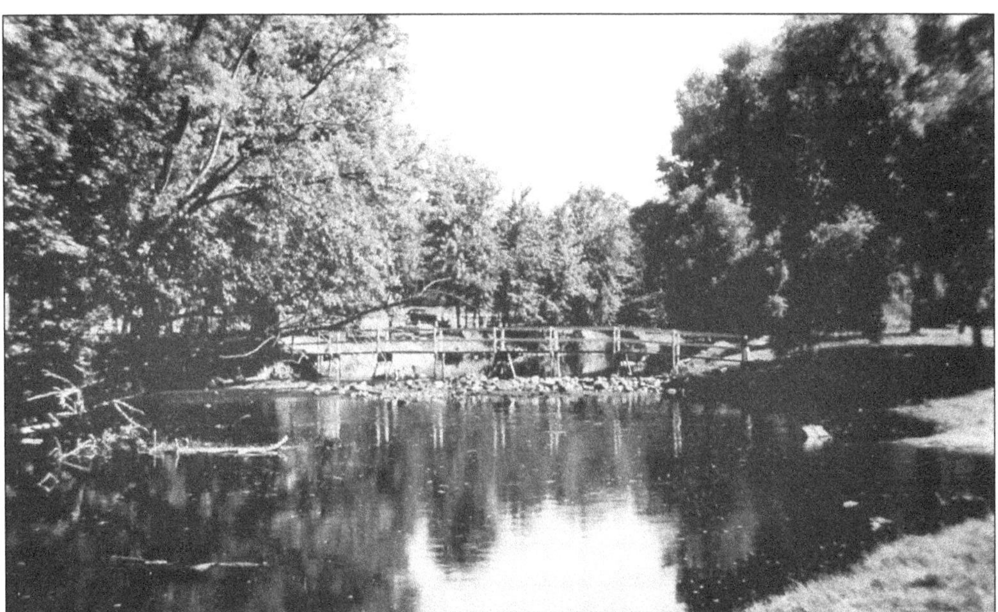

The lowlands on the west side of present-day Okemos Road had shallow banks that allowed easy access to the land. The first white pioneer to the area, Sanford Marsh, purchased land in the 1830s on the south bank of the river at that site.

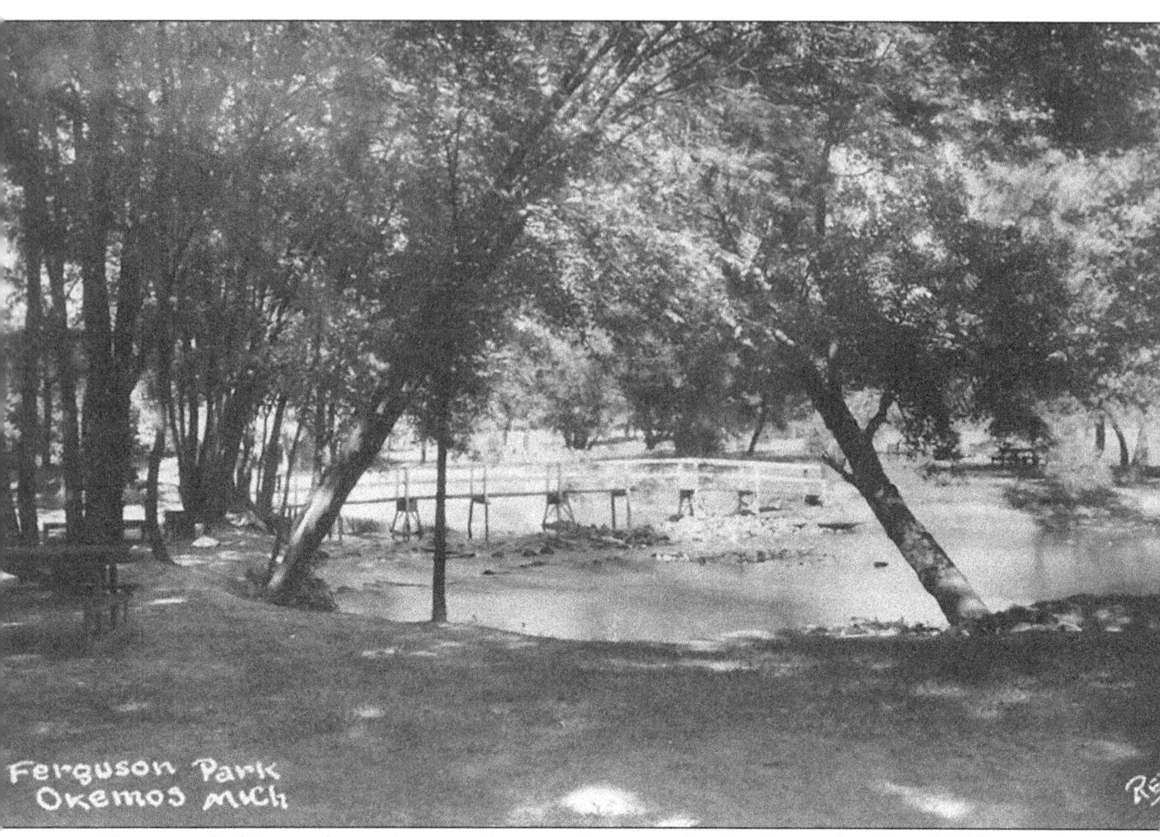

The second white settler to the area, Freeman Bray, sent his brother-in-law Joseph Kilbourne to the area to purchase prime property for his use. The property was on the north side of the Red Cedar River, across the water from Sanford Marsh. The bend in the river at that point provided an ideal location for a millrace to generate power for a mill. Remnants of the millrace can be seen from Ferguson Park on the east side of Okemos Road.

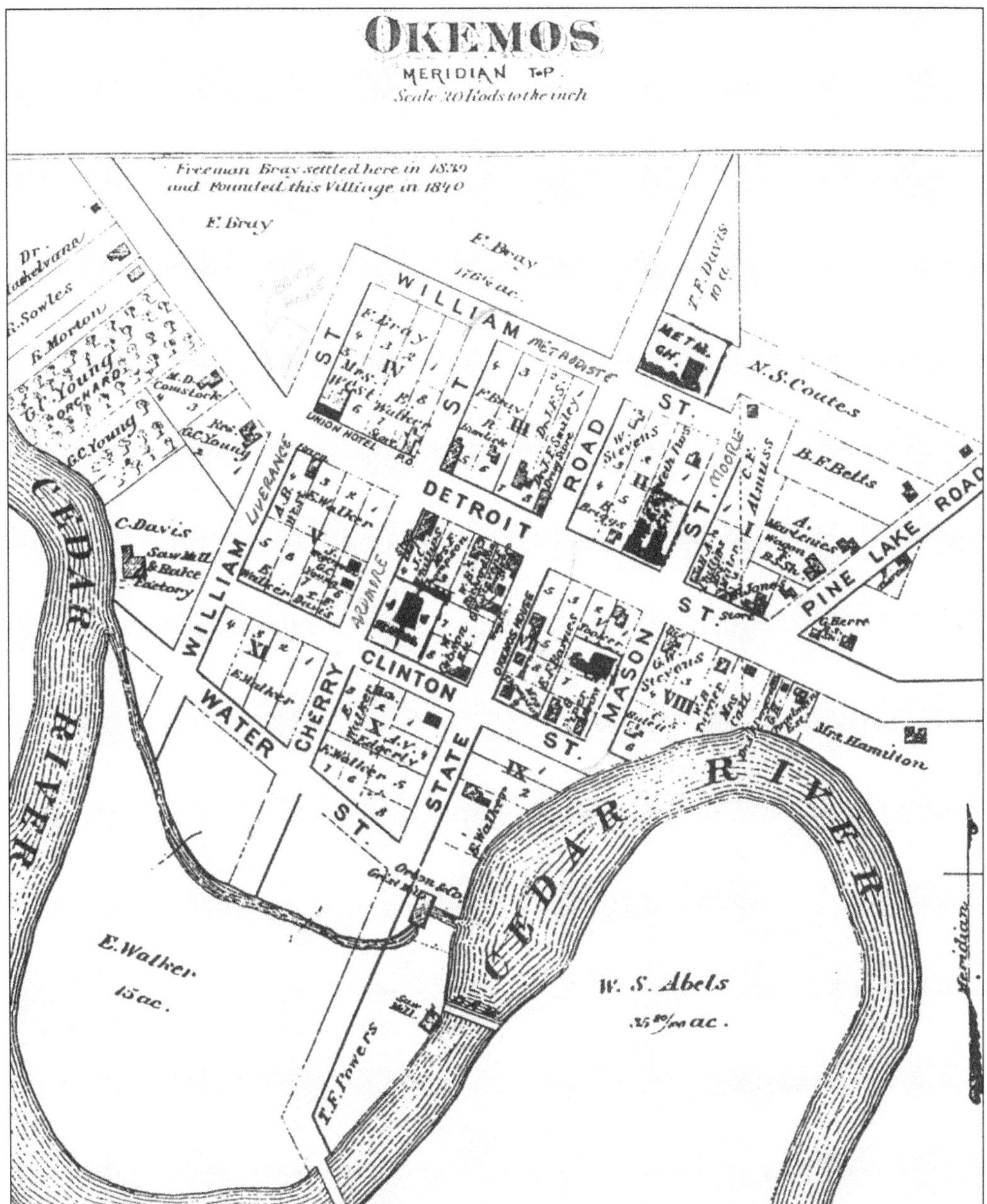

Bray settled on this property with his wife, Carolyn, and began clearing the land for farming. They platted out the southeastern corner of their acreage for sale to other families interested in taking advantage of the cheap land prices in Michigan. The above map shows where the millrace was cut in the lowlands between the two bends to allow for mills.

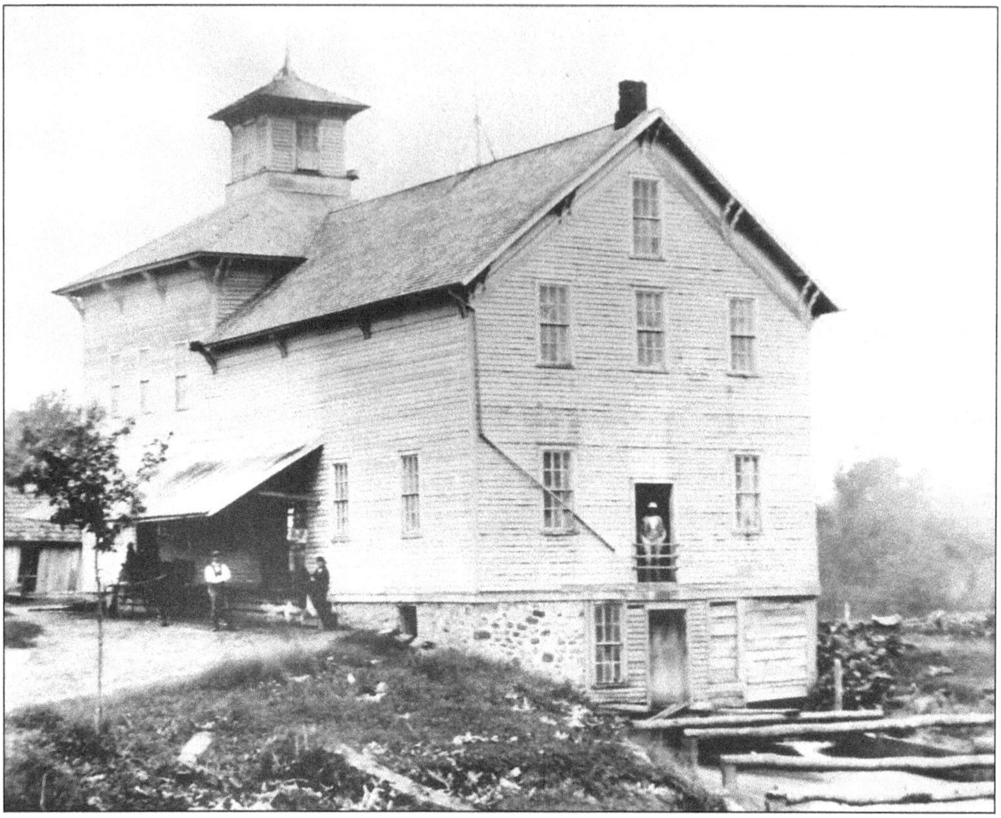

Bray built the original dam in 1843 and constructed his mill at the site shortly after. Ebenezer Walker purchased property from Bray and built a new mill in 1849, which burned down in 1863. The above mill was built in 1866 by Amos Morton. Charles Burtraw purchased the mill from Morton and, with his son William, operated it from 1879 to 1891.

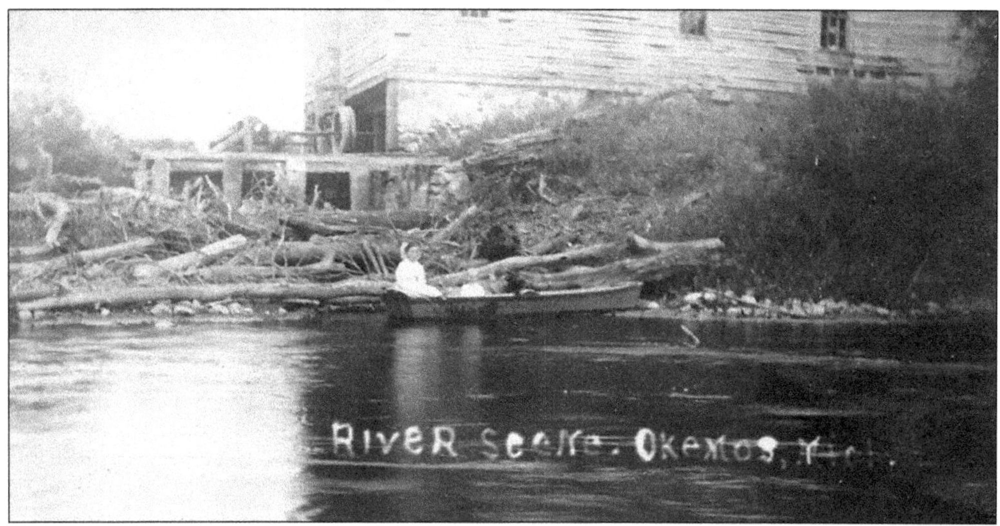

The river near the mill area proved a popular spot for boating during the warm summer months. The waters to the south of the dam were still and provided for a safe and pleasant waterway near low-lying banks.

Six

From Hamilton to Okemos

When the pioneers reached this area, they found members of native tribes already living here seasonally. Natives migrated throughout the year to take advantage of the best opportunities for hunting, fishing, and harvesting. One of their campsites was located along the river bends in the village of Hamilton.

The leader of these followers was Chief Okemos, a man who distinguished himself in battle several times and almost lost his life at the Battle of Sandusky in 1813. After recovering and fighting for the last time at the Battle of the Thames in October 1813, Okemos and others travelled to Fort Wayne in the spring of 1814 to sue for peace.

When Freeman Bray moved to the area in 1839, he began trading with Okemos and his band for furs. Bray was also known for plowing part of his land and allowing the natives to plant corn. Okemos became a frequent visitor to the Bray house until the mid-1840s, when authorities placed natives on reservations. Okemos and his family were moved to a reservation west of the capital nearby present-day Portland, Michigan. Even so, Okemos was known to travel back to Hamilton throughout the year and returned to his old camping ground each year to bring food for the dead in the burial ground.

Other village families developed friendly relations with Okemos, including the Turner family, who allowed Okemos to store supplies in their cellar when he went to Canada for his annual payments. The old chief always returned to the area and called Hamilton "Okemos City." He died in 1858, and the residents of Hamilton petitioned the Michigan Legislature to formally change the name of the village. On February 12, 1859, the legislature officially renamed the village "Okemos" in honor of Chief Okemos of the Chippewa.

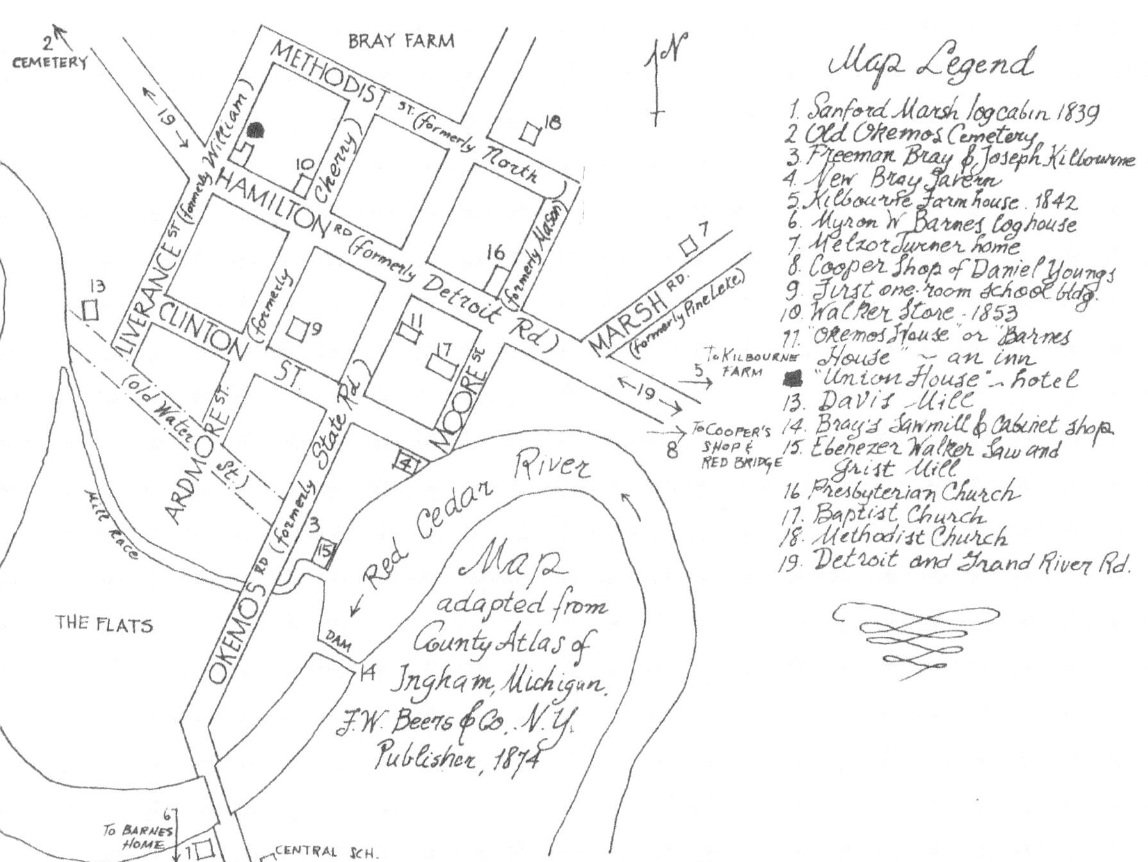

The little village of Hamilton continued to grow and, by 1853, boasted a minimum of eight businesses at the crossroads of State Road and Detroit Road. The local families continued to build private residences along the two routes and had numerous interactions with the local natives of the area, specifically Chief Okemos and his followers. Some of the business sites were located on property traditionally used by Okemos. The chief even referred to the camping area along the river as "Okemos City."

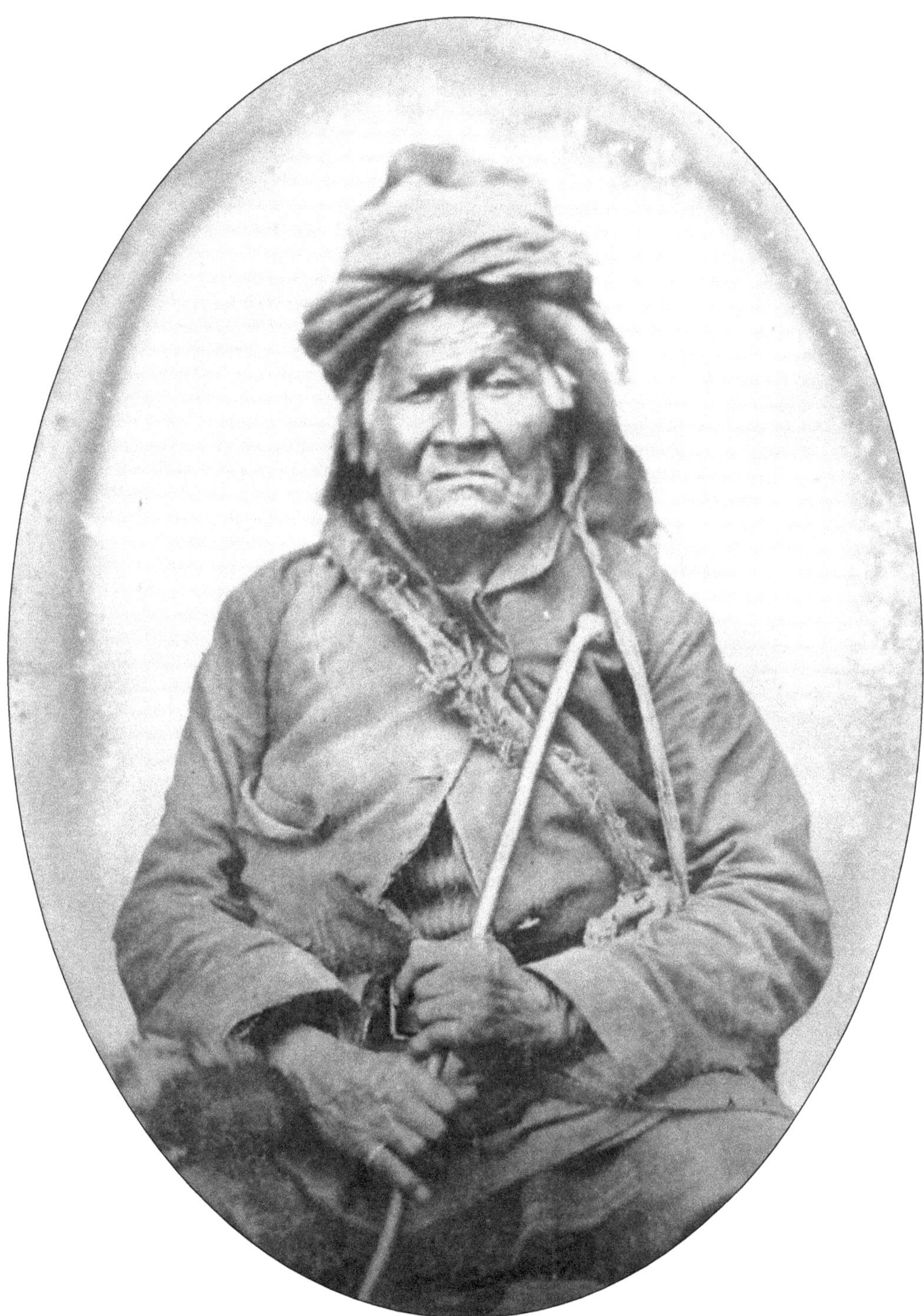

Chief Okemos of the Chippewa was highly respected by his followers and held in high regard by the white settlers. After his death in 1858, the village of Hamilton was renamed Okemos at the request of the citizens. His memory and bravery continue to be honored today.

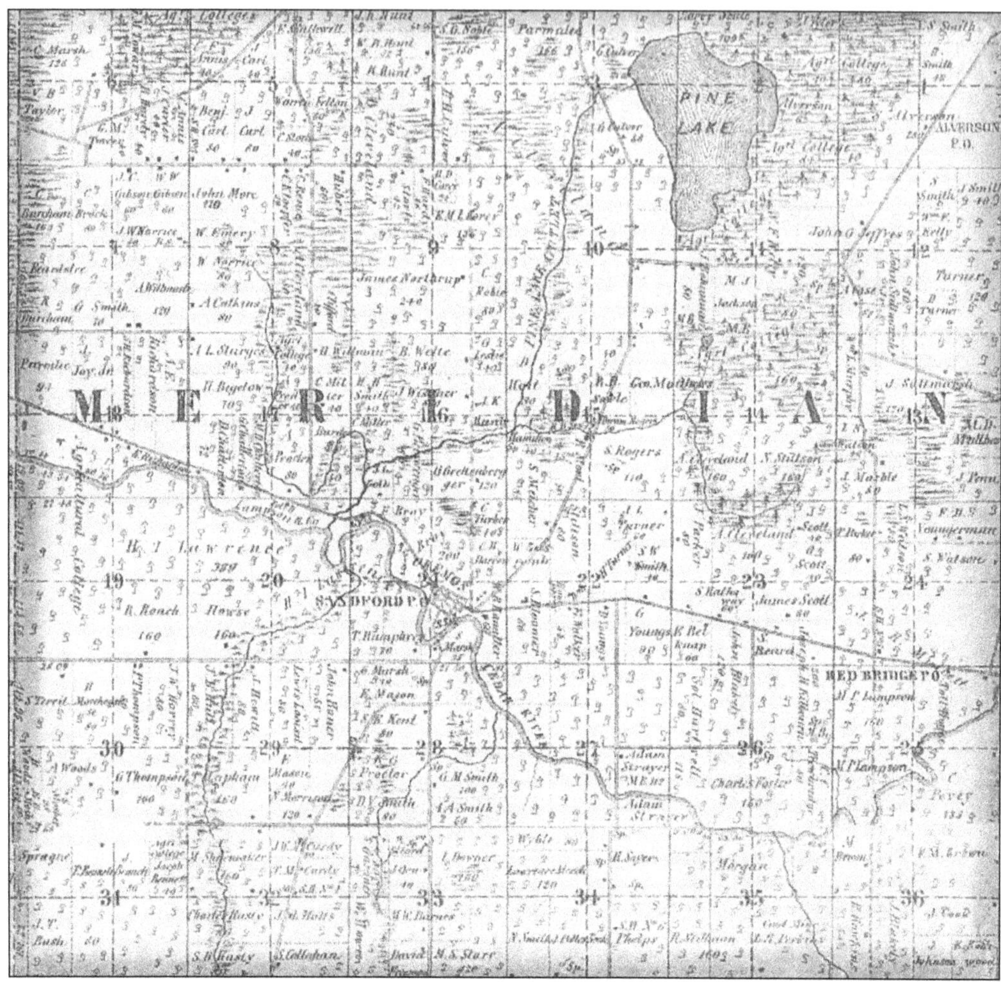

The above topographical map was printed in 1859, one year after the village was officially named Okemos. The map clearly shows the new village name in the center, along with "Sanford P.O." The post office for the area continued to be named after the first white settler to the river community until May 1862, when it was also officially renamed Okemos.

Seven

The Okemos Community Grows

The location of the village of Okemos just six miles to the east of the state capital along the Detroit Road put the community in an ideal location to serve travelers. Transportation in the 1840s was slow and tedious as drivers needed to steer their horses around ruts and avoid muddy dirt. Travel along the dirt roads from Lansing to Detroit could take anywhere from three to five days, depending on the weather conditions. As a result, the Michigan Legislature passed the General Plank Road Act in 1848 to standardize the construction and toll rates of wooden roads. The Lansing-Howell Plank Road was chartered in 1850. The portion from Lansing to the river community of Hamilton was completed in June 1851 and extended to Howell in Livingston County by 1853. Once completed, the road reduced travel time from Lansing to Detroit from three to five days down to 10 to 12 hours.

The Barnes House and the Union House served as hotels along the road. Performers stayed in the hotels and performed in the second floor of the nearby Heathmann-Herre brick store. Educational and social improvements were made in the mid-1800s. Churches were built in the village, rural one-room schools were erected throughout the district, and land along Dobie Road was set aside for the county poor farm to serve the poor, infirm, and mentally ill.

By 1874, there were three churches, three mills, two hotels, one tavern, and one store in the village. Eight rural schools were built to serve children in the greater Okemos area. Until the 1920s, there was no high school in Okemos, and students who wanted a higher education had to travel to Mason to the south or East Lansing to the west to attend the higher grades. The first consolidated school in Okemos was opened in 1923 and offered classes to intermediate and high school students.

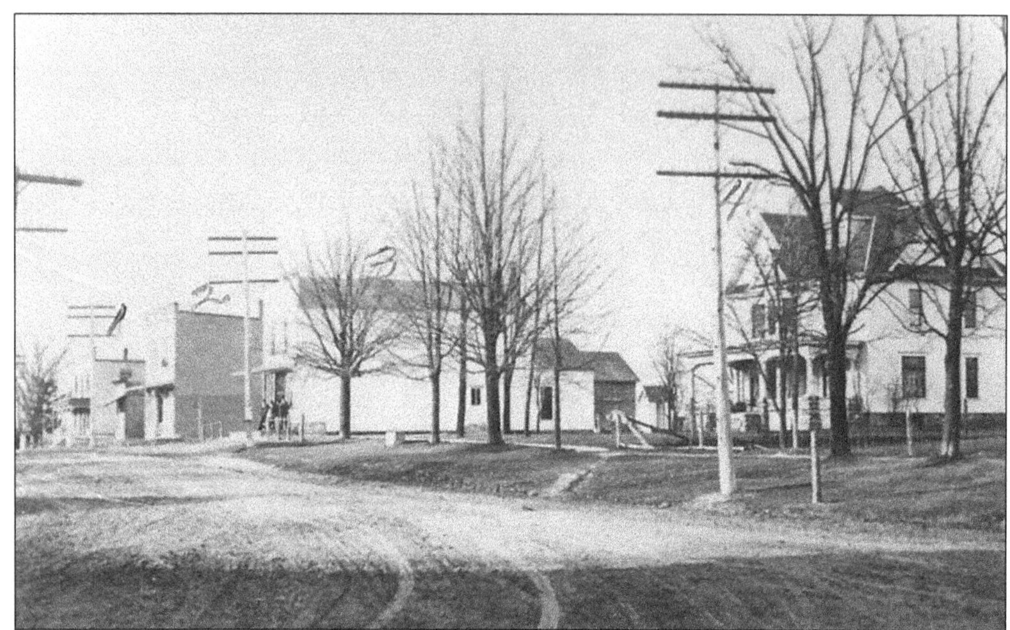

The four corners were the primary location for development within the village of Okemos. The above photograph shows former Detroit Road, now Hamilton Road, looking to the west toward the city of Lansing. The first building is the only mansion built in Okemos and was constructed by John Orin Grettenberger, the owner of the general store immediately to the west of the property. Past the store is the brick meeting hall for the Independent Order of Odd Fellows (IOOF), a "friendly society" organized to provide community service for members in need.

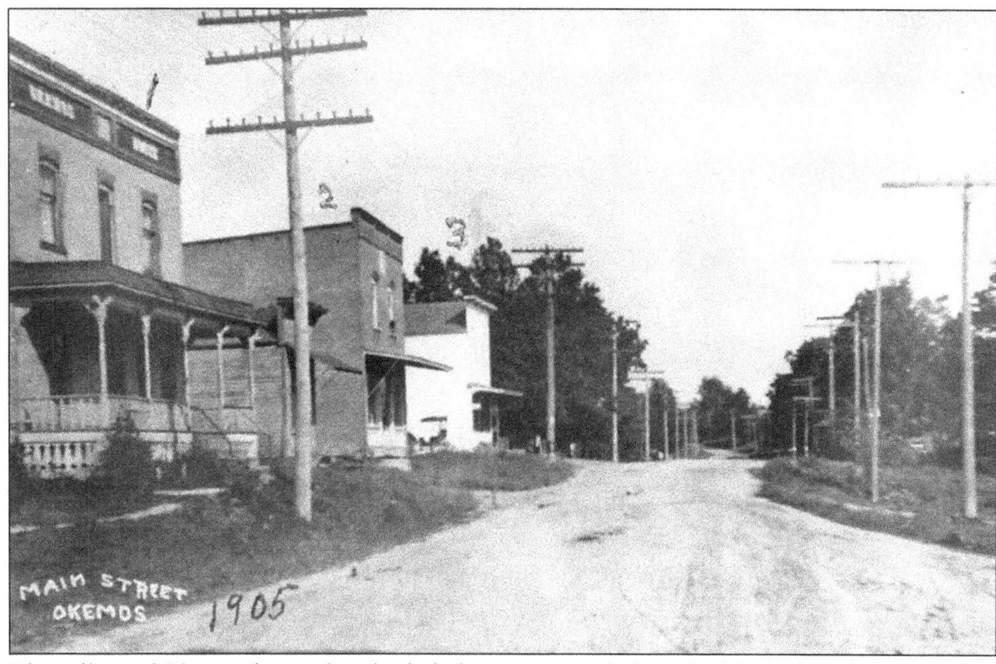

The village of Okemos boasted multiple lodging sites, including the Union Hotel, identified as "1" in the above photograph. Other businesses located along the four corners to serve travelers were the Okemos House and the Bray Tavern.

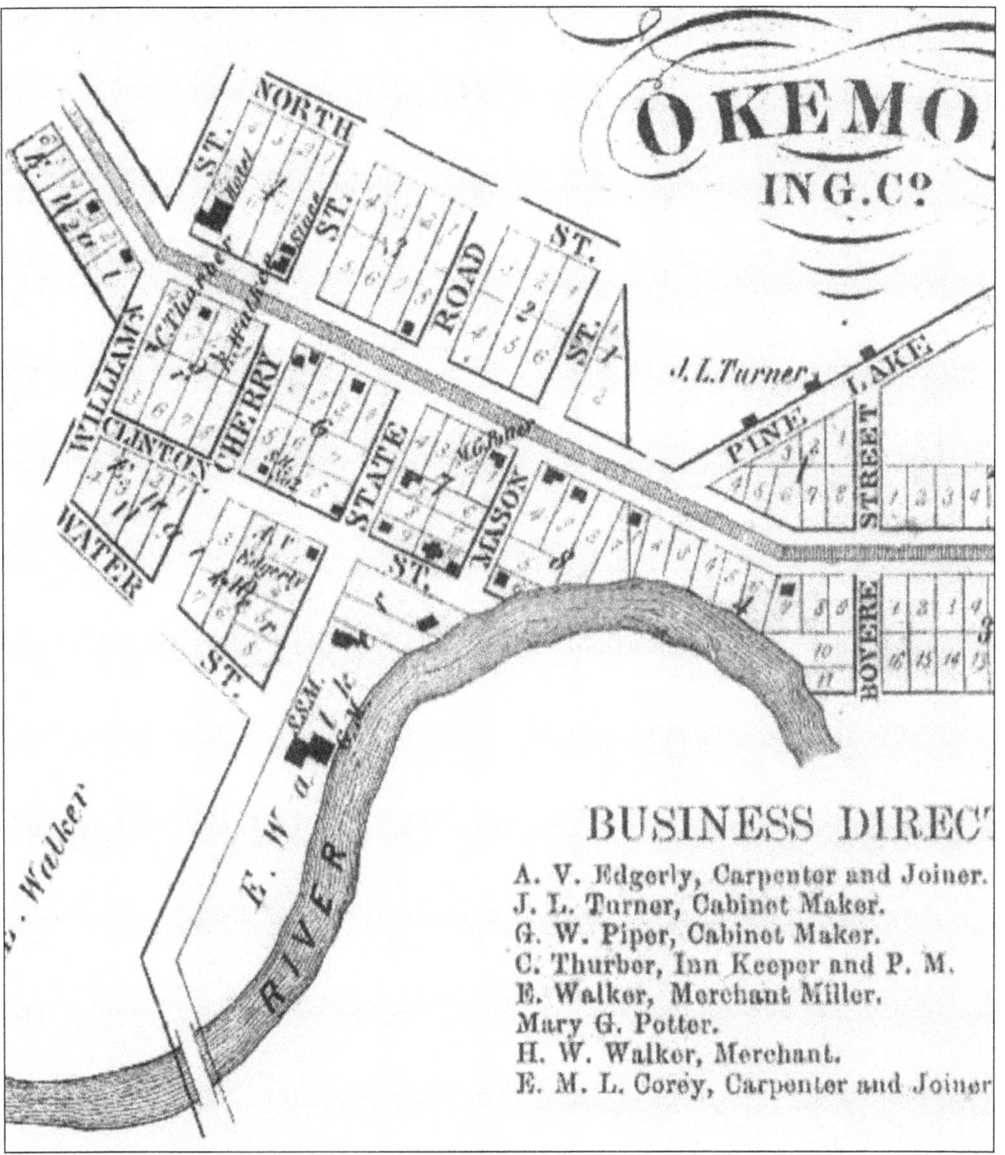

One of the reasons for the need for hospitality in Okemos was the construction of a modern wooden road through the heart of the village. The plank road was built to speed travel between the capital city of Lansing to the original capital site of Detroit. The trip decreased from three to six days along rutted or muddy dirt roads down to 10 to 12 hours along the plank road.

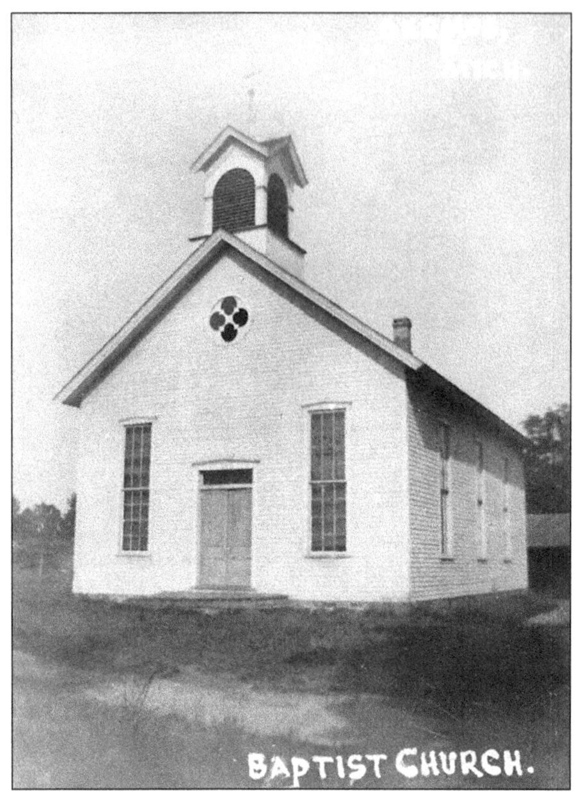

The 1840s saw a number of residents forming their own worship groups. The worshippers originally met in members' homes until a school was built large enough to hold the congregation. The Baptist church was built on Moore Street south of the main road, now named Hamilton Road. The original building remains on Moore Street; it was enlarged and is used for apartments.

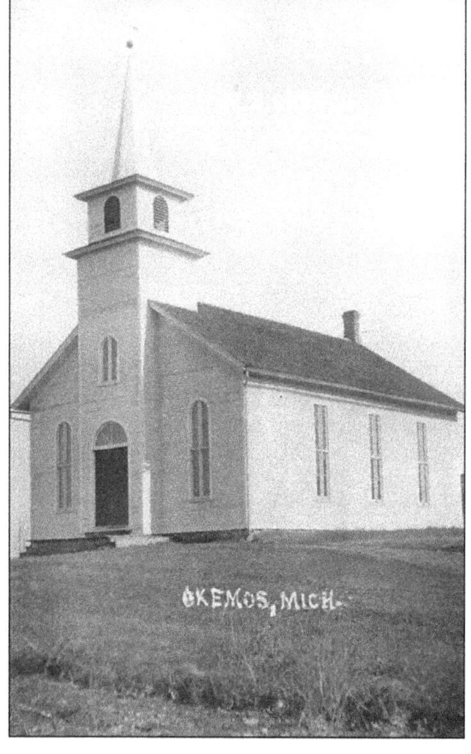

The Methodist Society formed as early as 1840 and also met in members' homes until 1849, when the school was built. The group continued to save and purchased property at the corner of Okemos Road and Methodist Street to construct its own worship site. Even so, the full amount needed to build the church was not available until 1869, and the new Methodist Episcopal church was erected on the site in 1870. The congregation outgrew the structure in the 20th century, and the building was razed in 1969 to make way for a new, larger facility. A replica of the building currently sits in the Meridian Historical Village in Central Park, Okemos.

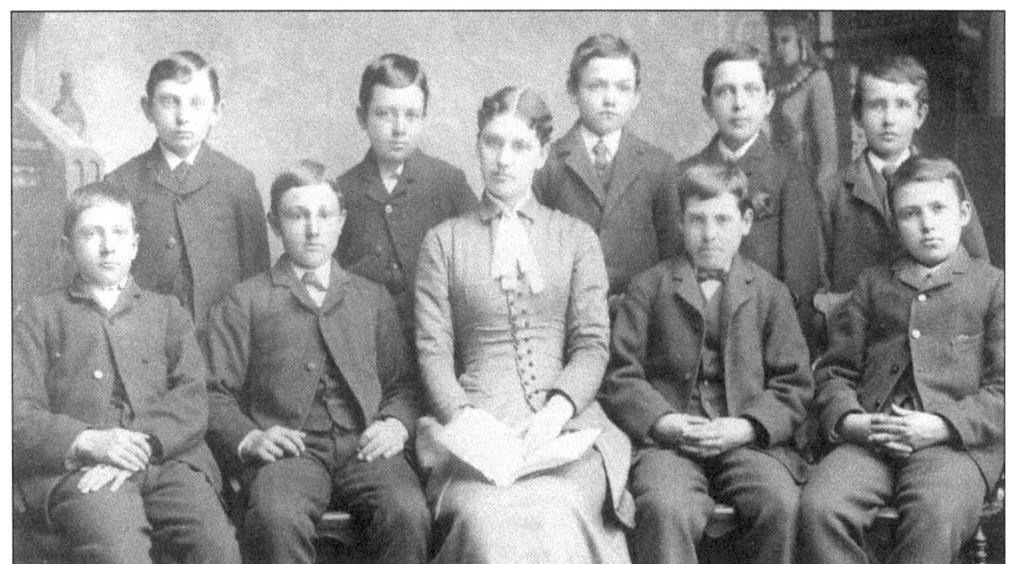

Pictured above around the late 1880s or early 1890s is the Sunday school class of the Methodist Episcopal church. The class met in the second-floor loft next to the belfry. The teacher was Pauline Herre. The students are, from left to right, (first row) Walter Allen, Freeman Washburn, Clyde Washburn, and Martin McNeal; (second row) Vern Proctor, Charley Grettenberger, Jake Kaiser, Dewey Slimmer, and Henry Wellman.

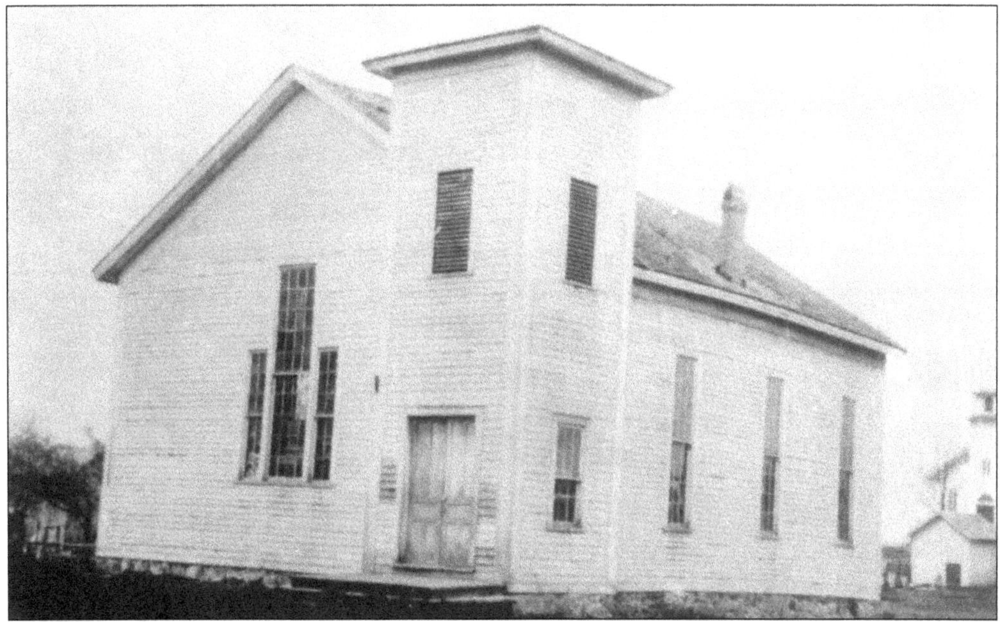

One religious society did not fare well within the village of Okemos and, despite its efforts, was not able to establish a long-term presence. The worshippers of the Presbyterian faith built a church at the corner of Moore Street and Hamilton Road on the northwest corner across from the current-day Wood's Marathon station. After the Presbyterian congregation moved from the location, the village acquired the property and used the building for the town hall. Numerous meetings and gatherings were held in and around the building for many years, including Independence Day celebrations and military drills.

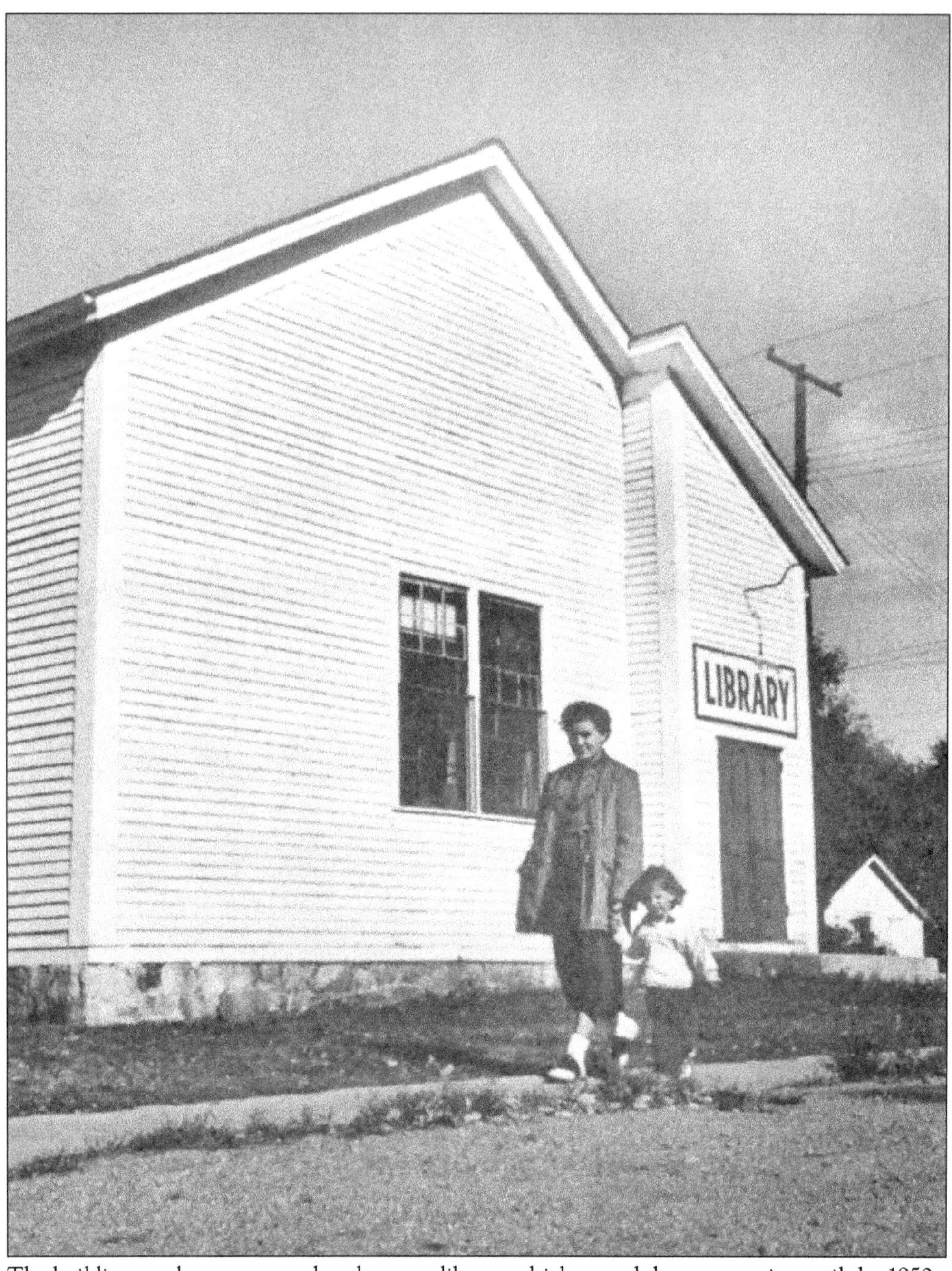

The building was later converted to the town library, which served the community until the 1950s. It was torn down in the 1960s, and a small group of local shops now inhabits the space.

Education was an important, basic need for the pioneers, and space was used where available. The first local school was convened in 1844 in a cooper shop owned by Daniel Young. The school was located east of Okemos along Hamilton Road, and Samantha Worden taught the children for $1 a week. A minimum of five children needed to be enrolled for the school to have legal status; two of the five children were enrolled at age three in order to meet the requirement.

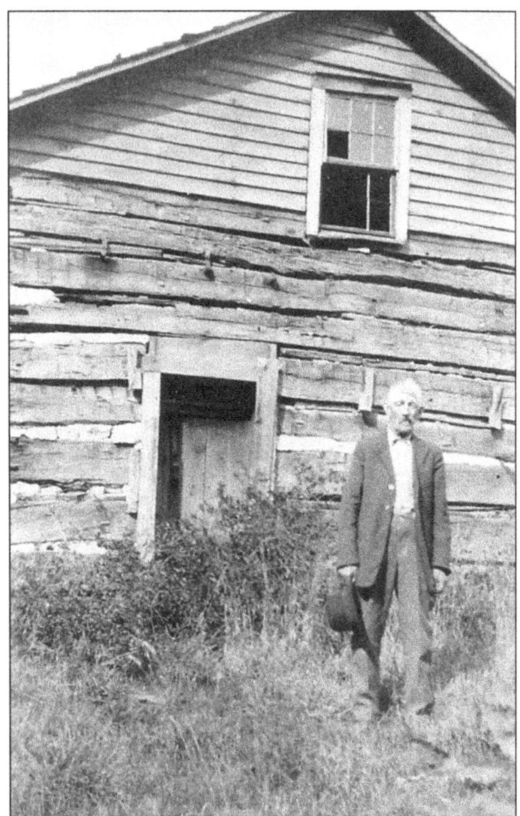

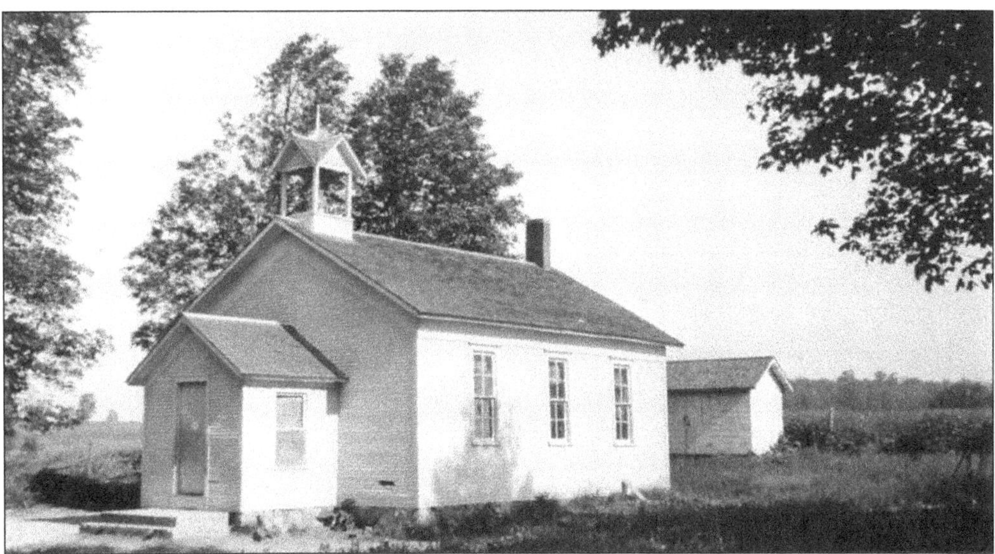

As was common for the time, numerous small schools were built throughout the township to allow children to walk to school. More often than not, the land was donated or loaned by a local family who had school-age children. The Bennett School was built at the corner of Bennett and Hagadorn Roads and continued in operation at that site until the consolidation of all rural schools into one central site in 1921. The superintendent of Okemos schools then moved the building to Mount Hope Road west of Okemos Road and converted it to a private residence.

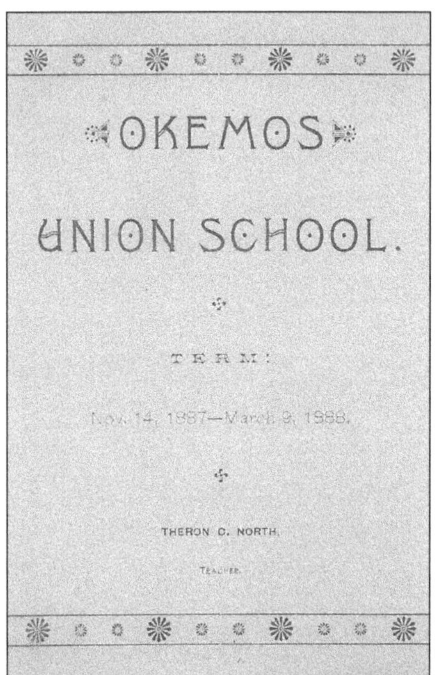

OKEMOS

UNION SCHOOL.

TERM:

Nov. 14, 1887—March 9, 1888.

THERON C. NORTH,

TEACHER.

Theron C. North, age 32, taught at the Union School during the winter term of November 1887 through March 9, 1888. School years were generally split into three terms: autumn, winter, and spring. Some larger communities also offered limited classes during the summer. Most communities preferred to hire a male teacher for the winter term, as this might be the only time of the year the older boys from the area farms could attend school. A stronger, male influence was seen as necessary in order to control the "big boys."

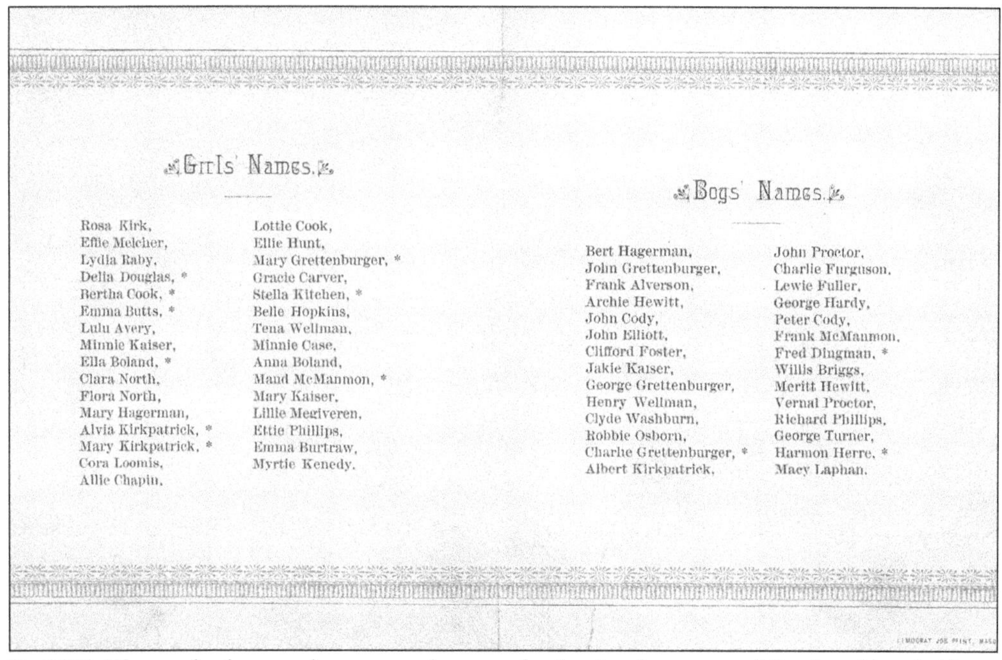

Girls' Names.

Rosa Kirk,
Effie Melcher,
Lydia Raby,
Delia Douglas, *
Bertha Cook, *
Emma Butts, *
Lulu Avery,
Minnie Kaiser,
Ella Boland, *
Clara North,
Flora North,
Mary Hagerman,
Alvia Kirkpatrick, *
Mary Kirkpatrick, *
Cora Loomis,
Allie Chapin,
Lottie Cook,
Ellie Hunt,
Mary Grettenburger, *
Gracie Carver,
Stella Kitchen, *
Belle Hopkins,
Tena Wellman,
Minnie Case,
Anna Boland,
Maud McManmon, *
Mary Kaiser,
Lillie Megiveren,
Ettie Phillips,
Emma Burtraw,
Myrtie Kenedy.

Boys' Names.

Bert Hagerman,
John Grettenburger,
Frank Alverson,
Archie Hewitt,
John Cody,
John Elliott,
Clifford Foster,
Jakie Kaiser,
George Grettenburger,
Henry Wellman,
Clyde Washburn,
Robbie Osborn,
Charlie Grettenburger, *
Albert Kirkpatrick,
John Proctor,
Charlie Furguson,
Lewie Fuller,
George Hardy,
Peter Cody,
Frank McManmon,
Fred Dingman, *
Willis Briggs,
Meritt Hewitt,
Vernal Proctor,
Richard Phillips,
George Turner,
Harmon Herre, *
Macy Laphan.

By 1885, Okemos had grown large enough to need a "senior department" for the older children. The senior department of the day did not necessarily refer to the senior class in a modern-day high school, but to the children who had progressed to the highest reading and study levels. The purpose of the asterisks next to student's names was explained by the teacher, A.R. Hardy, who said, "As an inducement to secure punctuality and good deportment, I promised to have the names of pupils printed at the close of the term, marking with an asterisk (*) those who refrained from whispering."

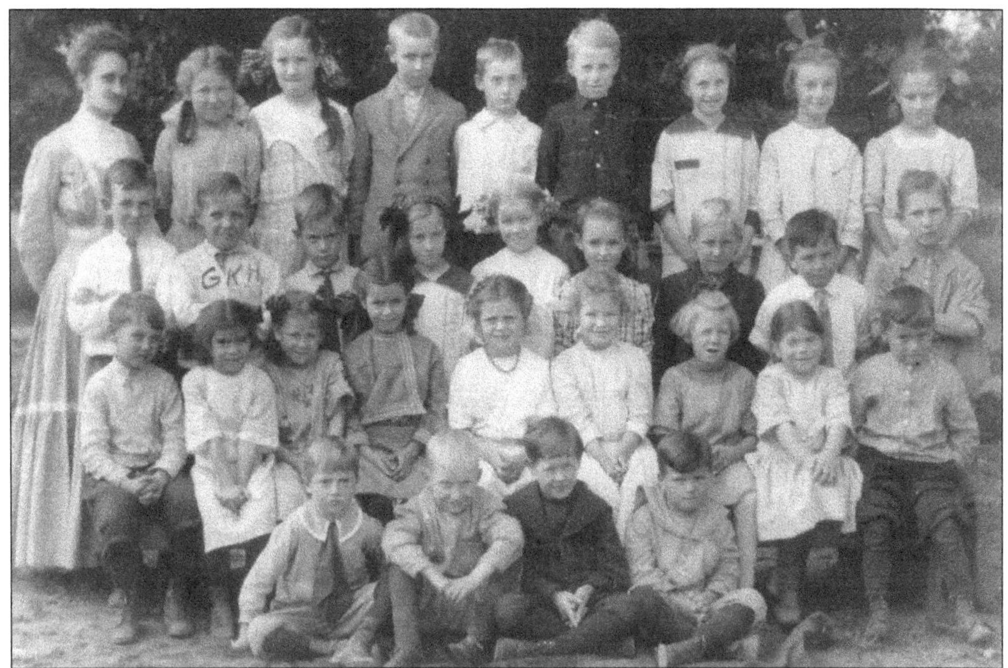

Emma Niebling served as a teacher for most of her adult life. Having never married, she could continue her career in the field. She primarily taught the younger students. The above photograph from October 1913 includes, from left to right, (first row) Orin Grettenberger, Harold Edgar, William McKane, and Gerald Allen; (second row) unidentified, Lavina Strayer, ? Baldwin, Anna Strayer, Rhea Eberly, Alice Heathman, Mildred Roberts, Ruth Sturges, and Glenn Torrance; (third row) Charles Deeg, Garnet Honsberger, Warren Brown, ? Brown, Carrie Hammond, Rosa Olds, Frank Evert, Larue Clark, and Russel Clark; (fourth row) Emma Niebling, Eva Allen, Leah Brown, Howard Hammond, Clair Smith, Leo Clever, ? Brown, Leota Holtz, and Florence Olds.

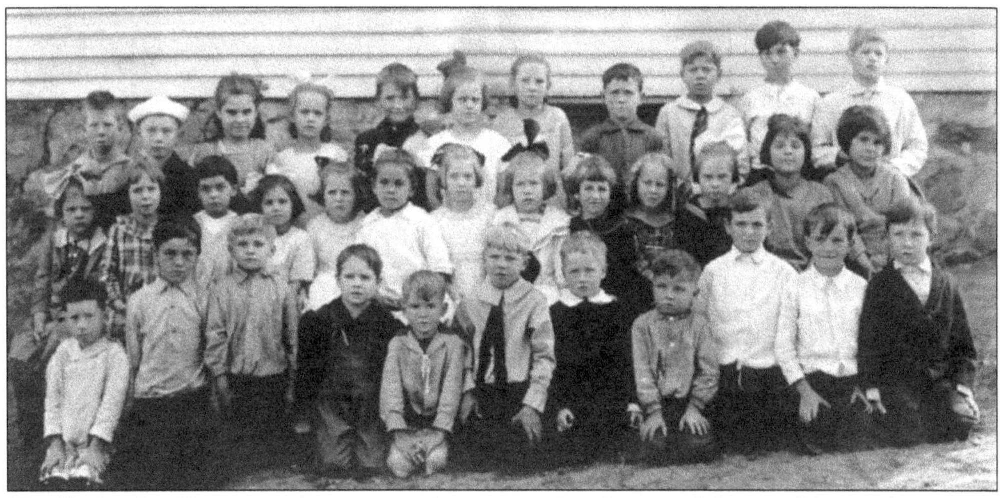

The "little school" continued to serve students even after the consolidation of the rural one-room schools into a central location in 1921. The little school served the youngest grades, and the students benefitted from the small classes in a less chaotic environment than could be found at consolidated school, with its multiple grades of older students. The students pictured above in November 1921 are not identified. Their teacher (not pictured) was Alice Moore.

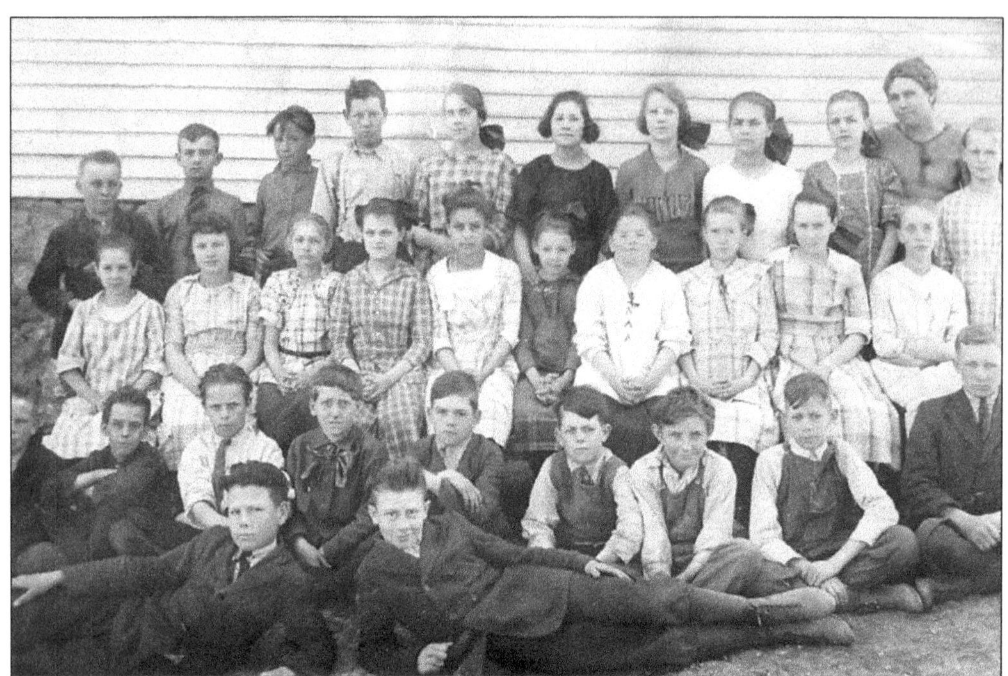

The above photograph shows the intermediate class of the old Okemos School prior to 1921. Student names are unavailable. The teacher, shown in the upper right corner, was Agnes Polhenins Young. Once the large, brick, consolidated school was opened in 1921, all intermediate classes were transferred to that building, and the old school became known as the "little school."

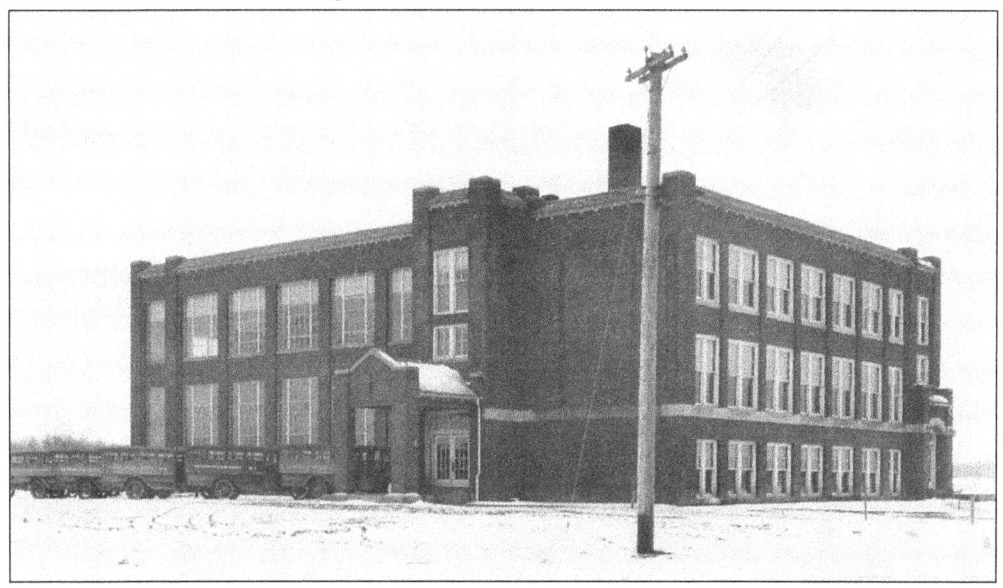

The quality of education received in rural one-room schools varied greatly depending on the resources of the community, and some graduates from eighth grade found entry into an area high school difficult. By 1920, Okemos followed the statewide trend of consolidating area schools into one central location to combine resources. The above photograph is of the Okemos consolidated school at the corner of Okemos and Mount Hope Roads. School buses were introduced to transport students living in far corners of the district.

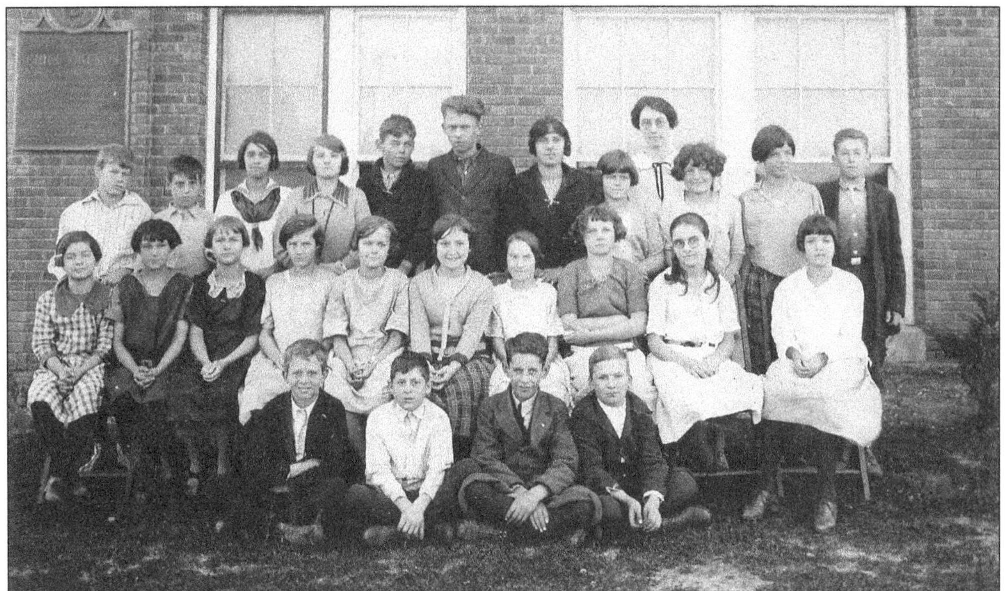

The intermediate students were now being prepared for higher education. Before the consolidation of schools in 1921, an Okemos student would need to travel either south to Mason or west to East Lansing to pursue a high school degree. Pictured above in 1924, Irene Beaumont taught the 10-year-olds at the sixth-grade level. Names of the students are unknown.

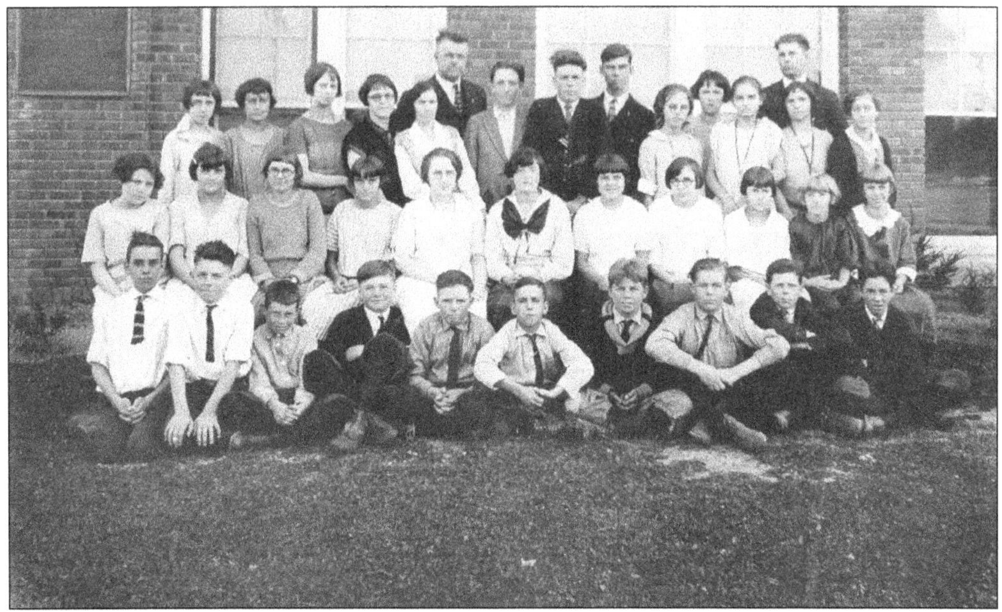

Another photograph from 1924 shows the combined classes of the seventh and eighth grades. As was common with the older students, a male teacher was employed to keep the male students in check. The students are not identified; however, the teacher is G.C. White.

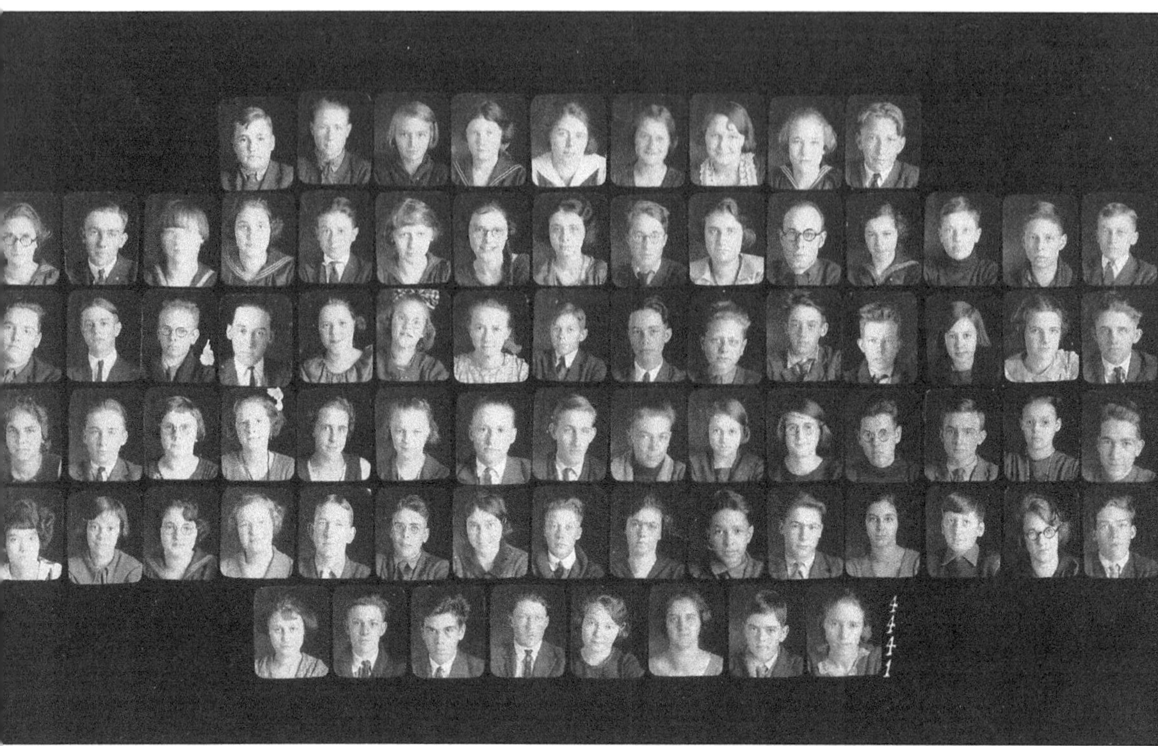

The above image from 1925 shows a full enrollment for the new high school at the Okemos consolidated building. Once the school was consolidated in 1921, local students could receive a high school education without having to travel to other cities. Pictured are, from left to right and top to bottom, (first row) Rex Beaumont, two unidentified students, Frances Hadley, unidentified, Velma Eberly, Wilma Kinney, Elsie Dietz, and Harold Edgar; (second row) Lucille McKane, two unidentified students, Vera Gubbins, Orin Grettenberger, Marie Blinn, Moneta Wilkins, Rhea Eberly, Howard Collins, Elsie Greenfield, Grant BeVier, three unidentified students, and Elton Daniels; (third row) Frank Coleman, three unidentified students, Irene Turau, Naomi Wilkins, two unidentified students, Carleton Beaumont, Bernie Hague, Howard McClure, Milton Stevens, Fannie Williams, Charlotte Hammond, and unidentified; (fourth row) Laura Woodworth, Maynard Eberly, three unidentified students, Bernie Fink, four unidentified students, Marjory Eberly, William McKane, unidentified, Ruth Huff, and Spencer Worthington; (fifth row) two unidentified students, Gladys Gubbins, unidentified, Merle Wilcox, Maynard Dietz, Alberta Russell, unidentified, Frances Turau, Eugene Williams, Ernest Jennings, Ida Strayer, Ralph Guile, Mildred Roberts, and Albert Dormer; (sixth row) two unidentified students, Philip Woodworth, Robert Hadley, Jessie Fink, two unidentified students, and Lois Webster.

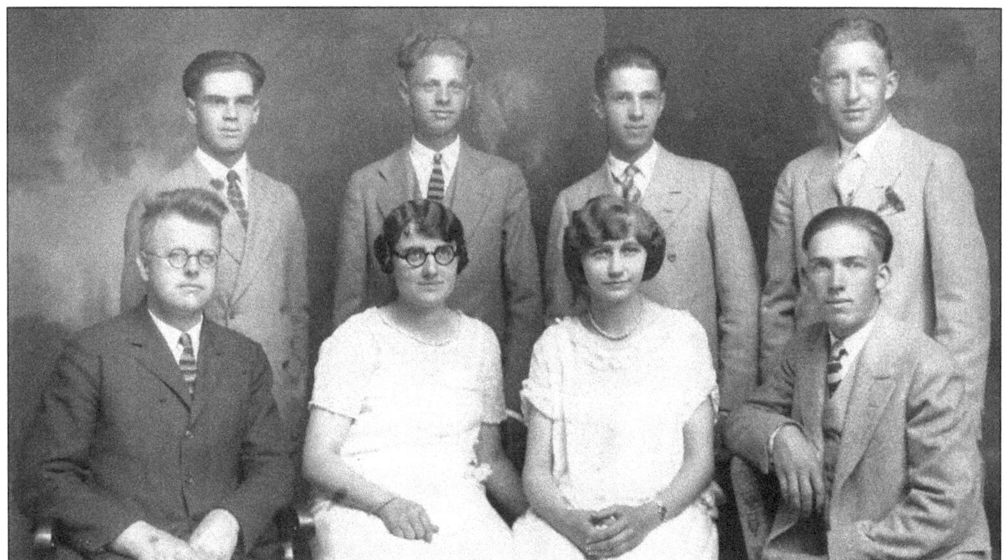

By 1925, G.C. White was listed as the superintendent. He oversaw the education of all the students and mentored those who wished to finish their studies at the highest level possible. The class of 1925 finished out the year with a total of seven (five males and two females) completing their exercises. Pictured here from left to right are (first row) G.C. White, Elsie Greenfield, Marie ?, and Albert Dormer; (second row) Philip Woodworth, Bernie Hague, Eugene Williams, and Harold Edgar.

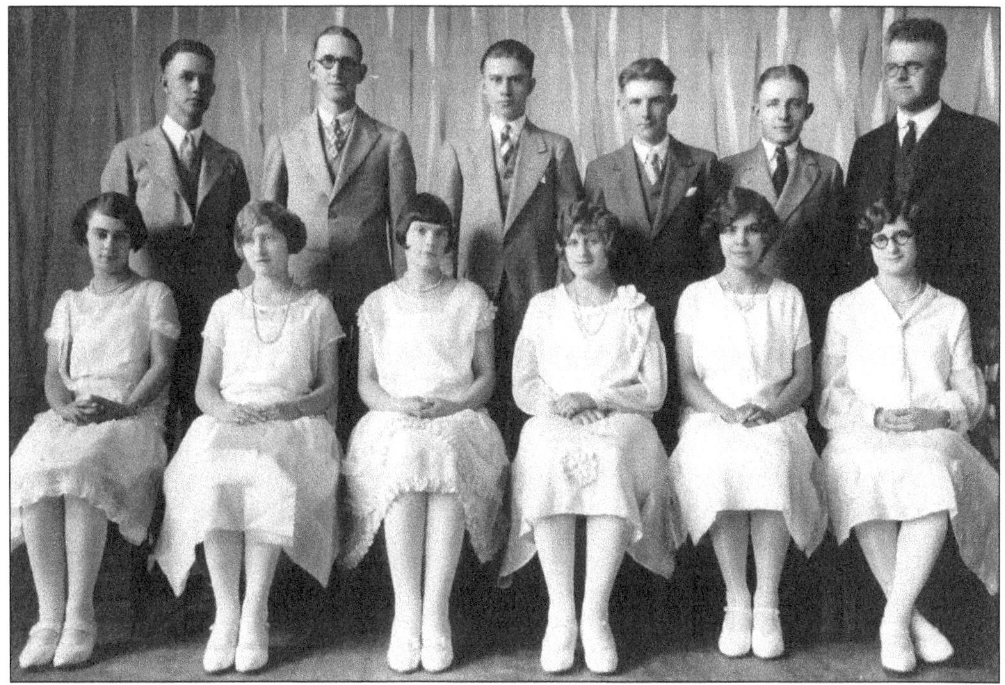

G.C. White also oversaw the graduating class of 1926. In the photograph above are, from left to right, (first row) Thelma McClure, Bernice Bitgood, Moneta Wilkins, Velma Eberly, Laura Woodworth, and Marjorie Eberly; (second row) Carlton Beaumont, Merle Wilcox, Orin Grettenberger, Lee O'Caroll, and Marion Kinney.

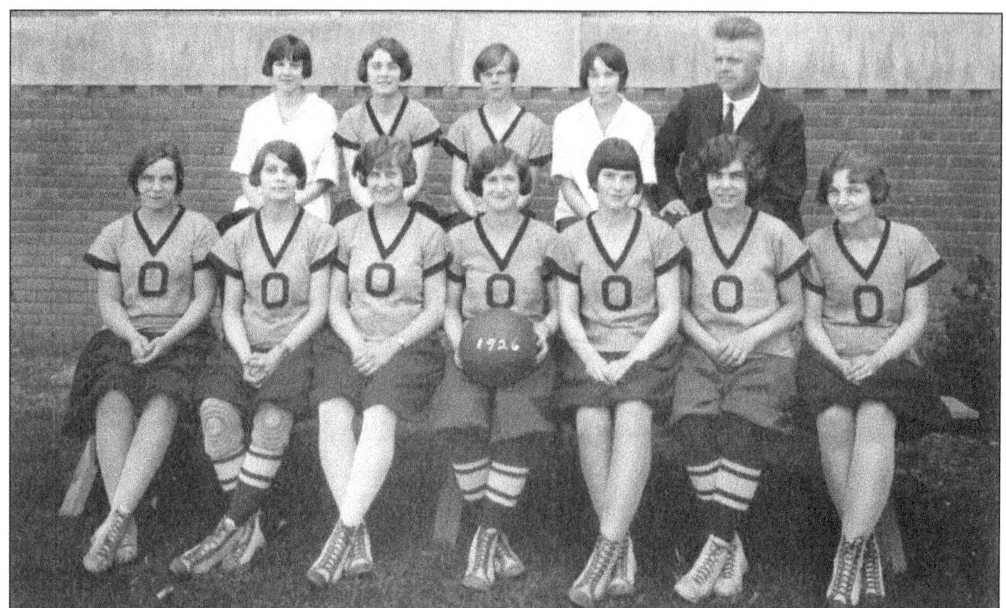

Prior to World War I, ladies' fashions limited the types of activities they could participate in. When the fashions changed after 1918, females became more active in sports. The trend of the time encouraged team sports for health and discipline. Pictured above are, from left to right, (first row) Jo Currier, Jennie R. (last name not listed), Velma Eberly, Marjorie Eberly, Moneta Wilkins, Laura Woodworth, and Wilma Kinney; (second row) Fannie Williams, Marjorie Woodworth, Delsie R. (last name not listed), Alberta Russell, and superintendent G.C. White.

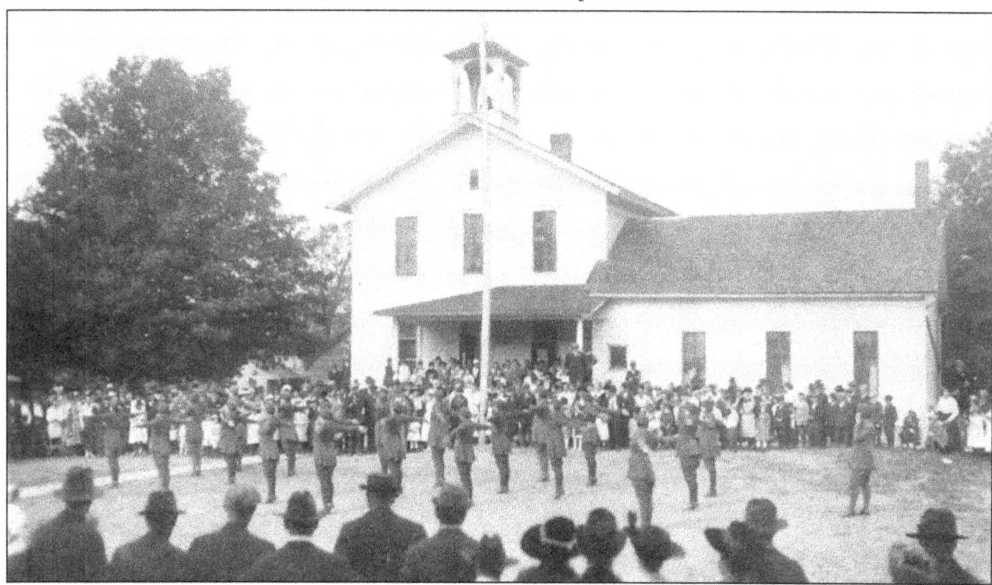

World War I had a major impact on the Okemos area, largely because many of the pioneer families were German Americans who wished to distance themselves from the German kaiser and his attacks on other European countries. Many local families stopped using the German pronunciation of their names and switched to the Anglicized forms; for example, "Georg" became "George," or "Johann" became "John." Military drills occurred in Okemos around the "little school" building. The above c. 1918 photograph shows the female soldiers standing at attention.

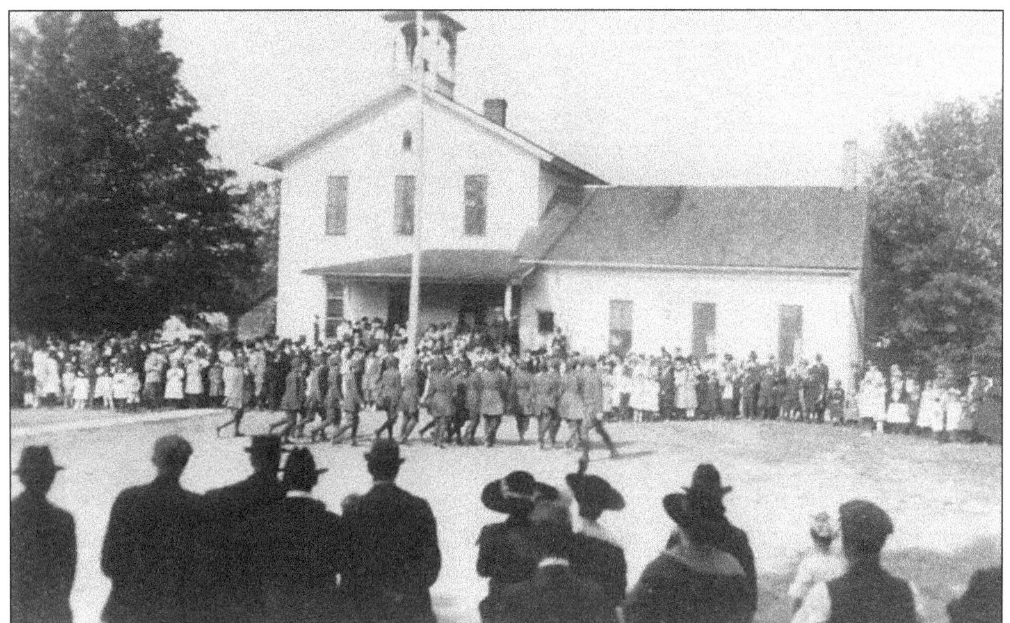

The female soldiers participated in drills at patriotic events to the delight of the local residents. In this c. 1918 photograph, they drill around the flagpole at the elementary school in Okemos.

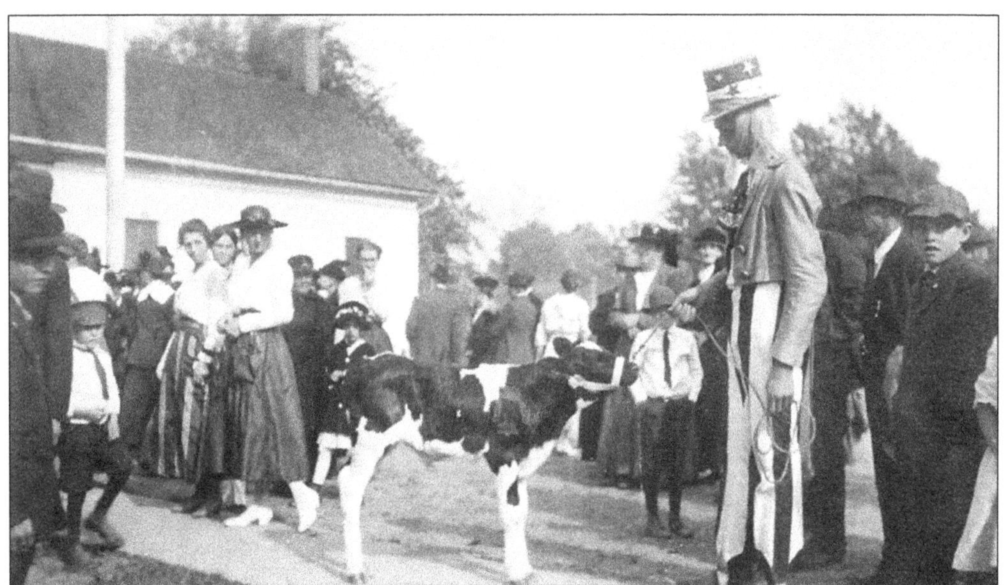

The year 1918 saw a surge of patriotism as the United States entered the Great War in Europe. Not yet called World War I, it was thought to be the "war to end all wars." Uncle Sam and his calf attended the Independence Day festivities at the Okemos Town Hall on July 4, 1918.

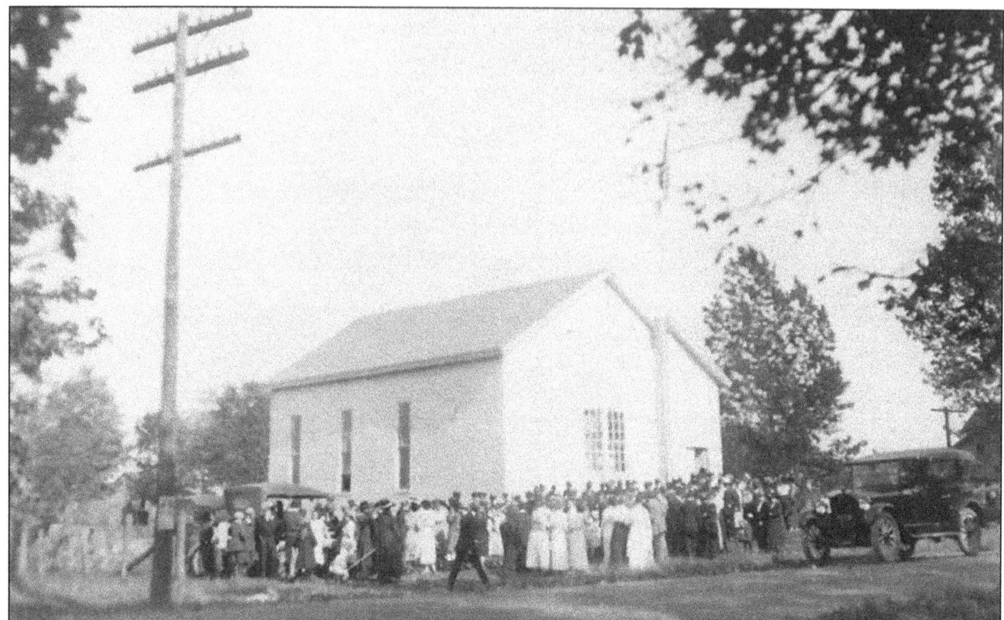

The town hall in the center of Okemos became a gathering spot for local residents interested in demonstrating their patriotism and voicing their support for American troops fighting in the war. The local German American residents were sensitive to their ancestry and were especially diligent in demonstrating their support for their adopted country. This photograph was taken around 1918 in front of town hall.

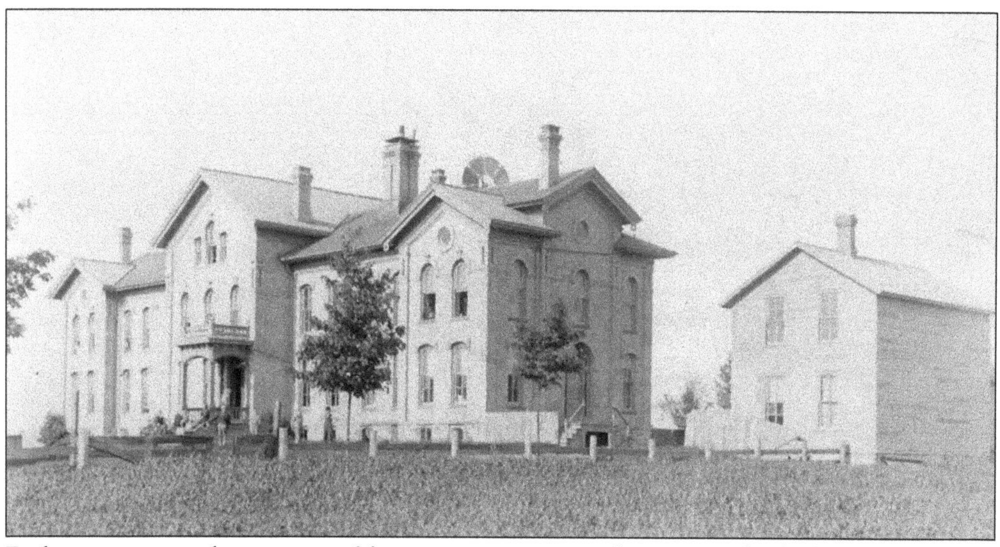

Each county set aside a portion of farm property to serve those in need. The homeless, ill, and indigent were housed on the farm, and those physically able would work the farm to help support the tenants. The poor farm was moved from Alaiedon Township to Meridian Township in 1878 and was located along Dobie Road, north of Jolly Road. A small cemetery is located on the property for those who died while in residence. Dates on the grave markers run from the 1890s to 1942. There is no evidence of graves dating to the 1920s because a university offered to pay for bodies to be used for research. The former poorhouse is now Carriage Lanes Apartments on Dobie Road.

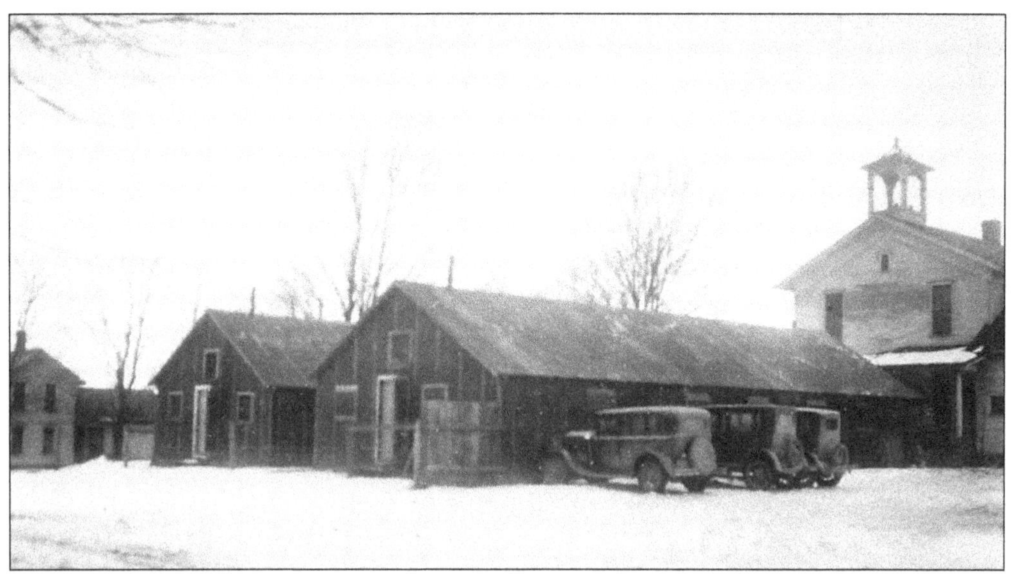

The poor farm burned down in 1885, and a number of residents perished. A later building was constructed of brick to decrease the possibility of destruction. Over time, and especially after veterans returned home from the World War I, the county changed the focus to serve the ill and infirm rather than the destitute. The farm became a county hospital for those who could not afford the care offered in the larger cities. The expanded focus required a modern hospital facility, which was constructed about 1930. The above photograph shows temporary barracks to house the ill during the construction.

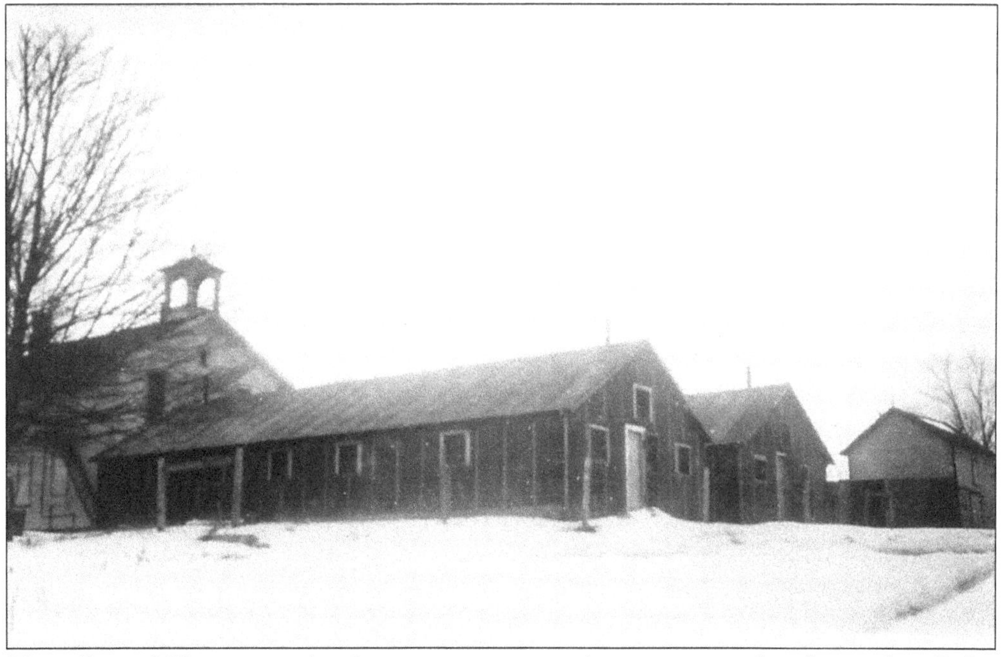

The village of Okemos was the closest community to the county poor farm/hospital on Dobie Road and served as the host for those in need of temporary housing. Temporary barracks were constructed in the center of Okemos near the old elementary school in 1930. The above photograph shows the temporary location at the corner of Clinton Street and Okemos Road.

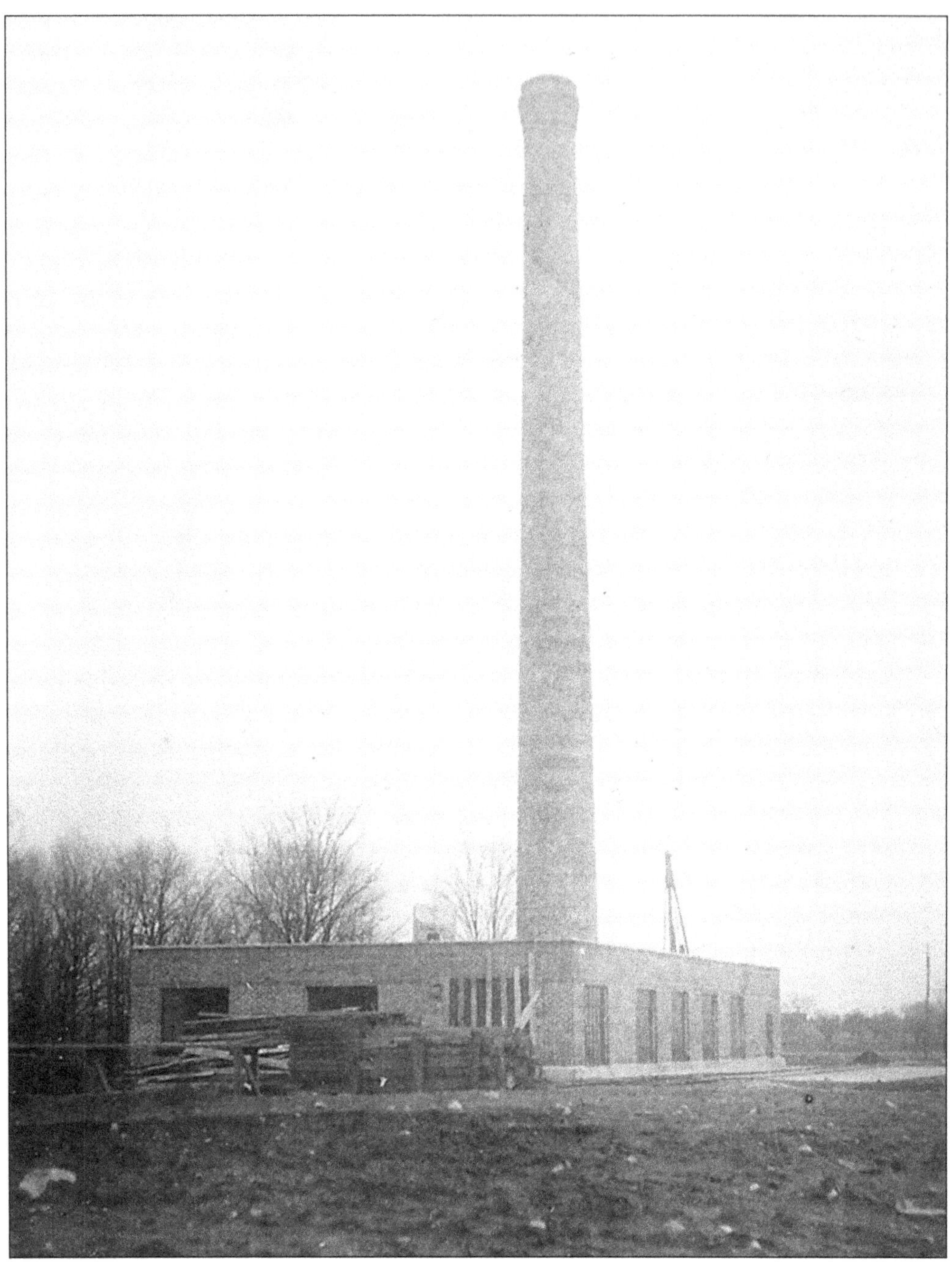

The area along Dobie Road became known as the location of buildings related to human services. A movement began in the 1920s to construct a prison along the road for female prisoners only. The closest area prison was located to the south in Jackson and provided cell housing for men and also separate buildings for women. The supporters of this idea pushed the governor to build the prison, and construction proceeded with the erection of a building intended to generate the power necessary for the facility. Because of the economy and lack of resources, the governor put off construction until there was no longer enough support to move forward. The power plant in the above photograph has been removed.

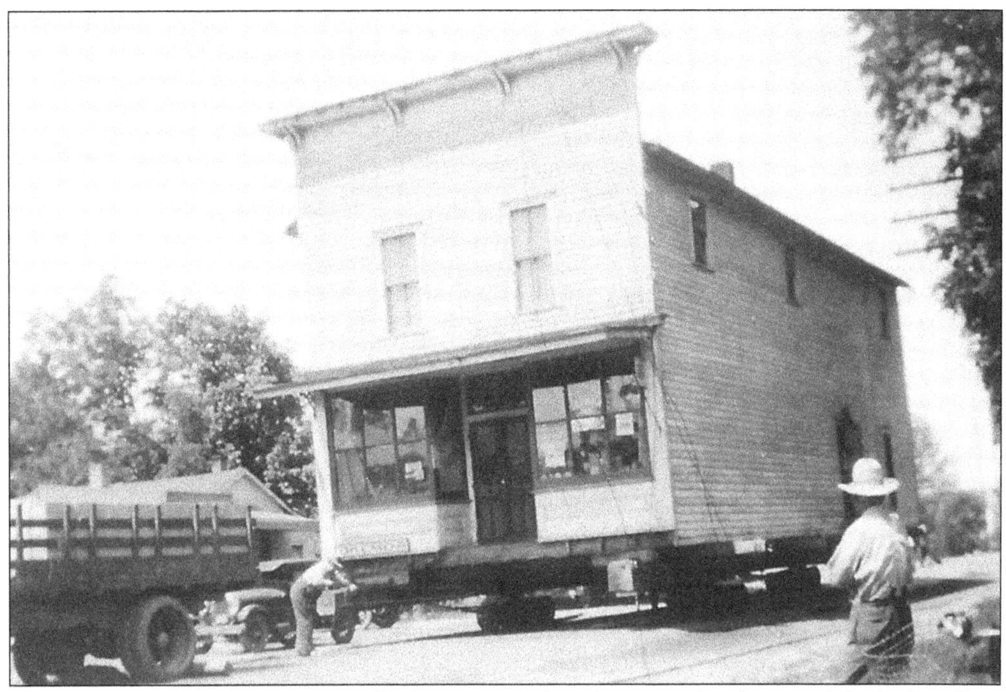

The Michigan Bureau of Highways built a state road in the 1920s that bypassed the little village to improve the flow and speed of traffic. It was built north of Hamilton Road and cut through the farm property of the Bray family. Savvy businessmen such as John O. and Orin K. Grettenberger realized that, if their business was to survive, they would need to move to the main four corners of the village.

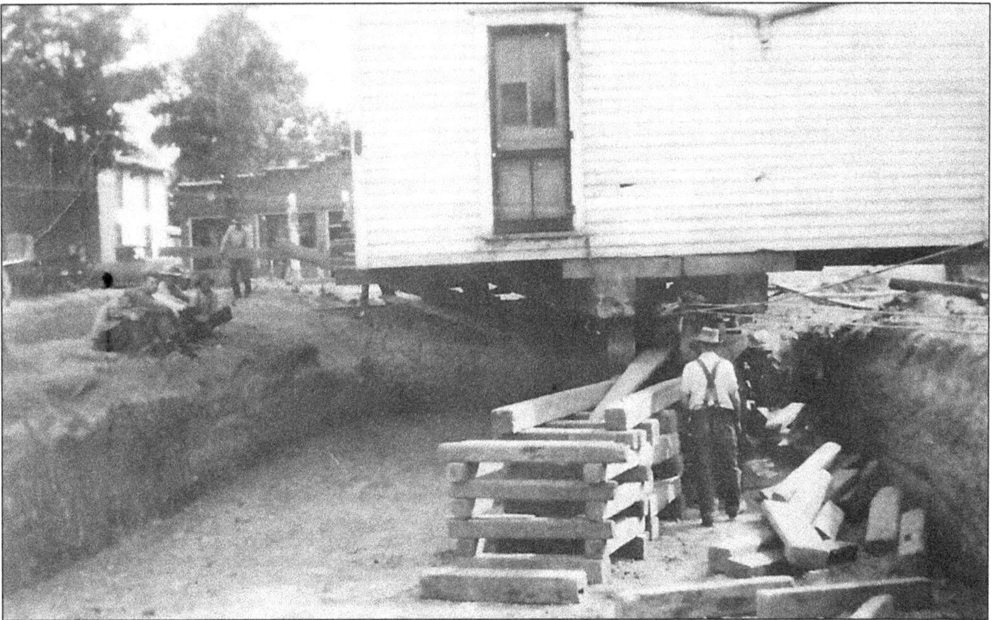

Rather than abandon the building that had housed their business for years, the Grettenbergers arranged to move the structure to the new site. The above photograph shows the excavation to raise the building to allow for transport.

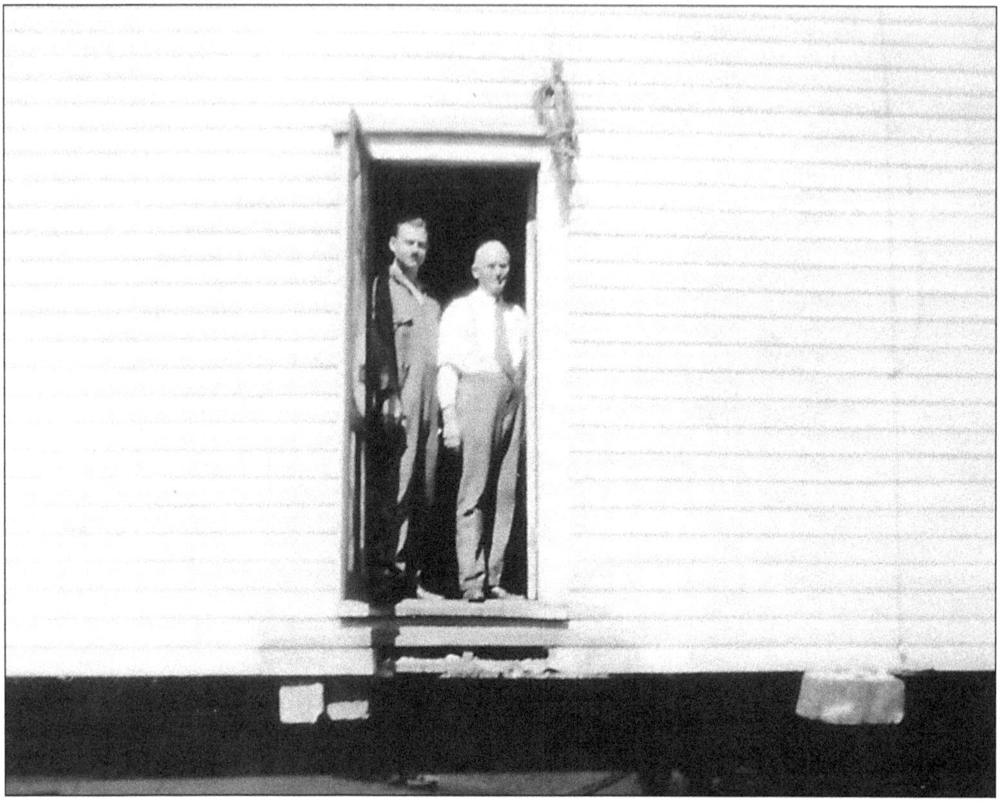

The building was moved just one short block east from the corner of Hamilton and Ardmore Roads to its new home at the corner of Hamilton and Okemos Roads. The new owner, Orin K. Grettenberger, and his father, John O., are shown enjoying the ride to their new site.

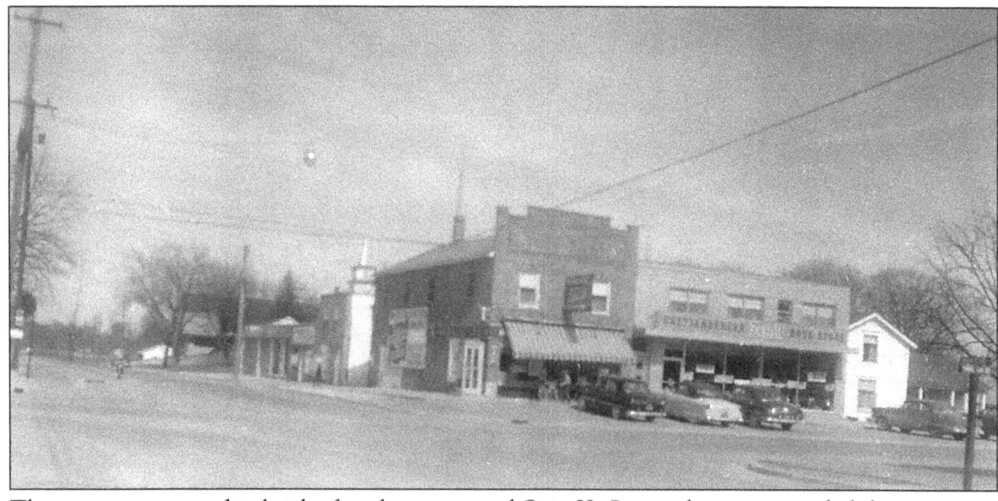

The store was covered in brick after the move, and Orin K. Grettenberger expanded the operation to include a pharmacy and soda fountain. The store continued in operation into the 1980s, and the building remains at the site today and houses a martial arts studio.

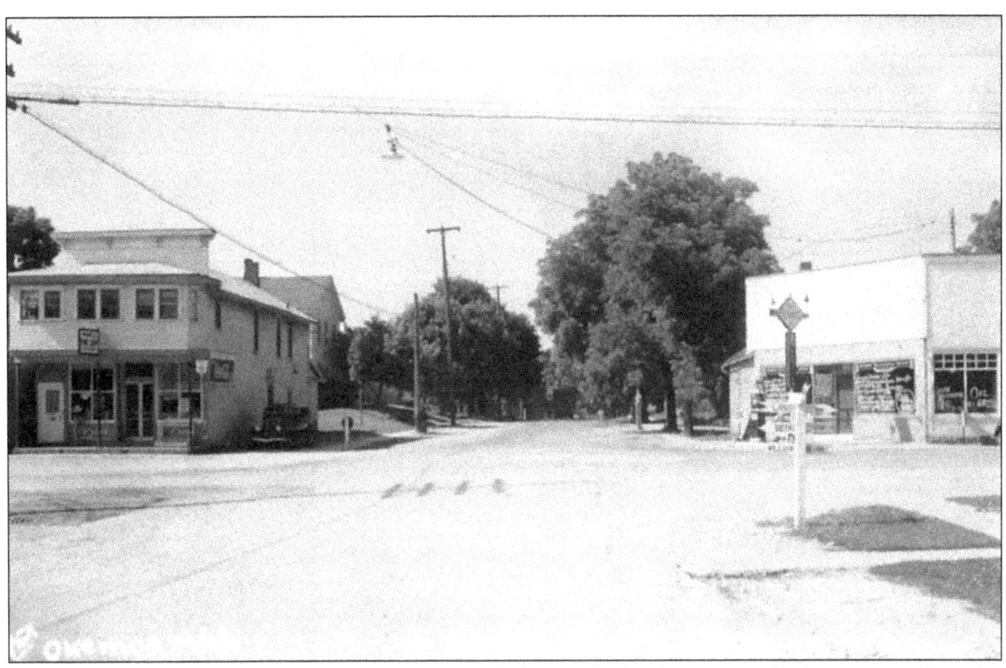

The same corner of Okemos and Hamilton Roads housed other businesses looking to weather the decreased traffic when the road bypass was built in the 1920s. A grocery store was located on the southeast corner (left side of photograph), and a Sunoco gas station was located on the southwest corner. In the foreground of the photograph is the signpost directing travelers to Lansing to the west and Williamston and Detroit to the east.

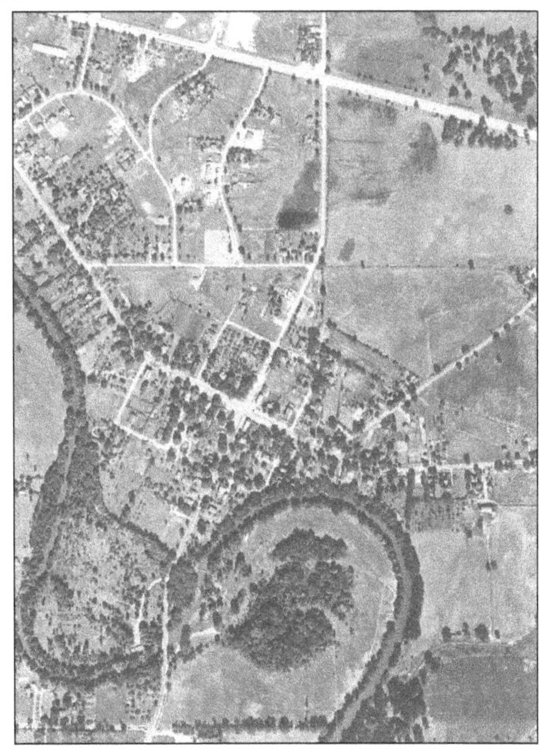

An aerial photograph taken by Talbert "Ted" Abrams of the village of Okemos shows how construction of the road bypass affected the growth and development of the area. The new road, built in the 1920s, cut Bray farmland in half, making it very difficult to farm on both sides. Bray chose to plat the portion of his property south of the new road, Grand River Avenue, to be sold for residences. The new neighborhood was named Cedar Bend Heights. Even so, the area remained largely rural, with farmland and pastures abutting the little village until rapid development began in the late 1960s and early 1970s.

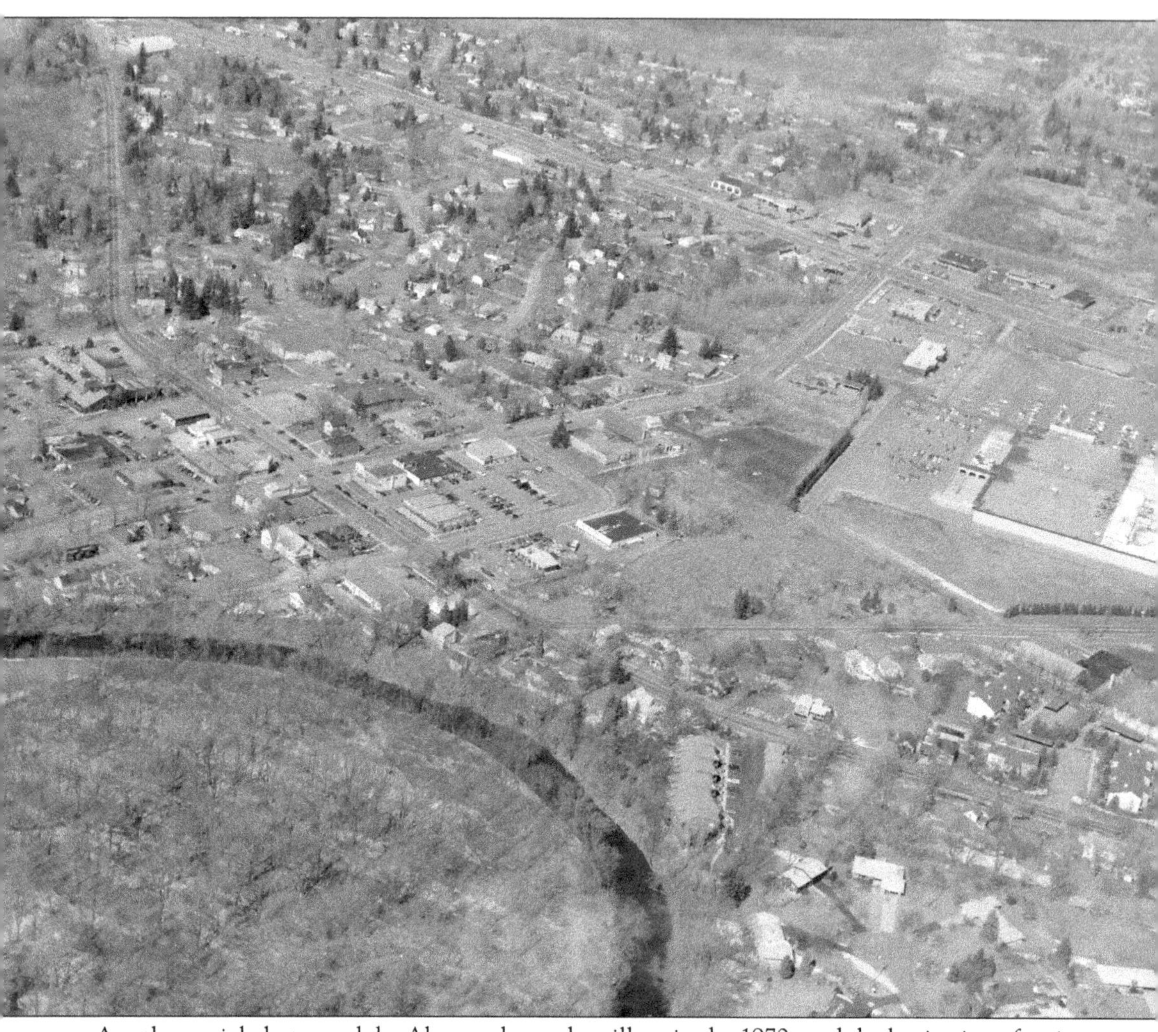

Another aerial photograph by Abrams shows the village in the 1970s and the beginning of major development of Okemos. The large parking area in the upper right portion of the photograph served the new Meijer store built in the 1970s. The Michigan-based company started with two area locations, one in Okemos and another in south Lansing. In recent years, the company has added three more stores to the Greater Lansing area, one in Delta Township, one on the north side of East Lansing, and the most recent addition in Bath Township just north of Haslett.

Eight

PIONEER FAMILIES

Meridian Township attracted many families looking for inexpensive land during the time of the "Michigan Fever" of the 1830s. Descendants of several early pioneer families continue to reside in the township and talk of their deep roots in the community.

The Babbit, Elliott, and Foster families were instrumental in the development of the Haslett area around Lake Lansing. The first postmaster of the Pine Lake Post Office was Edward Elliott. Several of the photographs in this book were donated to the Friends of Historic Meridian by his granddaughter Mary Elliott.

The area along the river in Okemos was settled by the Marsh, Bray, Kilbourne, Turner, Proctor, and Grettenberger families. Mary Turner, called "Aunt Mary" by many, was the first white child in the area when she moved with her family in 1842. Aunt Mary voted in a local election for the first time in 1927 at the age of 94. The Proctor family was instrumental in overseeing the use of the wooden plank road through the community and maintained a tollhouse along the route. The Grettenberger family arrived in the 1850s and established farms and businesses. The LorAnn Oil Company was started in 1962 by Orin K. Grettenberger and has continued to expand with customers from around the world.

Social clubs were formed by members of these families, and two organizations remain today. The Haslett Woman's Club was formed in 1906 and still meets monthly. The Okemos Pioneer Society began with informal gatherings of the daughters of the original pioneers and still holds meetings today. The commitment of these pioneer families to settle, develop, and improve the area has resulted in communities that continue to thrive.

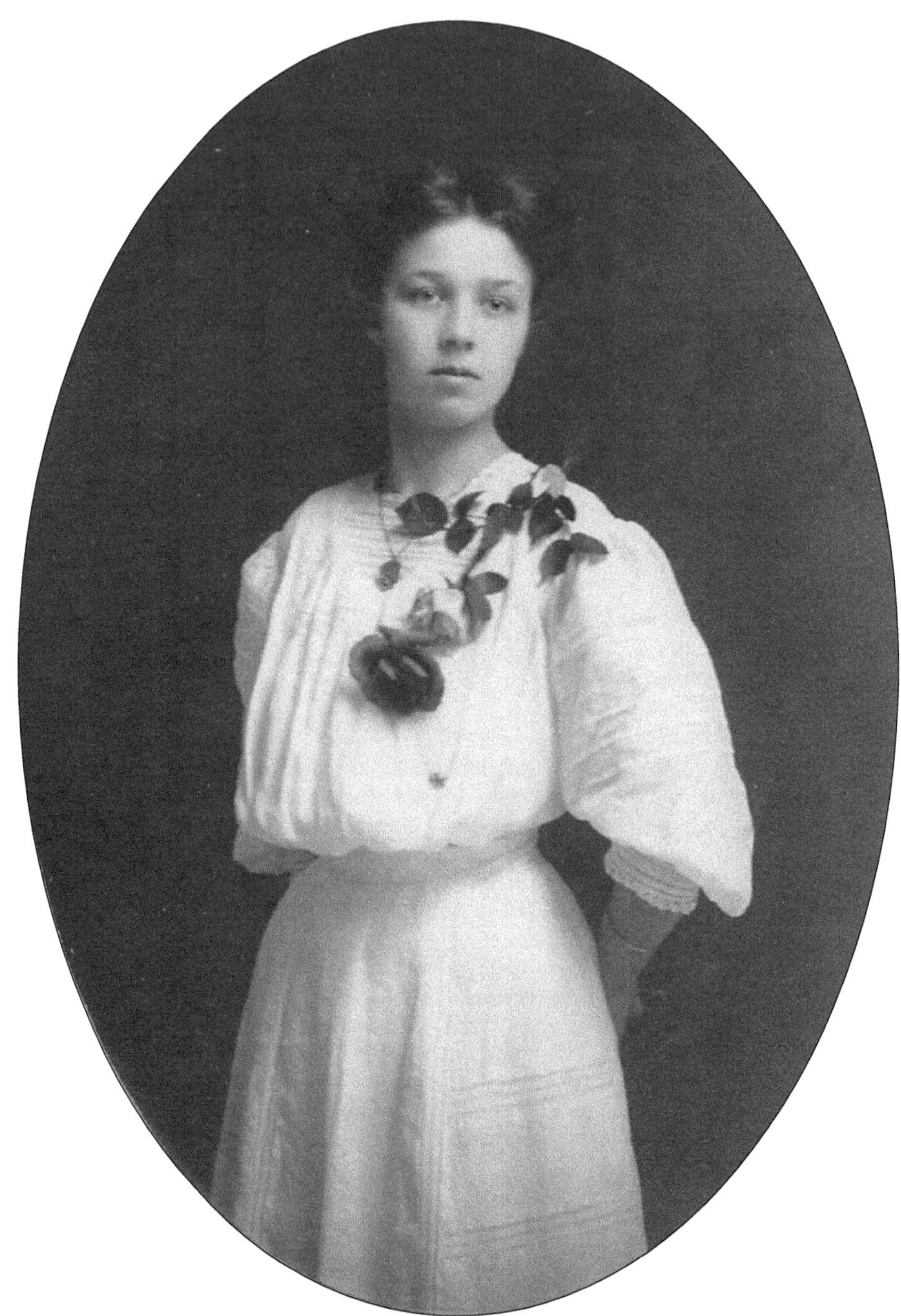

Mary Elliott was a lifelong resident of Haslett, graduating from the new brick school building in 1907 and joining the family business along the village's main street. The Elliott family had a store along present-day Haslett Road near the railroad tracks. Mary's grandfather Edward was the original postmaster of the old Pine Lake Post Office when the first bag of mail was thrown off the train in 1879. Later, in 1902, his son E.K. Elliott took over the postmaster duties, followed by his wife, Cynthia, until 1915. Mary took over the position in 1915 and continued to serve as postmistress until the end of 1954.

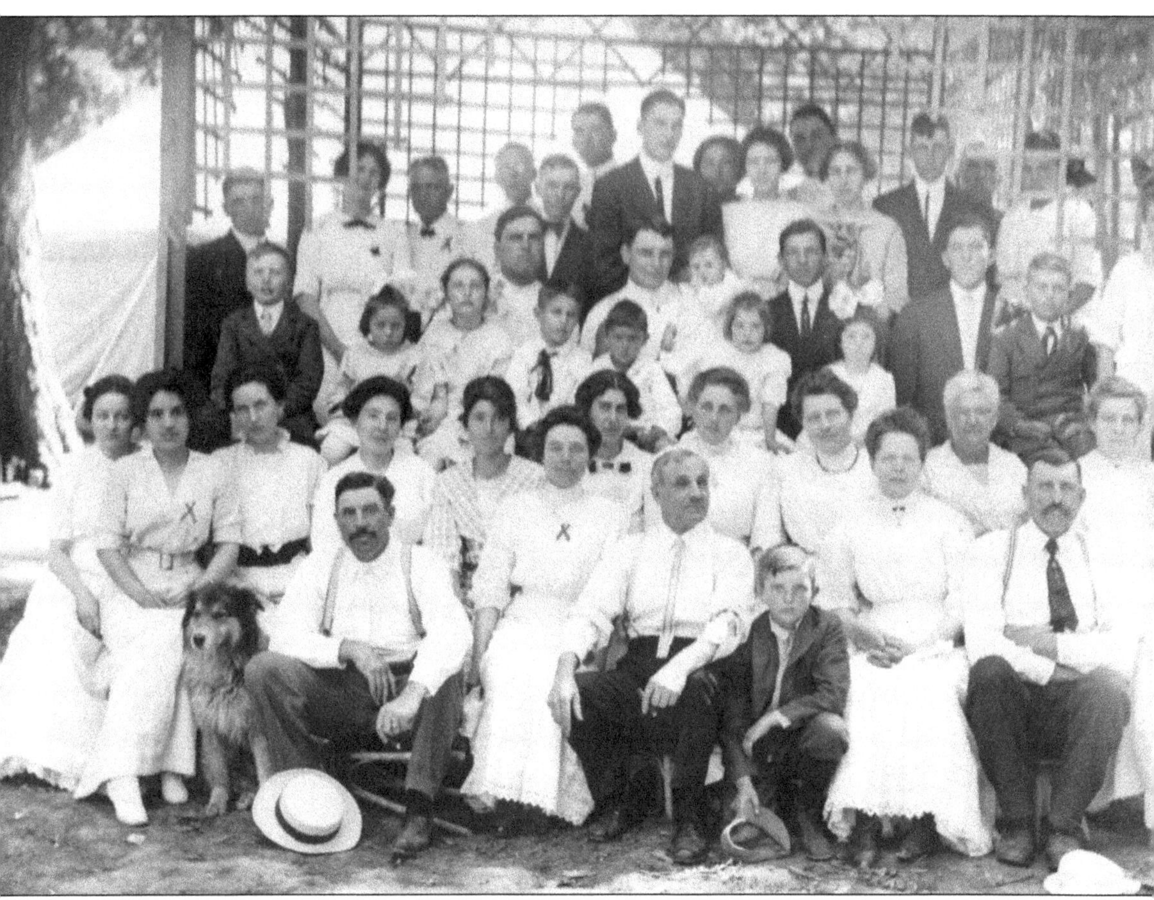

The Charles S. Foster family came to Meridian Township in 1850 and helped settle the Haslett area. Since 1900, they have had a yearly family reunion at Lake Lansing Park South on the last Saturday in July. The family celebrated their 114th consecutive reunion in 2014. This image shows the 1913 reunion. (Courtesy of Foster descendant Rebecca Adams Blair.)

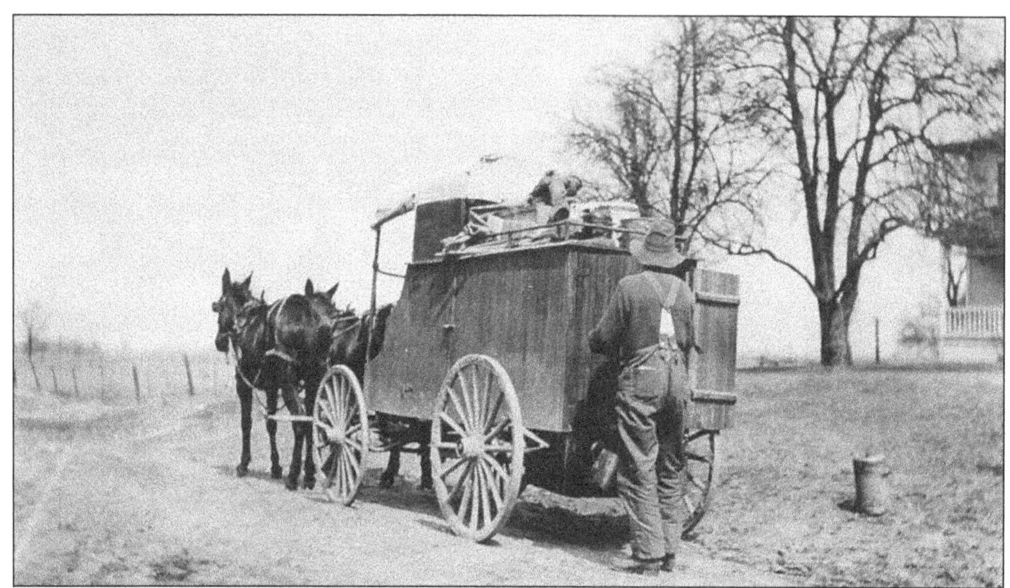

Another Haslett resident, Walter Buxton, bought a local grocery store in 1909. In addition to operating the store, he also operated a grocery wagon, which he took around the township drawn by his two mules. Buxton travelled as far south as the Netzloff farm at the corner of Hulett and Jolly Roads. The above photograph shows Buxton at the Netzloff property.

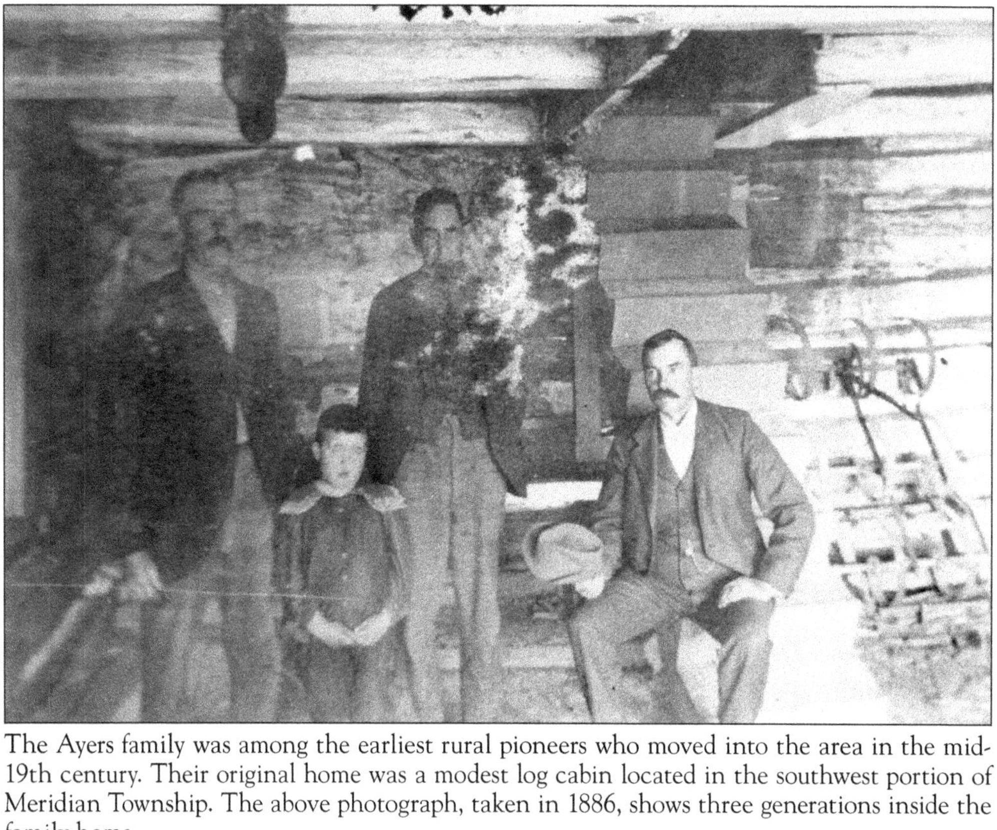

The Ayers family was among the earliest rural pioneers who moved into the area in the mid-19th century. Their original home was a modest log cabin located in the southwest portion of Meridian Township. The above photograph, taken in 1886, shows three generations inside the family home.

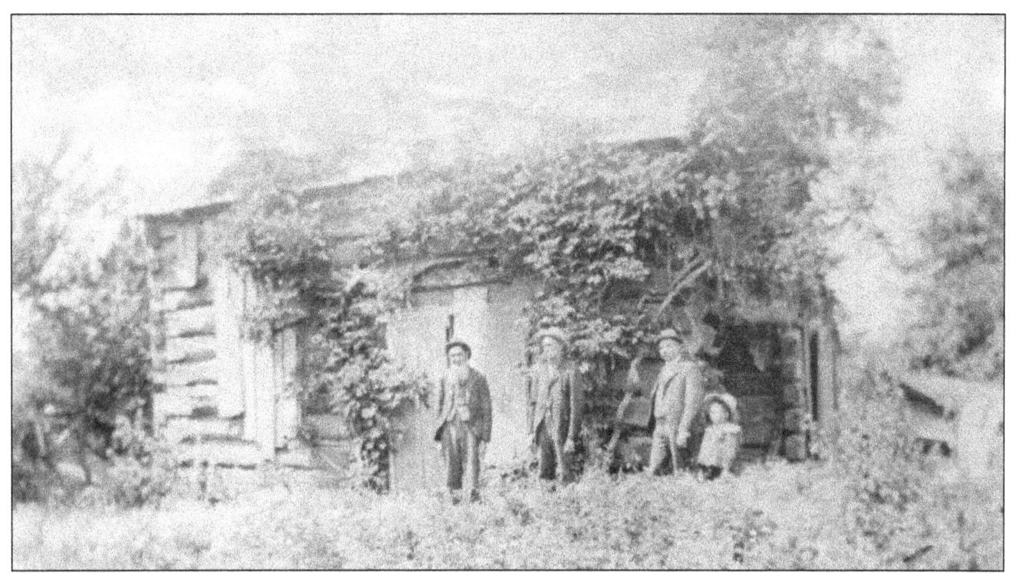

The exterior of the Ayers cabin was overgrown when Charles Ayers and family returned to the old homestead for this photograph in 1886. The property was sold, and the family moved into the city of Lansing, where they established a solid business reputation and opened a boardinghouse to serve travelers.

Date	Name	Amount	Date	Name	Amount
Oct 31	M Bray	1 35	13	Chas Hewitt	1 00
Nov 3	M Bray	1 65	13	Weaver	90
4	Henry Eckner	1 55	13	Ed Sutherland	50
4	Jas Morrison	1 50	15	Melcher	2 30
4	Wilhalf	60	15	Israel Wood	40
1	Johnson & one Barrel	1 12½	15	Del Felton	55
7	Jod Smith	1 00	16	Dan Mead	55
7	M Bray	1 65	16	Henry Eymer	1 20
8	M Bray	1 20	17	Herman Hulse	1 [illegible]
8	Richards	1 65	17	Samby Hulse	10
8	Foot	85	17	Jod Smith	1 75
8	Bigelow	1 50	17	Proctor	85
9	M Bray	65	18	E Ringman	85
9	E Hoskins	70	20	Jno Pattison	35
9	Proctor	1 13	21	Calkins	3 75
10	Richards	85	21	Kent	80
10	1 Barrel cider	1 25	21	Watson	1 40
12	Stringham	1 50	22	Martin Redman	45
12	Chas Bognes	95	22	Sturgis	60
12	A Proctor	65	24	Smith & Gardner	85
	Total	23 90			

While still living on the family farm in Meridian Township, Charles Wesley Ayers produced and sold apple cider from his orchard. The above ledger from 1876 shows transactions with other locals, such as Charles Hewitt, Mahlon Bray, the Foot family, the Proctors, and the Weavers.

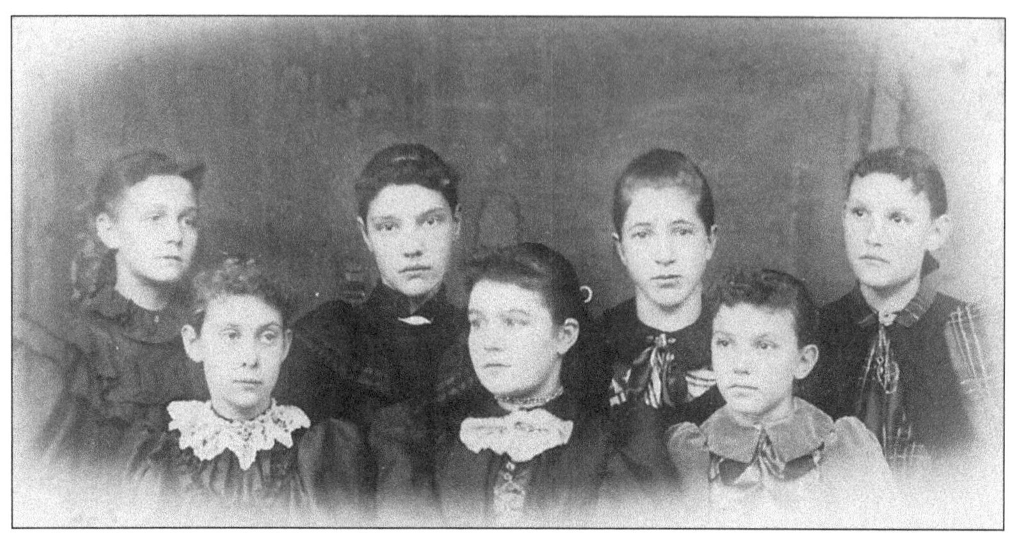

A small group of girls who grew up in Okemos became lifelong friends and eventually formed a club for children of the original pioneers. As adults, the friends met frequently in each other's homes to visit and work on homemade quilts. The above photograph from before 1918 includes, from left to right, (first row) Statie Hammond and two unidentified young ladies; (second row) unidentified, Fannie Williams, Grace Weaver, and Orpha Williams.

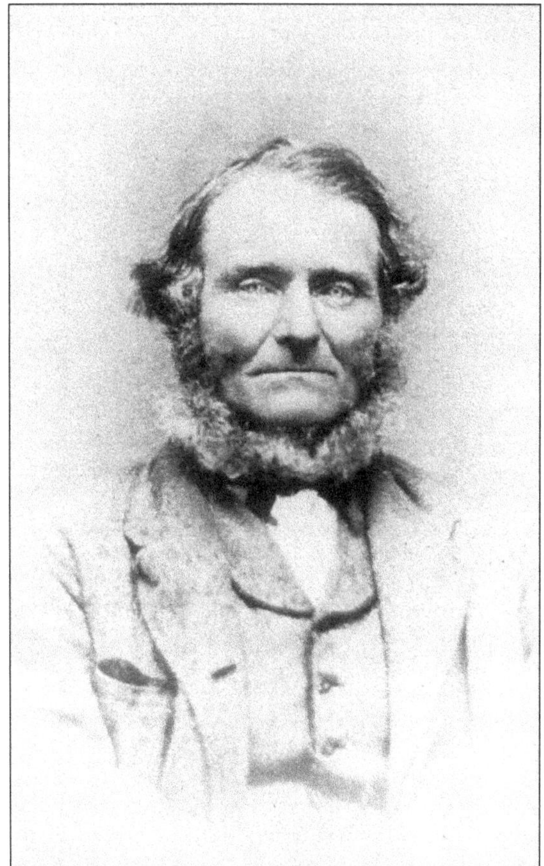

In 1864, Ezekiel Barnes purchased the house originally built in 1849 by Melzor Turner. The structure had been converted to an inn, and Barnes added a one-story wing on the south side to use as a dining room. The building also housed the post office in the northwest room on the first floor. It continued to be used as an inn into the early 20th century.

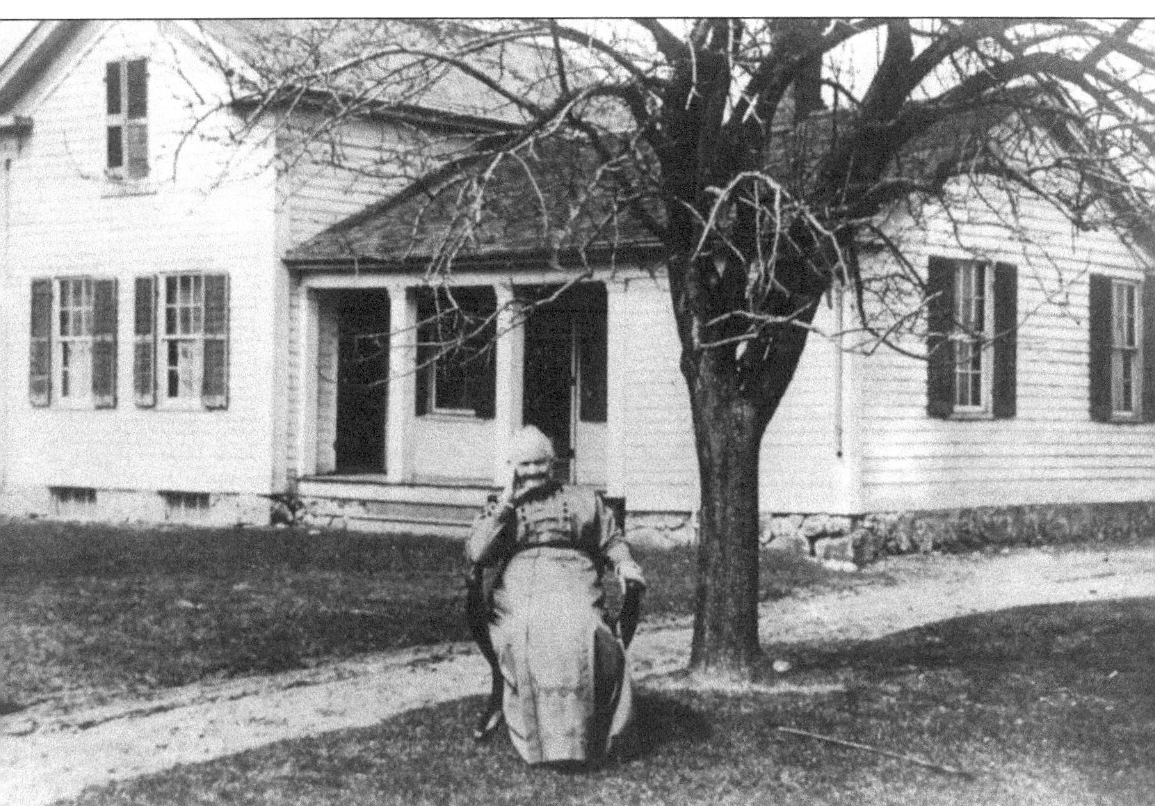

The Grettenbergers were among the pioneer families who helped settle the Okemos area. Johann Georg Grettenberger arrived in the area in the 1850s. He started a farmhouse in the early 1860s to help his son Jacob get settled in the area. The house stood along Marsh Road south of Grand River Avenue next to the present-day Pilgrim House Furniture store. The lady pictured above is Jacob's wife, Catherine Helwig Grettenberger.

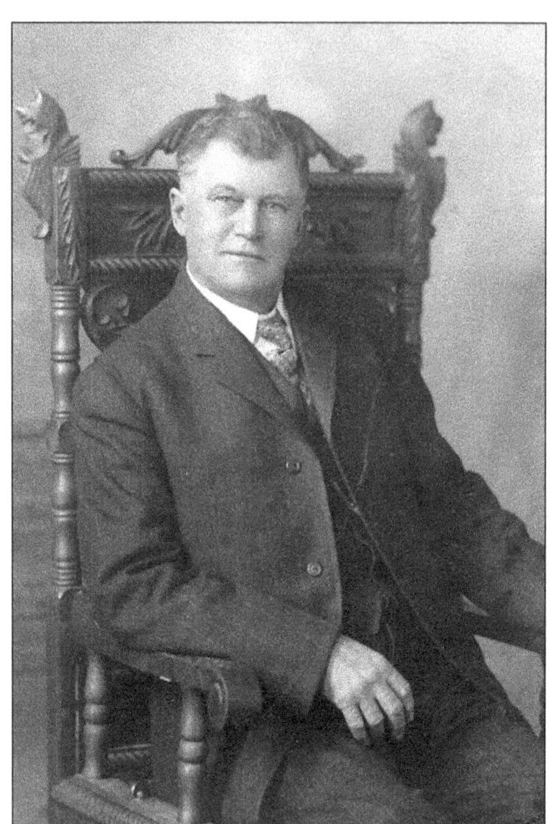

The Proctor family arrived in the area very early in the settlement. Alonzo Proctor and his brother came to improve a farmstead and build a home. Once completed, Alonzo returned to retrieve his young wife, Sara, and the rest of the family. The family farm was located on the west side of Park Lake Road north of Grand River Avenue. When the plank road was constructed from Lansing to Howell, tollgate operators were needed to collect and record tolls. Alonzo's father, Asa, took on the task until his death, and then Alonzo assumed the duties. Pictured is Alonzo's son, Asa Proctor II. The younger Proctor built his own home, which still stands today at the corner of Park Lake and Heather Street.

As noted earlier, Freeman Bray was the second white settler to arrive along the river. Nellie Bray, pictured, was his granddaughter, the daughter of Mahlon Bray.

Another child of the Bray pioneer family was Nellie's brother Charlie H. Bray. This photograph was taken when Charlie was 19 years old. Charlie's father, Mahlon Bray, was the son of the original pioneer Freeman Bray.

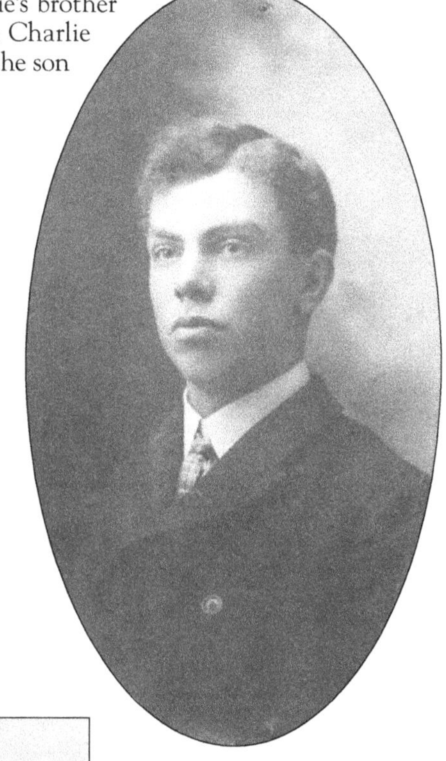

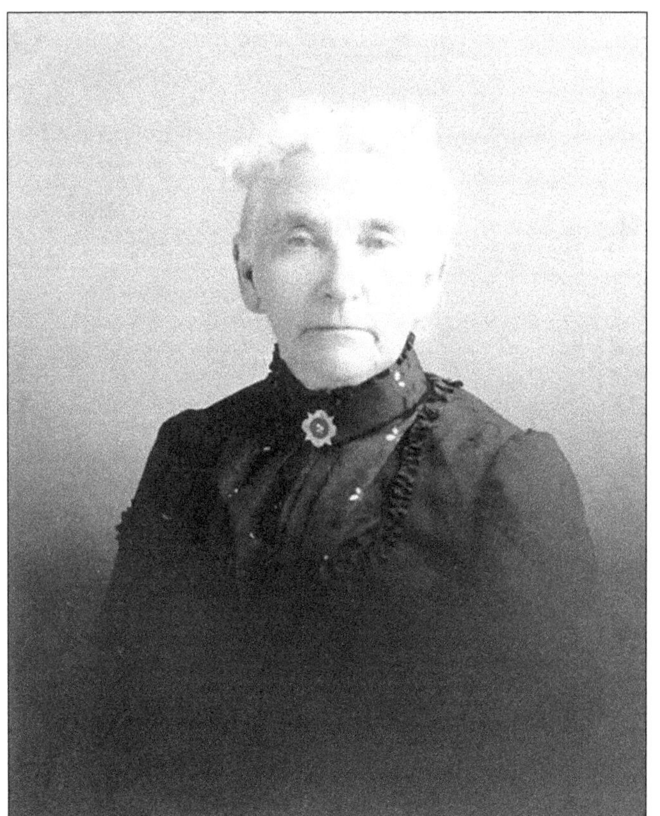

Melzor Turner moved from New York State in 1842 with his family. His 10-year-old daughter, Mary, was the first white child to move to the area. Turner found a small pioneer settlement consisting of log buildings for both residences and inns. He built the first frame house in the village in 1849 at the corner of Okemos and Hamilton Roads. This photograph shows his daughter Mary at age 68 in September 1900. After moving out of the area for a time, Mary returned to Okemos to live out her life. She was able to vote for the first time in 1927, at the age of 94.

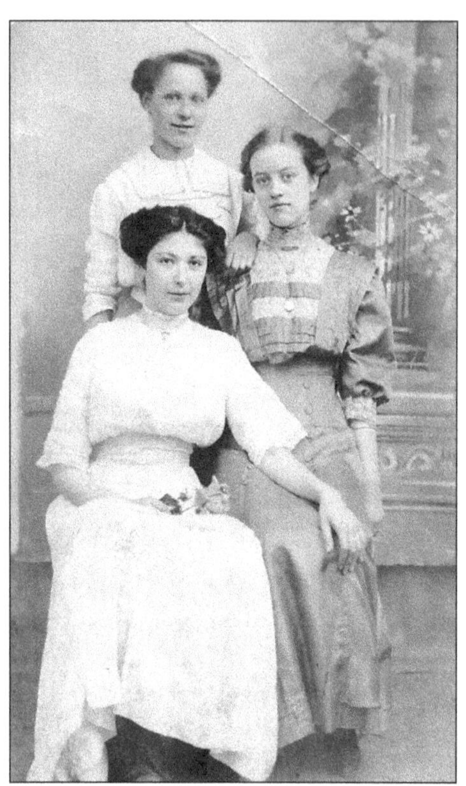

The Turner cousins were great-grandchildren of Melzor Turner and grew up in the village of Okemos. Melzor's son, William Henry Turner, had several sons who married, had children, and remained in the area. Pictured are cousins Cora (back), Jessie (middle), and Daphne Turner (front).

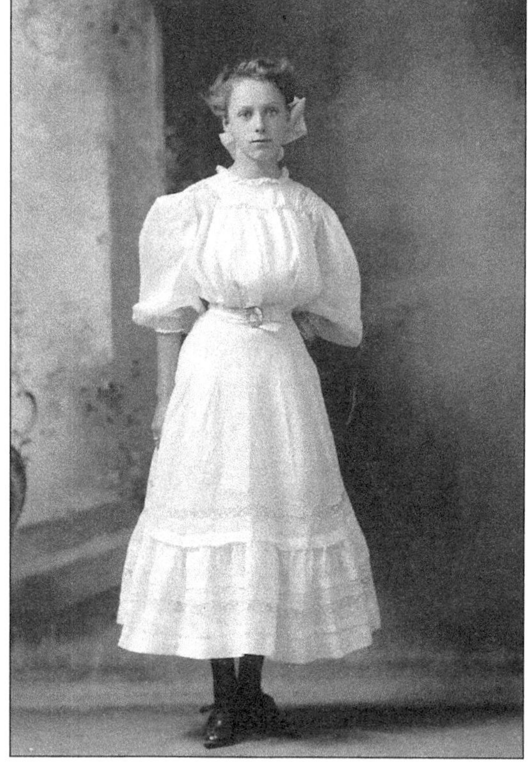

Turner cousin Jessie is pictured at age 14 in 1907. Jessie graduated in June 1908 from the 10th grade, the highest grade attainable in the Okemos schools at the time. The traditional high school of ninth through 12th grades was not available to Okemos students until 1921. Jessie lived a long life as an active and well-known community member. Her home was located at 2043 Hamilton Road, the current site of the Erickson Learning Center.

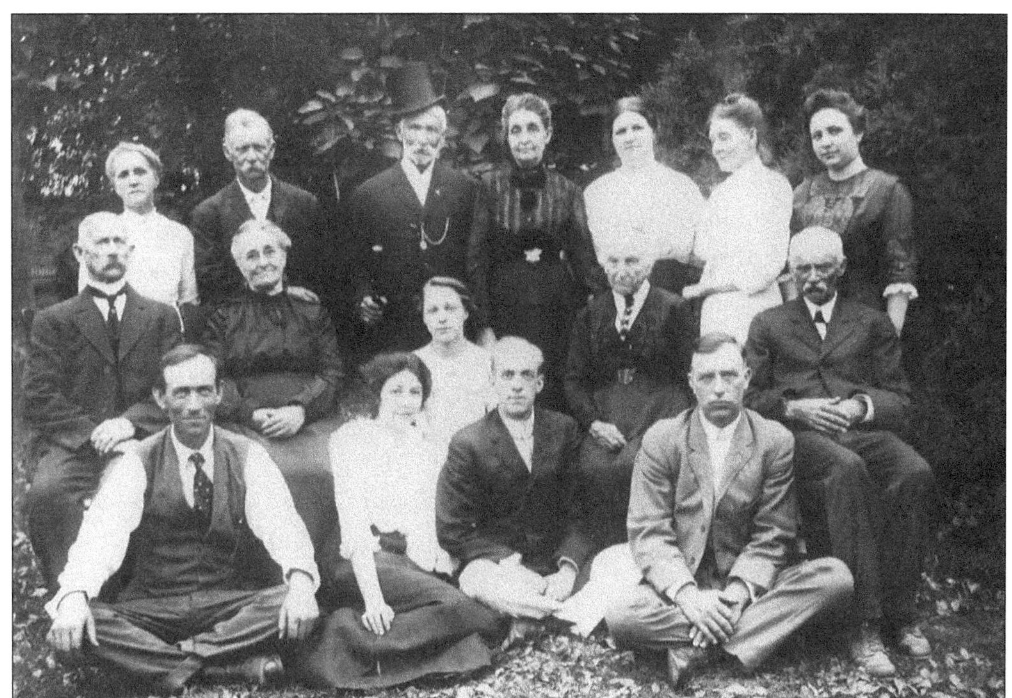

The Turner family continued to hold reunions for many years. The undated image above includes Mary Turner (second row, second from right), the daughter of pioneer Melzor Turner and the first white child to move to the Okemos area. Seated in the center is Cora Turner, and in front of her are Daphne Turner and Ray M. Hardy.

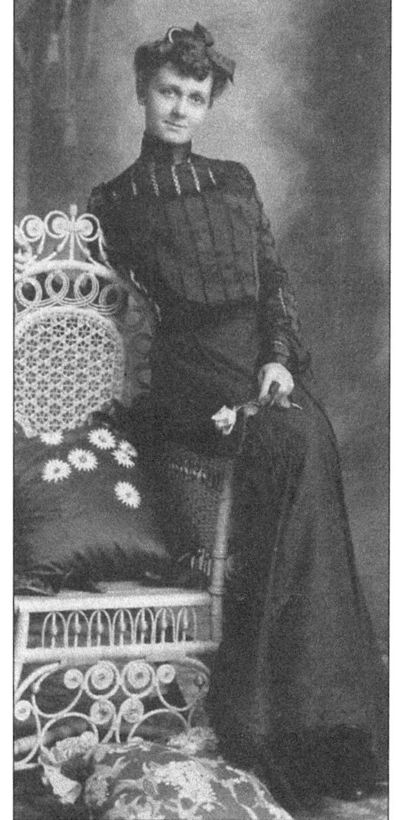

Ethel Honey of Okemos, pictured, operated a millinery shop from 1900 to 1912 in what was the Barnes House Inn and Tavern on the corner of Hamilton and Okemos Roads. The building eventually was purchased by the Breckenfeld family and used as an antique shop. A group of attorneys purchased the building in the 1980s before it was excavated and moved to the Meridian Historical Village.

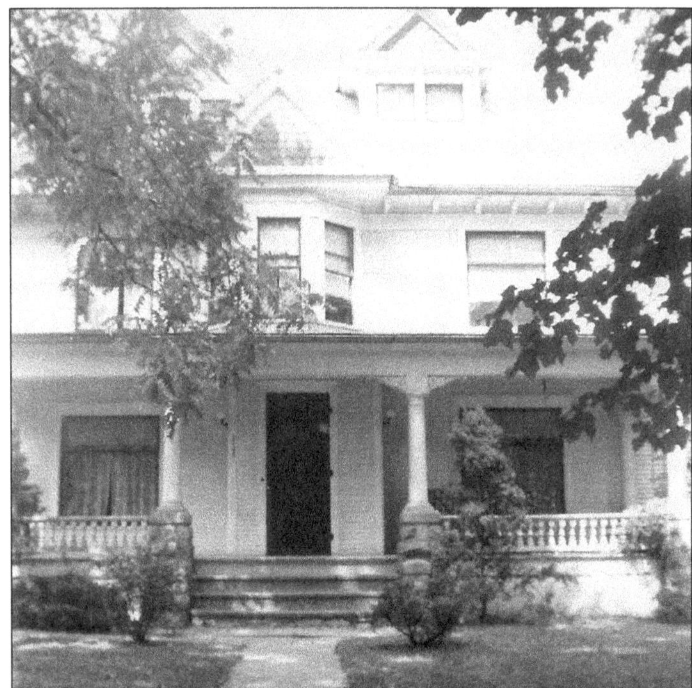

John O. Grettenberger owned a store along Hamilton Road in the village of Okemos and built his home on the lot to the east of the store. The size of the home and the care taken with construction made it the largest, grandest house in the village.

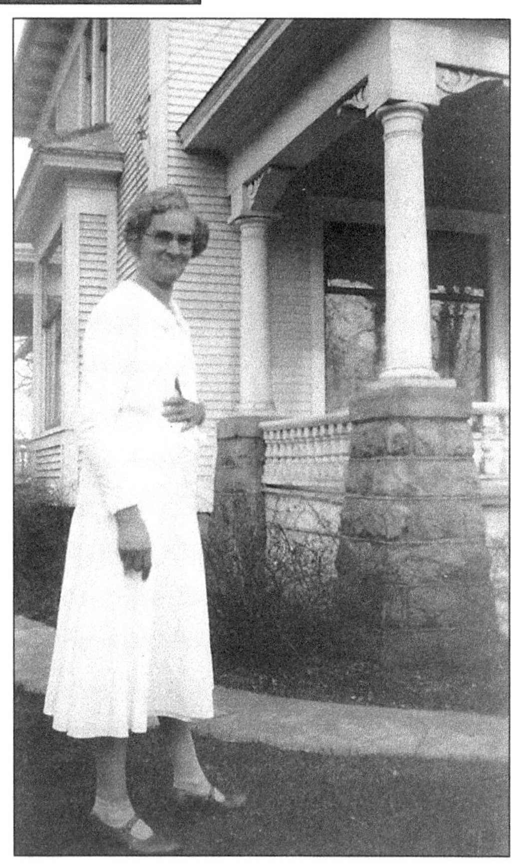

Minnie Grettenberger, wife of John O., is shown in her front yard along Hamilton Road. The house was torn down in the 1950s to make room for a service station.

The Grettenberger family gathers on the front porch of the Hamilton Road house. John O. Grettenberger is seated at front left. In the back row are Laura Woodworth Grettenberger (fourth from the left) and, to the right of her, Minnie Grettenberger.

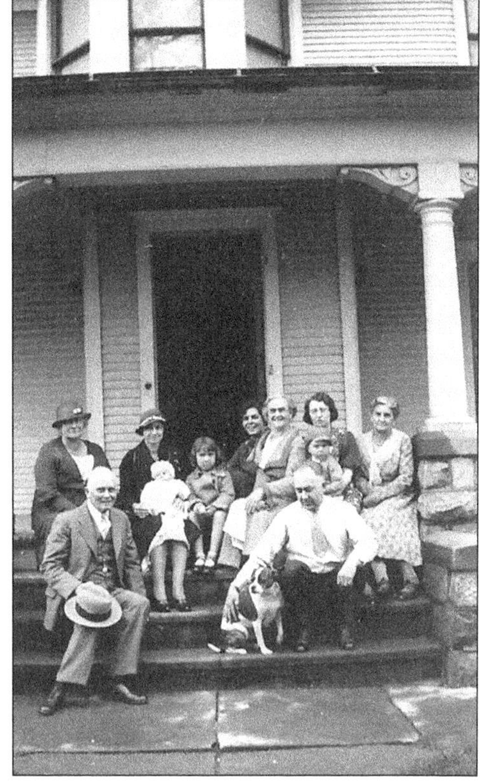

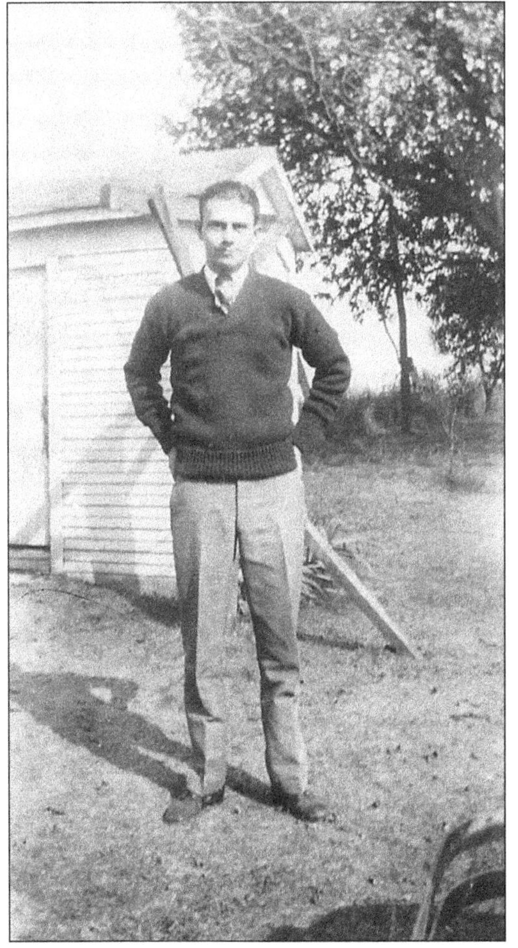

The son of John O. and Minnie Grettenberger, Orin Kaiser Grettenberger is pictured in the backyard of the family home. Orin took over the apothecary and general store from his father in 1935 and moved the store to the four corners of the village at the corners of Okemos and Hamilton Roads. Orin was a pharmacist and owned the only drugstore in the village. He began packaging essential flavoring oils in small containers for sale to local housewives who needed small quantities for cooking. The operation eventually became the LorAnn Oil Company, which is still operated by the Grettenberger family.

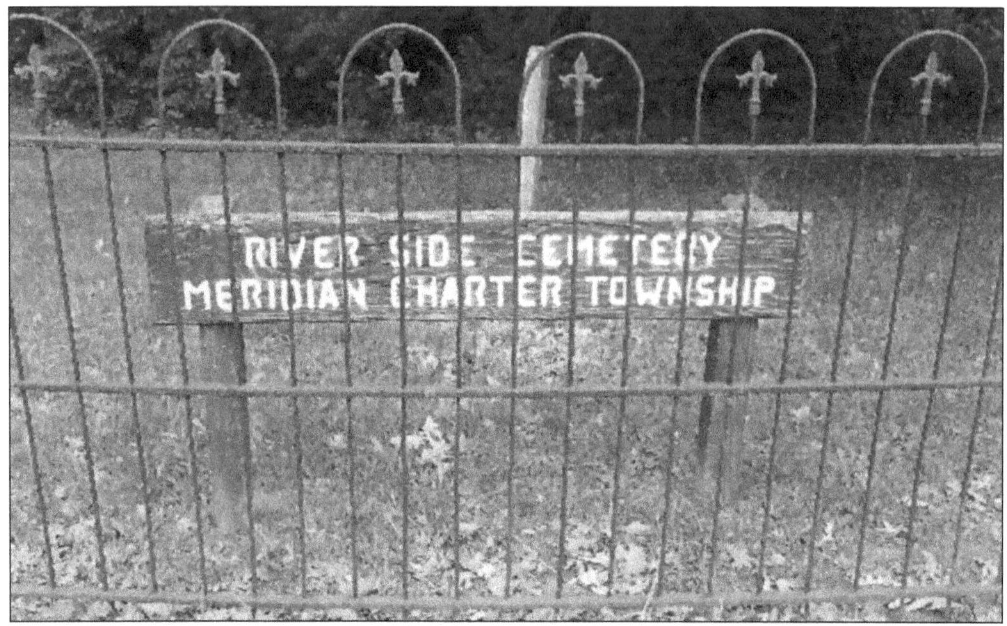

Many members of the original pioneer families were buried in the local Riverside Cemetery. The property originally was owned by Freeman Bray. The earliest burials took place around the existing Okemos churches until the 1850s, when Bray donated the property. The earliest interments were for residents who died in 1841, 1842, and 1847. There is evidence these graves were relocated from church grounds within the village. The cemetery is located south of Grand River on Little Acres Lane.

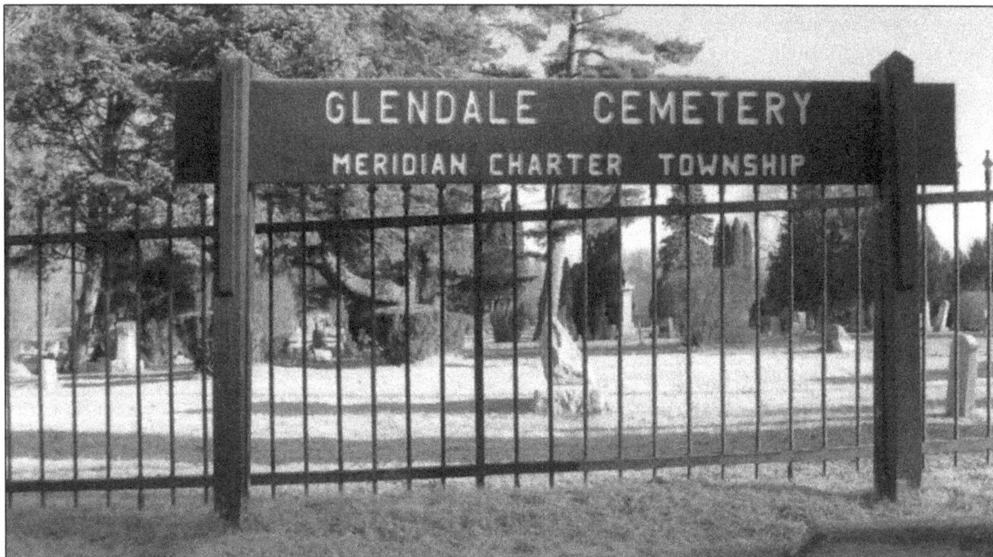

The small cemetery located along Red Cedar River had limited space, and most lots were sold by the 1880s. Another site needed to be designated for burial purposes as the community continued to grow. Mount Hope Avenue is a major east-west road that runs from Okemos Road all the way to the west side of Lansing. Property on the north side of the road was purchased in the 1880s and made available for use in 1887. The cemetery also serves as the burial place for numerous pioneer descendants.

Nine

A Forgotten Hamlet

As railroads became the primary mode of transportation in the 19th century, a line running southeast from the city of Lansing was built to connect the community with the city of Detroit. The line crossed the easternmost north-south road in Meridian Township, and a railroad office was built. The site also acquired a post office named for the north-south road, Meridian Road.

Much like the Haslett community, businesses and homes were established at the crossing. With the establishment of the post office, the small community was named "Meridian Post Office." The community grew large enough to build its own little church on the west side of the road, just to the north of the railroad tracks.

Still, the little community could not compete with the growing areas of Haslett and Okemos. The site had neither a waterway nor a recreation site to attract development. As improved roadways made rail travel less important, the population dwindled and the church was closed and finally removed.

What remains today is a small hamlet of homes at the crossing on the eastern border of Meridian Township.

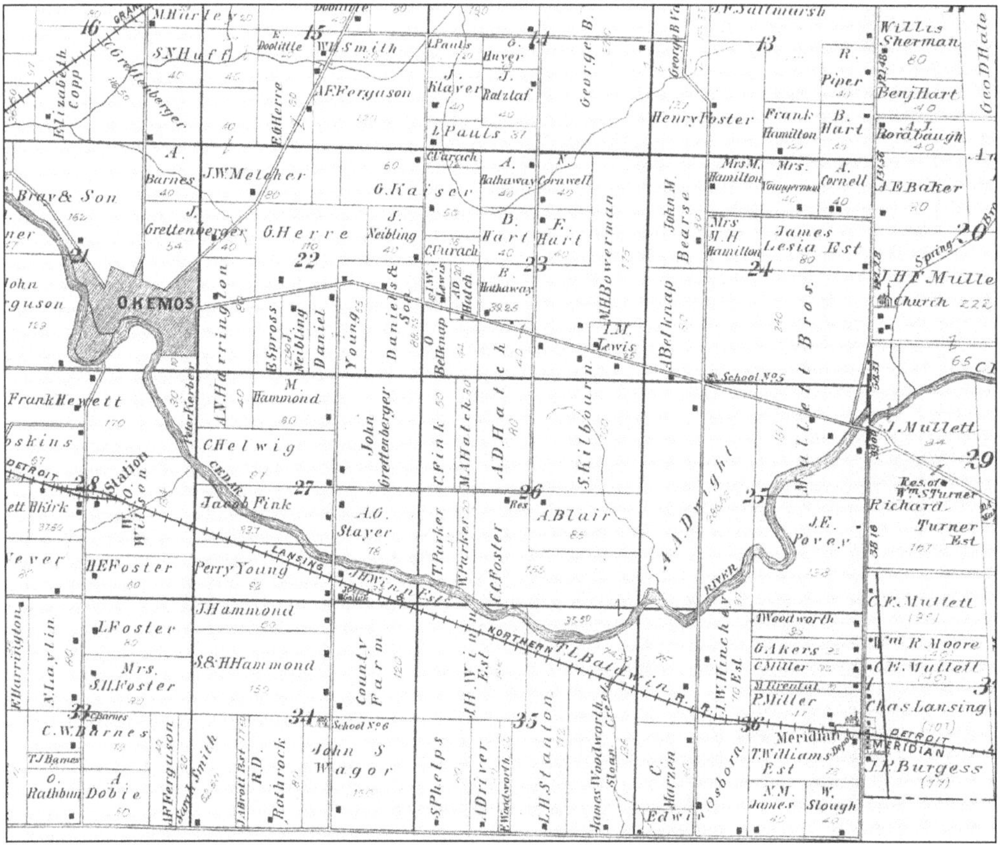

The construction of railroad tracks in the mid-19th century brought major changes to local communities. A small community formed next to the tracks built by the Detroit, Lansing & Northern Railway where the track crossed Meridian Road. No village was platted; however, buildings sprang up to serve the needs of the railroad. A rail depot was built on the south side of the tracks on the west side of the road. By 1878, A.A. Dwight built a lumber business there; a telegraph station was added in 1879; and a steam sawmill introduced the manufacture of boat oars in 1880.

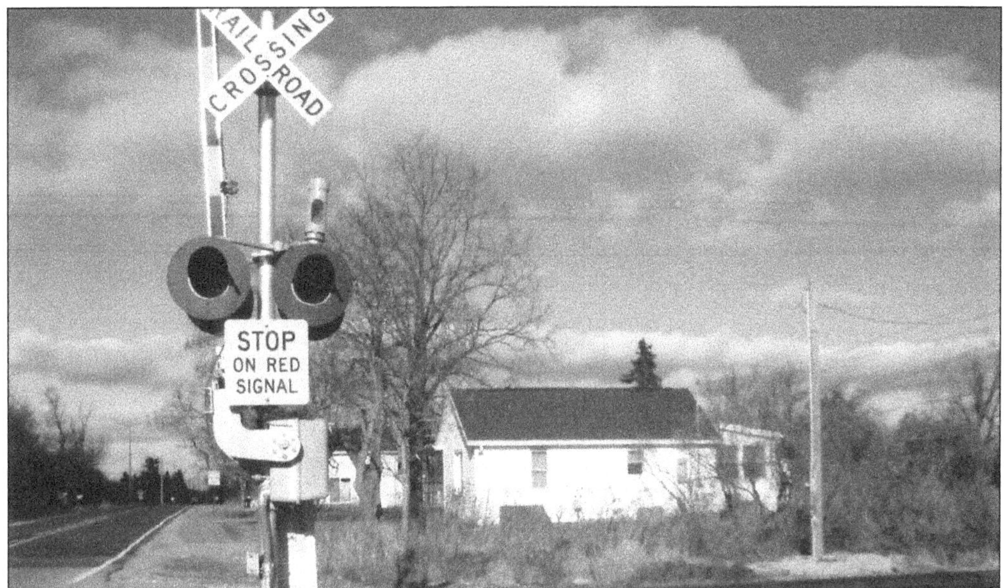

The tracks of the Detroit, Lansing & Northern Railway were built in 1871 and were used to transport work crews up and down the line for necessary repairs. Convicted prisoners were used in the 19th century to maintain and repair of the tracks. Temporary labor camps were established for the prisoners nearby the Meridian Road site.

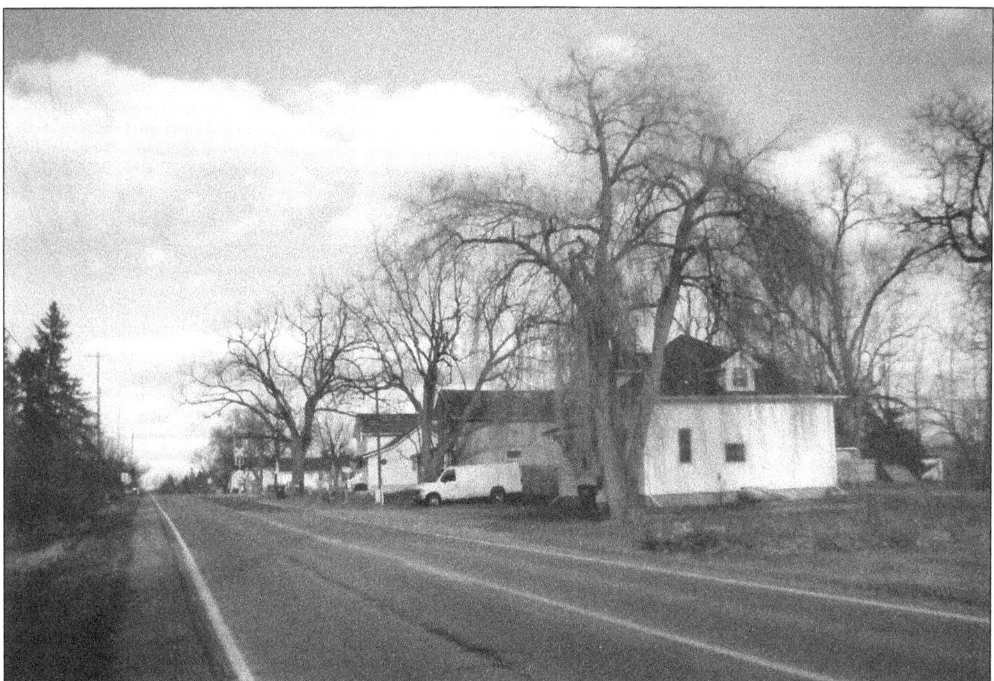

By 1874, the Meridian Road community had grown large enough to warrant its own post office. The community built its own church, the Wesleyan Methodist Church, in 1877 with some 50 members. The church was sold around 1920 after attendance dwindled, and the building was moved away. A one-room school was erected on the east side of the road prior to 1895 to serve the small community.

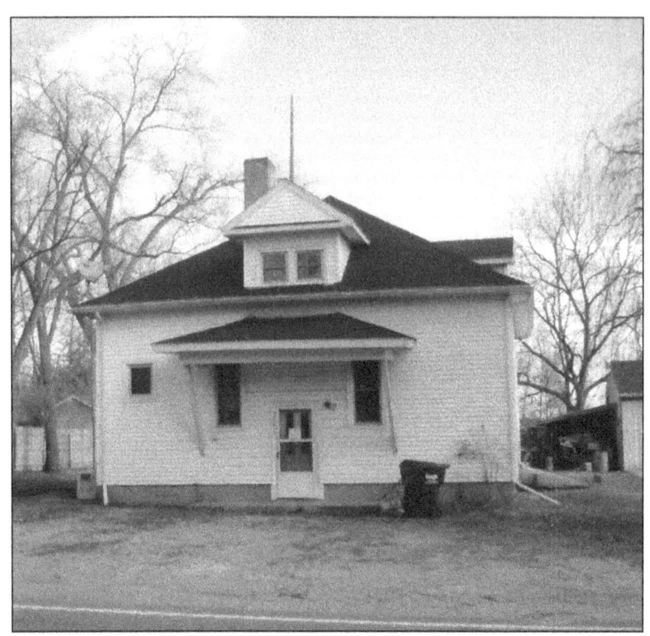

The railroad agent's house and school remain as private residences. Although the railroad brought life to the little community, the population dwindled after roads were improved and the importance of rail transport diminished. Okemos continued to grow thanks to the proximity of the Red Cedar River and the improved road to Detroit. Haslett was a resort community along the shores of Lake Lansing. Competition with other township communities prevented the little neighborhood from becoming a full-fledged village in the township.

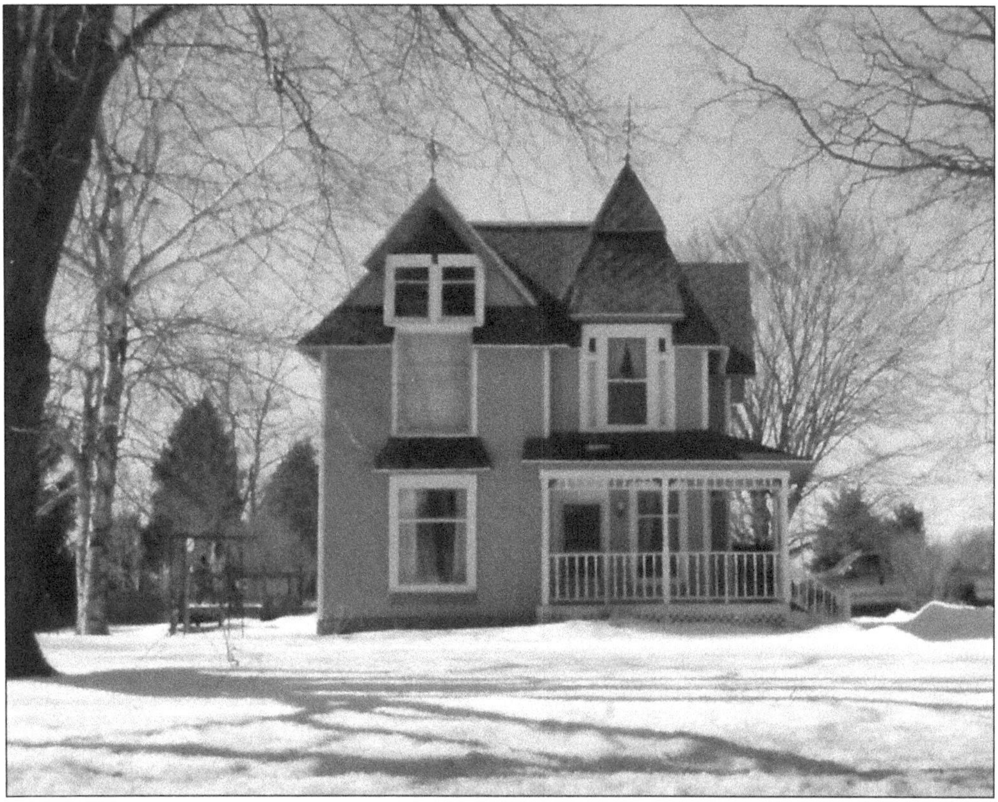

William Slough served as the telegraph agent at the Meridian Railroad Station, located on Meridian Road. He built this house in 1893–1894 just south of the train crossing. The building replaced an earlier structure erected in the late 1860s. It remains occupied today on Meridian Road just north of Jolly Road in Okemos.

Ten

Preserving Local History

Residents in Meridian Township have long valued the quiet—even rural—nature of the area. Commitments were made decades ago by the township to preserve large areas in the most natural condition possible. Sections have been set aside as parks and others as natural areas. Residents have financially supported these efforts with the creation of the Parks and Recreation Department and the Land Preservation Board. This support was encouraged during the 1970s and 1980s as residential and commercial development expanded at an increasing rate.

After the Michigan Legislature enacted legislation in 1970 authorizing historical conservation regulations, Meridian Township established a Historic District Study Committee in 1972. Members of the committee conducted an inventory of 19th-century buildings throughout the township and submitted the first report on the village of Okemos in 1972. Reports on the village of Haslett and the rural area of the township soon followed.

These reports highlighted the rich history of family homes and buildings and led to the creation of the Friends of Historic Meridian in 1974. The members realized the rapid development of the township was removing much of the area's past, and the organization was formed to create and sustain an active appreciation of local history.

As inventoried buildings fell into disrepair and risked being razed, the members raised funds to rescue the structures and have them moved to a central site and restored to their original condition. The site became known as the Meridian Historical Village and now houses eight historical buildings and three structures from the Haslett and Okemos areas.

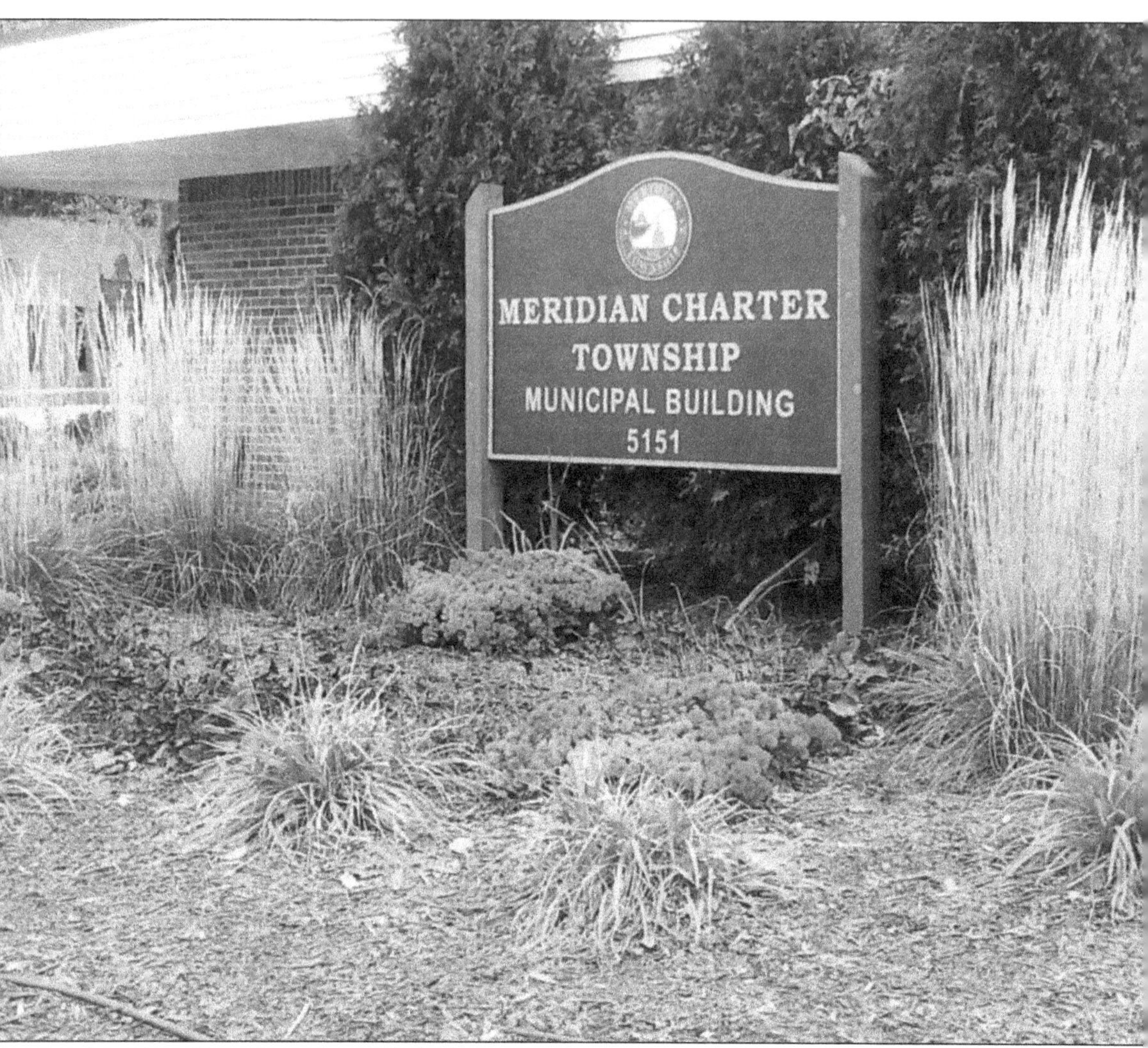

Meridian Township was established in 1842, and early meetings and officers included residents from Haslett, Okemos, and rural areas. Development in the 20th century put an ever-increasing burden on public utilities and required a new approach on the part of the government to meet those needs. The 1970s saw changes that resulted in Meridian Township switching its legal designation to the Charter Township of Meridian. (Courtesy of the Charter Township of Meridian.)

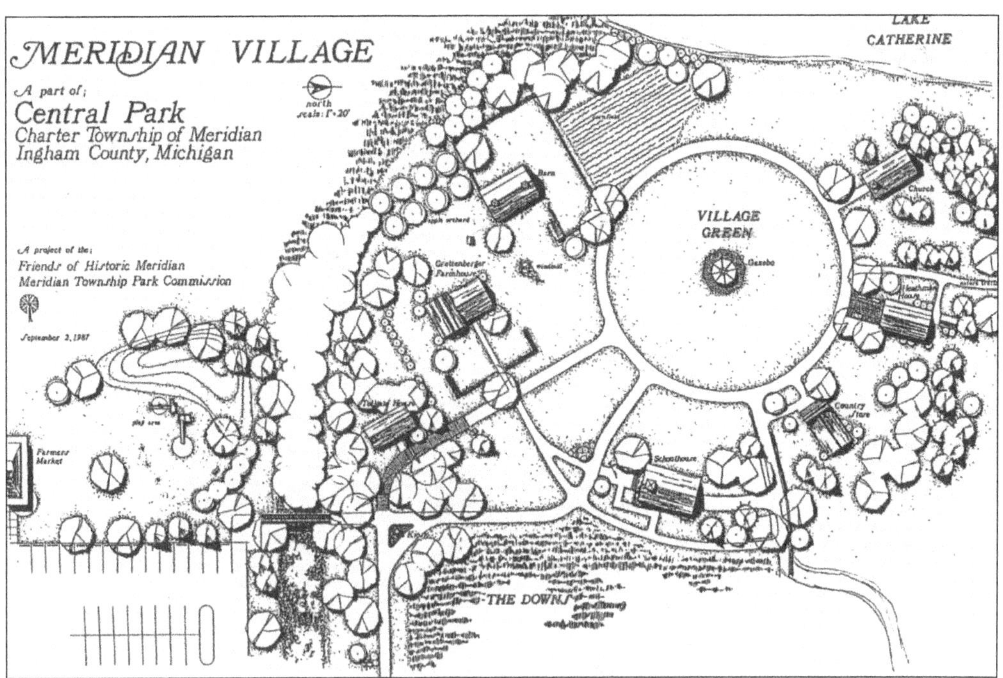

Township planners worked out a vision for the future use of the Central Park. The project was a joint effort between the Friends of Historic Meridian and Meridian Township Planning Commission. The "Meridian Village" noted on the map is not the same "forgotten hamlet" of the Meridian Post Office, which was located along Meridian Road north of Jolly Road. (Image courtesy of the Charter Township Planning Department.)

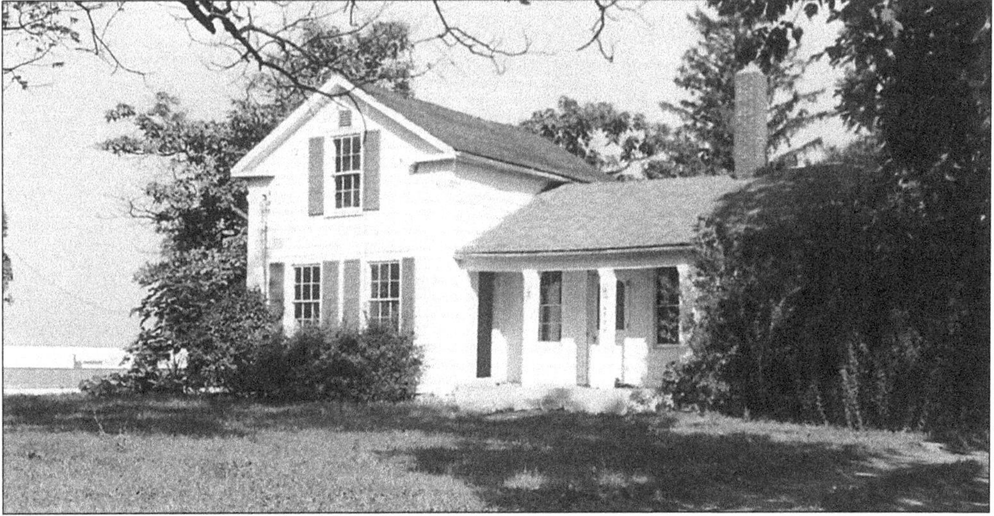

The Grettenberger farmhouse originally was located along Marsh Road between Grand River Avenue and Hamilton Road. It was built in the 1860s by Johann Georg Grettenberger for his son Jacob. The property was acquired by subsequent generations and eventually was owned by Orin K. Grettenberger, owner of the drugstore in the village. The last Grettenbergers to live in the home were John Grettenberger Sr. and his wife, Jane. Later, the house was used as rental property and fell into disrepair. This was the first building secured by the Friends of Historic Meridian for preservation.

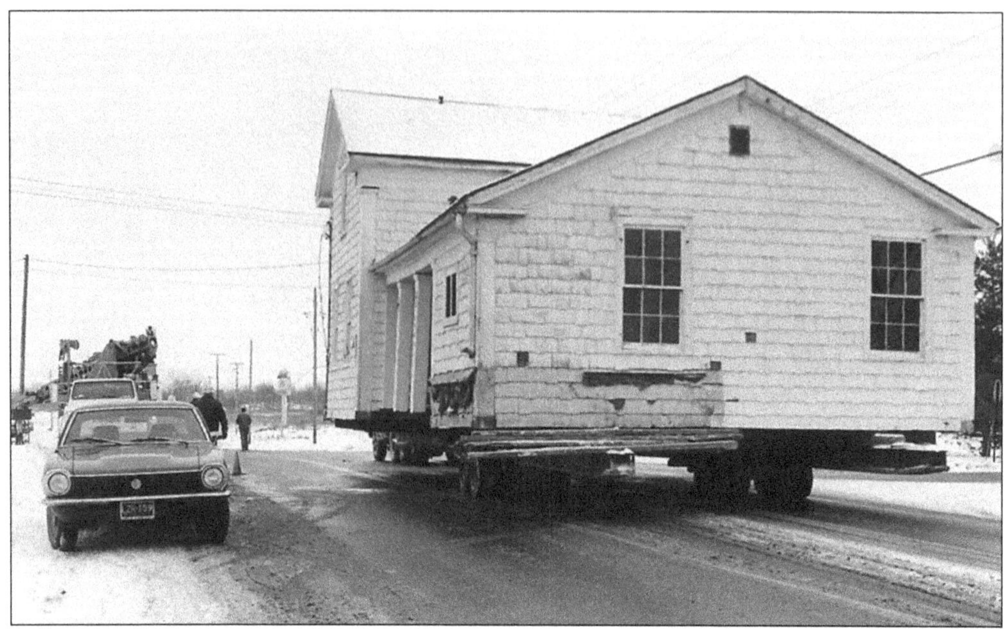

Orin K. and John O. Grettenberger Sr. donated the building to the Friends of Historic Meridian in 1973, and in January 1974, the building was excavated, placed on a flatbed truck, and moved a half-mile downhill to the new Central Park. The building stood alone in the snowy park field for months before funds could be secured to begin the restoration process.

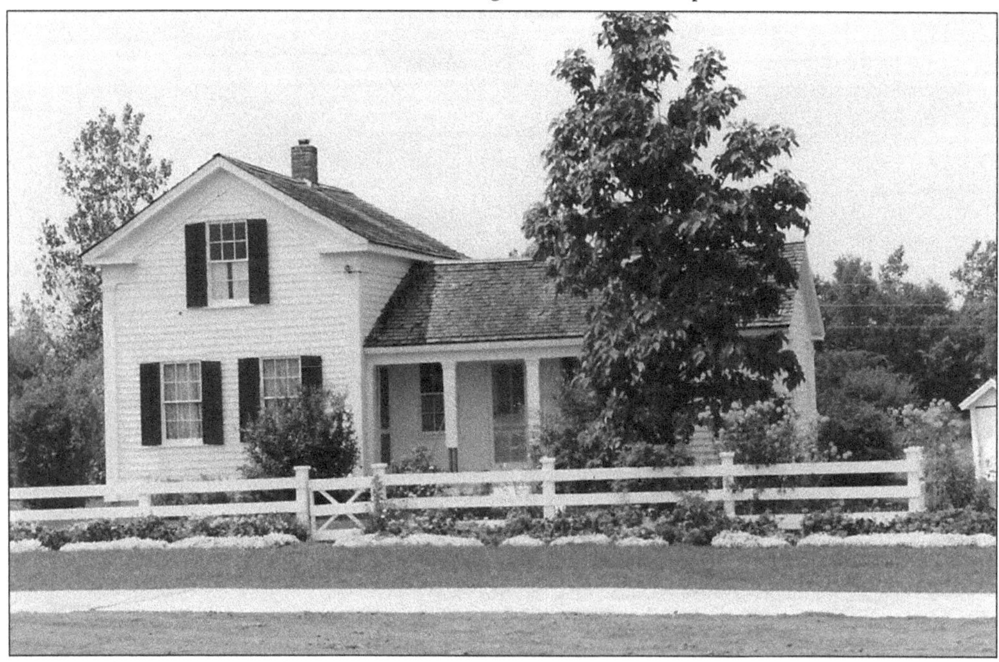

The farmhouse was initially set on an inadequate foundation, which needed to be replaced before the building could be restored and opened to the public. A gardening club formed in the 1970s, and members offered their valuable assistance to the Friends of Historic Meridian. The Meridian Garden Club planted and continues to maintain the beautiful gardens in front of the farmhouse.

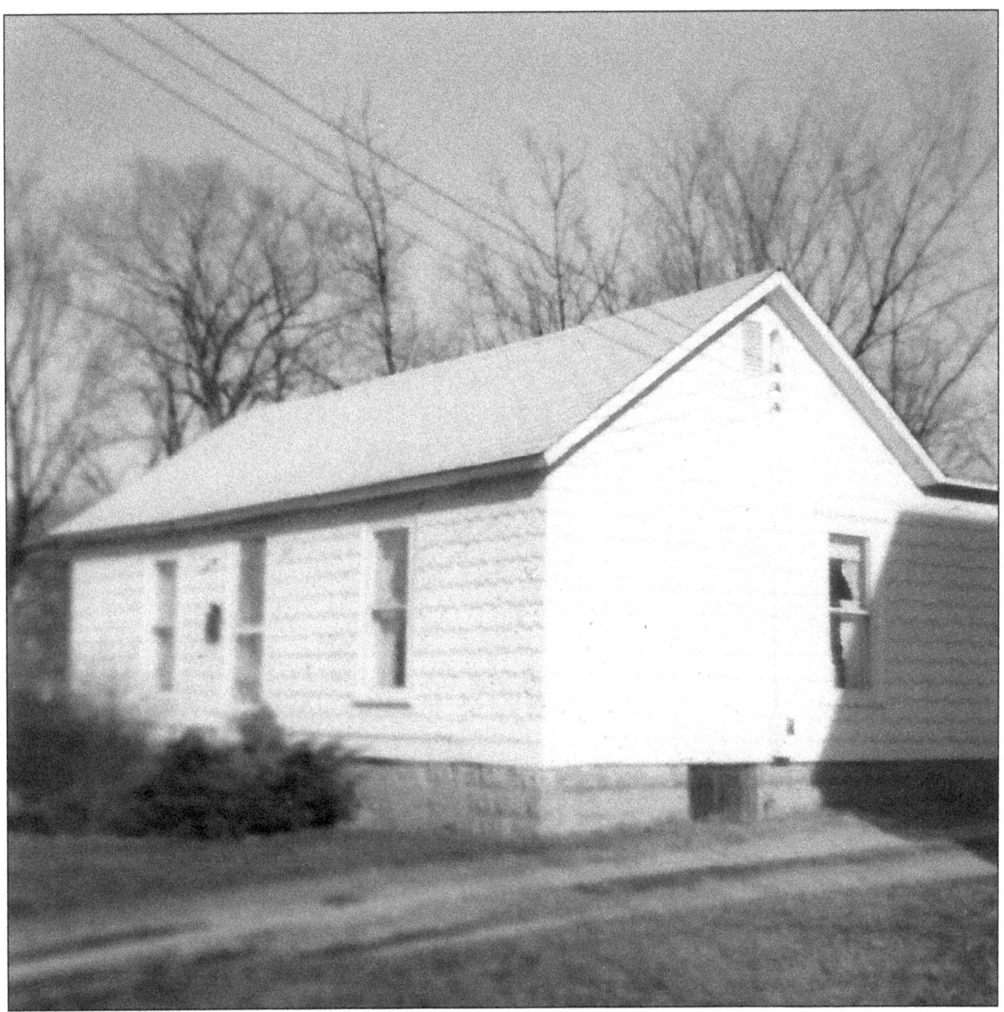

The frame building pictured above was erected in 1850 and used as a stopping point along the Lansing-to-Howell plank road. The Proctor family, initially Asa and then his son Alonzo, collected tolls from travelers and reported the earnings to the parent company, the Lansing to Howell Company. The original location of the building was on the south side of Grand River Avenue at Park Lake Road. The building remained at the site and, after it was no longer used as a tollhouse, served as an outbuilding for the Proctor family. It was located immediately next to the road and had to be moved when the Highway Department widened the road in the 1920s. The owners of the property at the time moved the building west and north into East Lansing along Hagadorn Road. The house was rented to students from Michigan State University for many years until road improvements again required the building be moved or torn down.

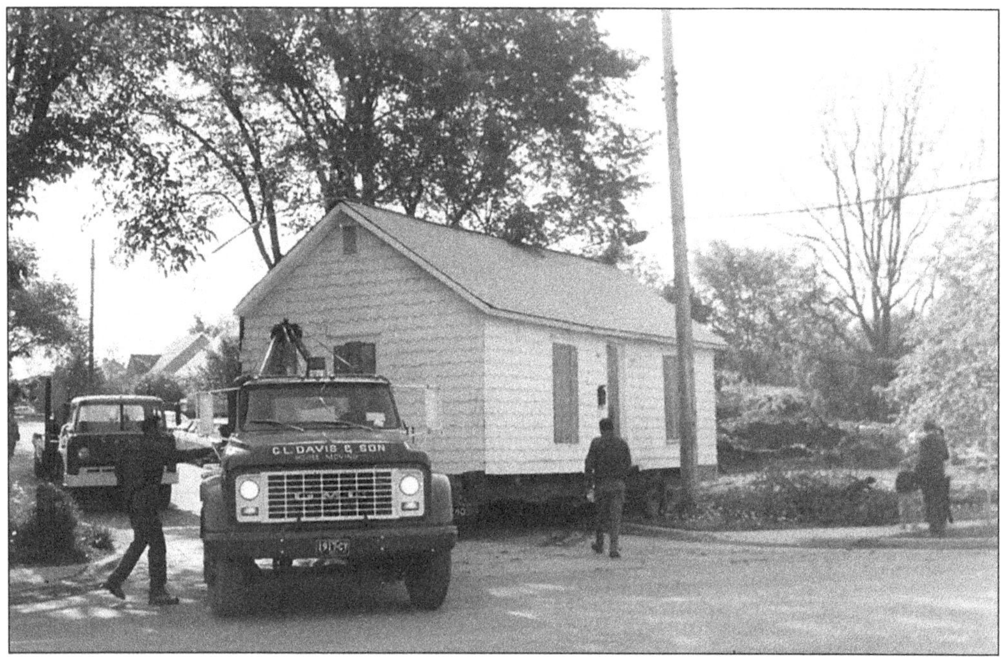

The rental house was acquired by the township and, with the assistance of the Friends of Historic Meridian, was moved to Wonch Park along Okemos Road. The location was less than ideal, as the park was in a floodplain along Red Cedar River. In July 1974, the building was moved a third time, joining the Grettenberger farmhouse at the Central Park site.

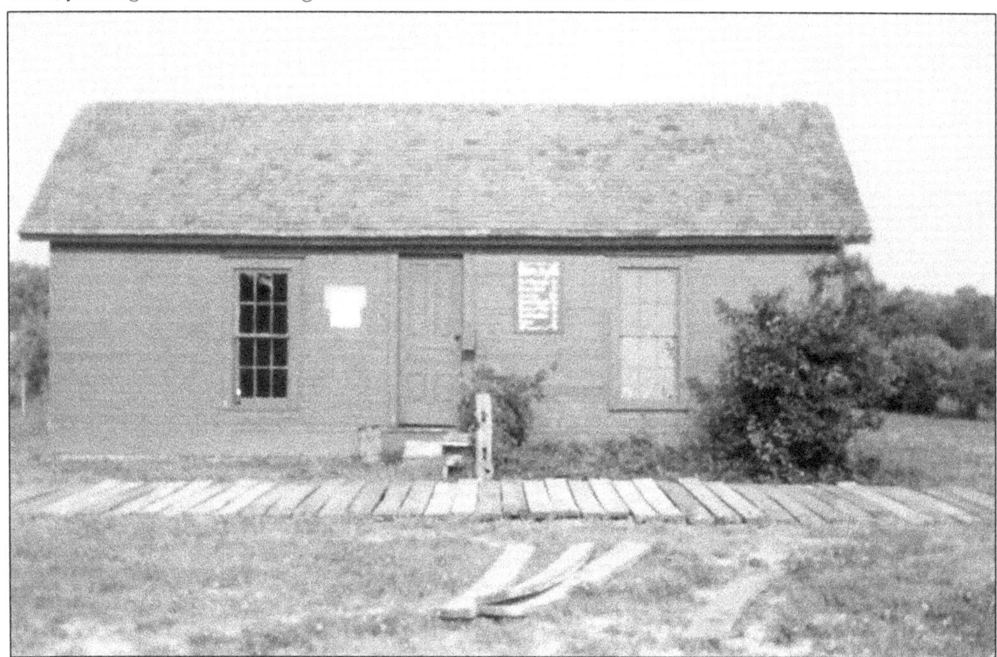

The Proctor tollgate house was located in the village just to the south of the Grettenberger farmhouse. The modern shingles were removed, and the walls were stripped down to the original beadwork paneling. The Friends of Historic Meridian also constructed a walkway in front of the building to serve as an example of the old plank road that ran through the center of Okemos.

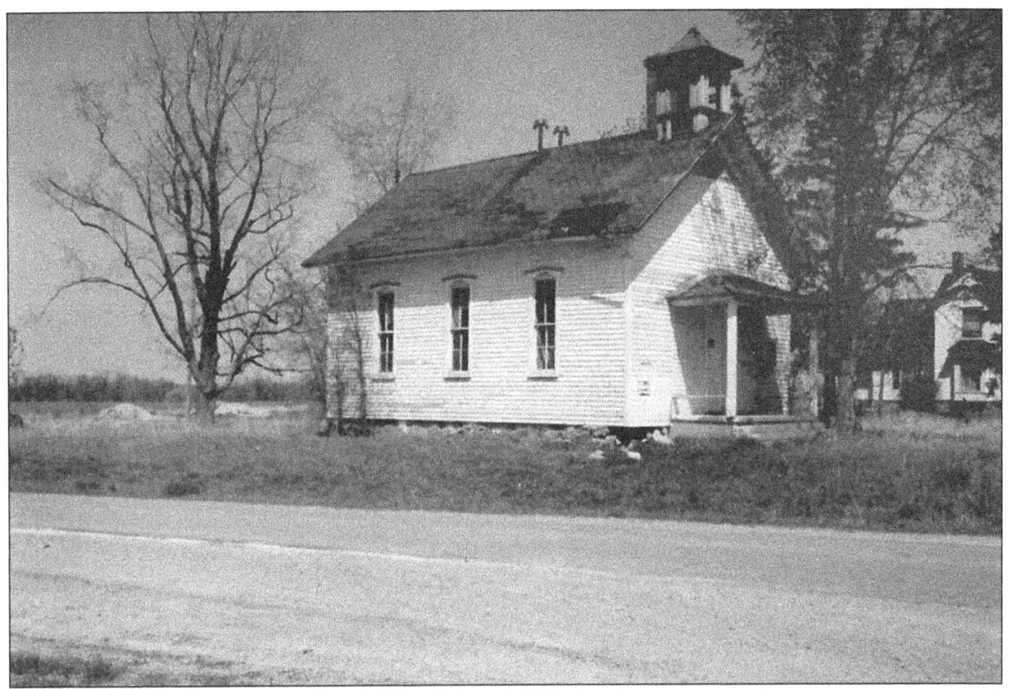

The Friends of Historic Meridian searched the township to find an existing local one-room school to add to the village. The few remaining school buildings were privately owned and used as homes. An abandoned school was found north of Fowlerville in Livingston County, and the owner agreed to donate it.

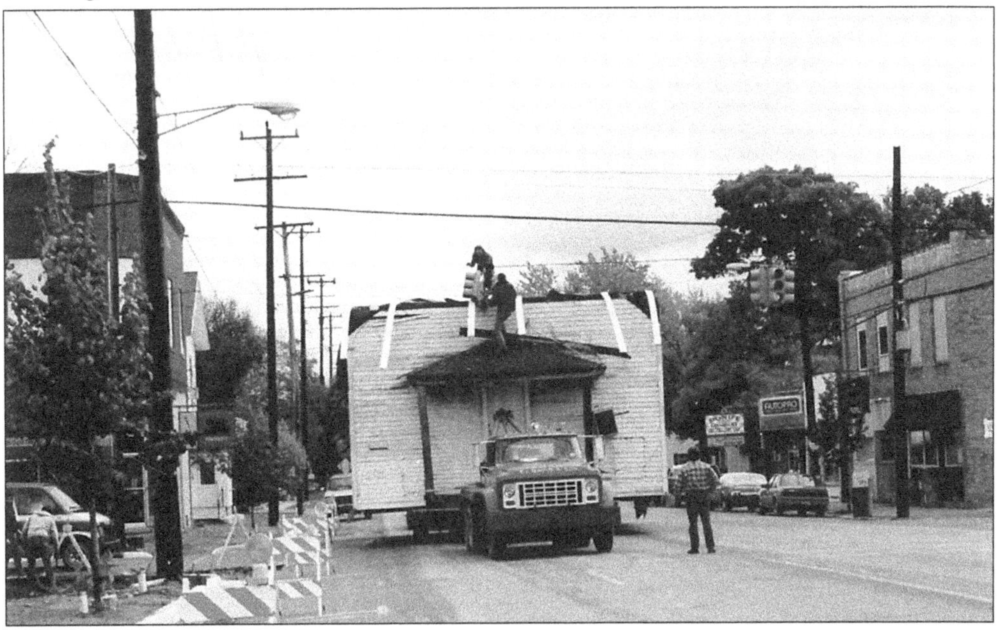

The schoolhouse had to be excavated and transported from Fowlerville to Okemos along the Grand River Avenue route. The belfry was removed for restoration, and the badly deteriorated roof was removed. This allowed the building to be moved through the towns but still required public utilities to be raised to allow the structure to travel beneath.

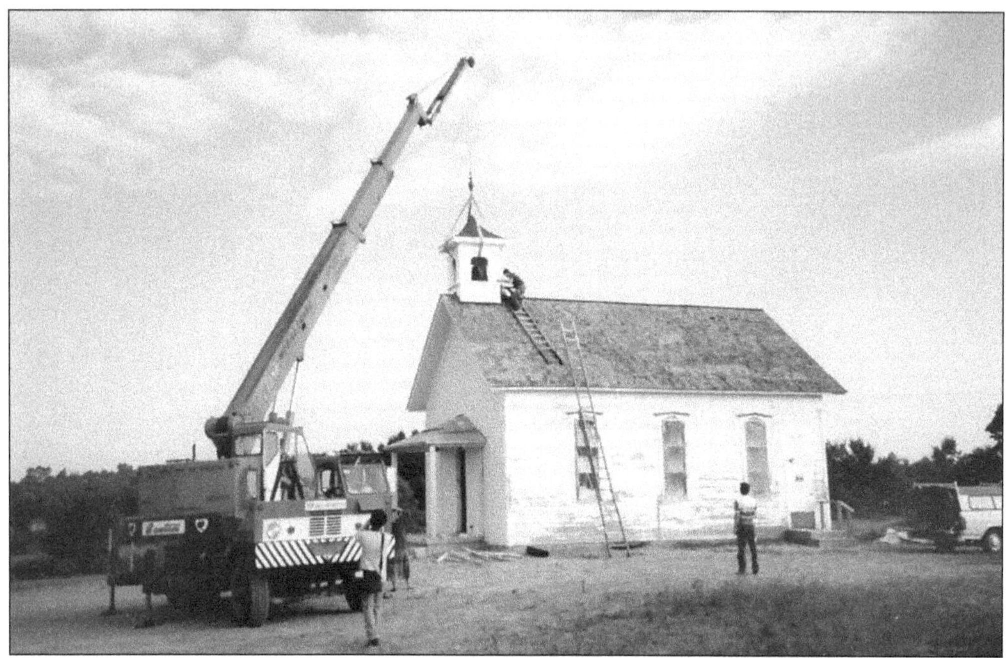

The schoolhouse was placed in the village atop the first basement built at the site. The belfry was restored and added to the building once a new roof was placed. The school is located directly across the green from the farmhouse. The three buildings in place—the farmhouse, tollhouse, and schoolhouse—provide a rich teaching opportunity for school groups who visit the village.

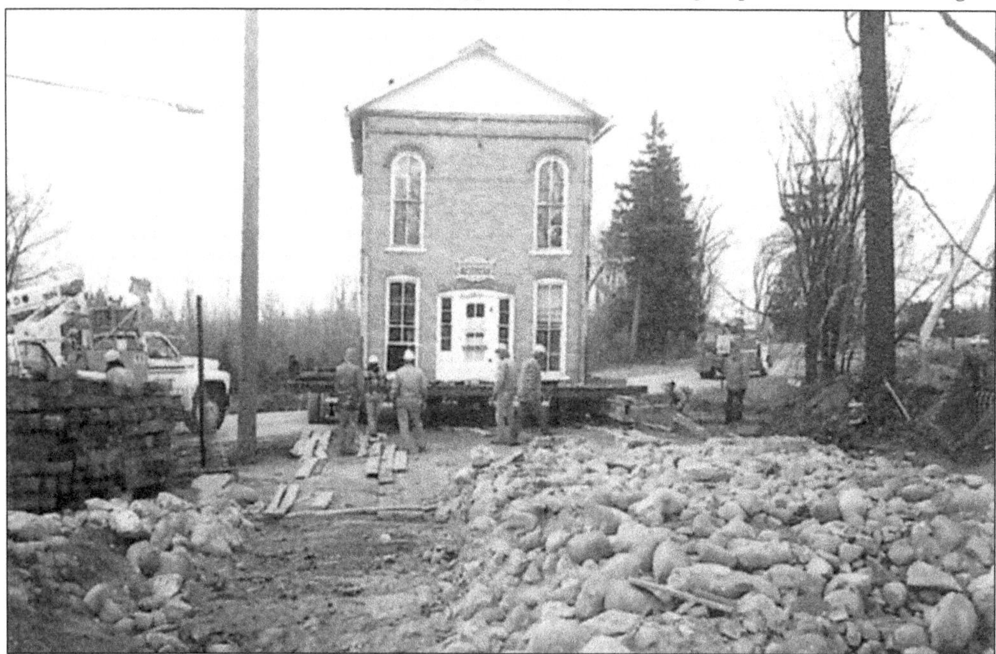

The Heathman-Herre house was originally built as a blacksmith shop. Its construction is unique in that the walls are two bricks thick, held together by iron rods running the length and width of the building. Both the Heathman and Herre families called the structure home for years. The last owner of the property was Keith Bartow, who operated a music studio there.

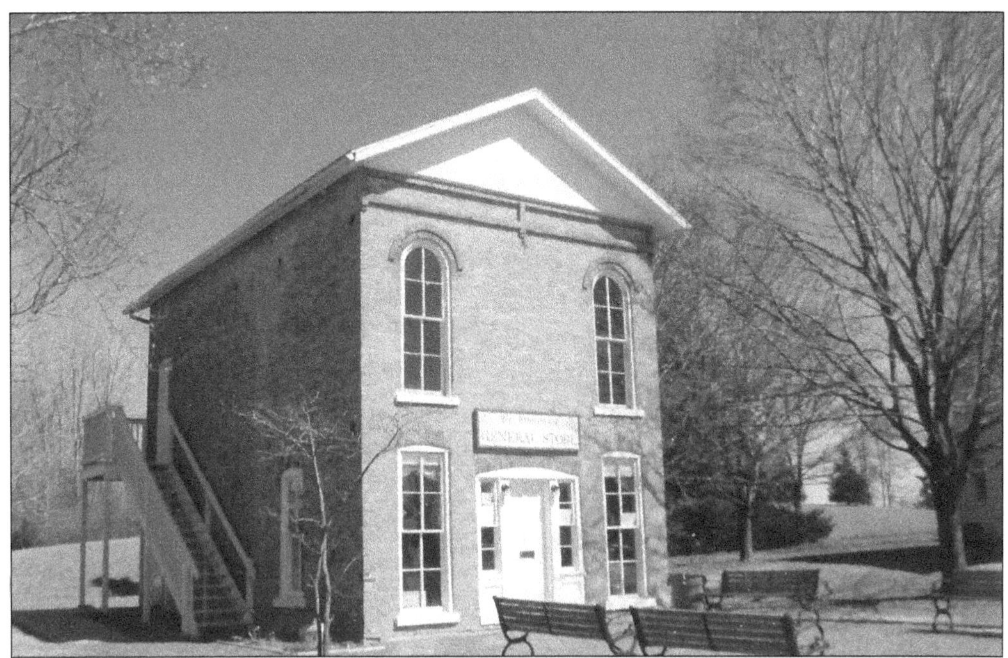

Newly relocated to the village, the building was restored for use as a warming house. It was never used for such purposes, and the Friends of Historic Meridian assumed the responsibility for restoring the building to its 19th-century condition. The building currently houses the gift shop, a general store exhibit, and the village office.

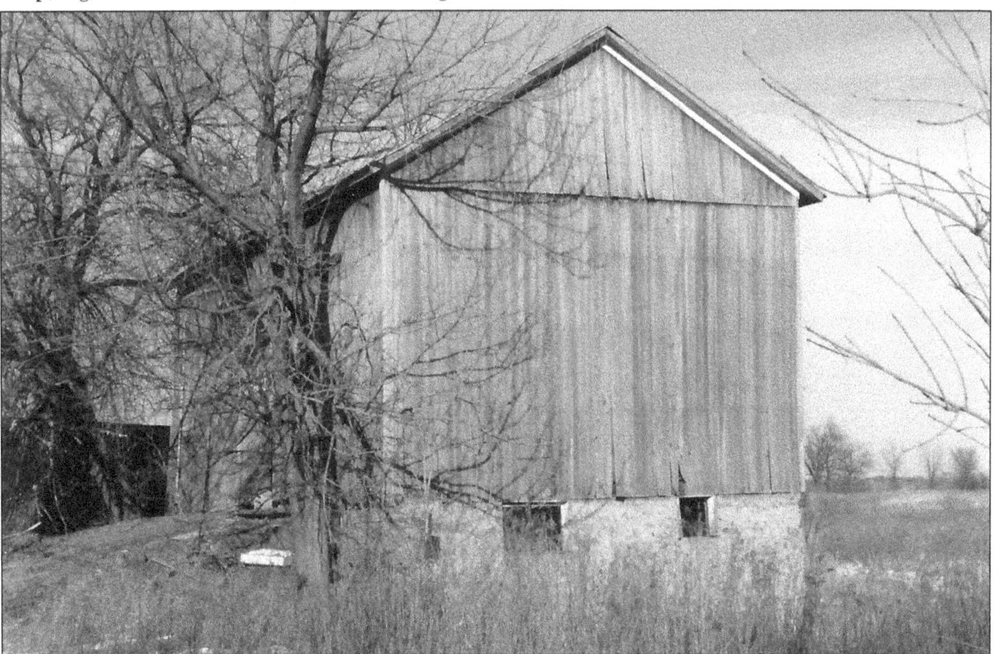

The rural nature of Meridian Township meant there were multiple farms in the township. One farm was purchased in the 1980s by a local developer, and the barn was scheduled to be torn down. The Friends of Historic Meridian approached the developer and the township for permission to rescue the building and relocate it to the village.

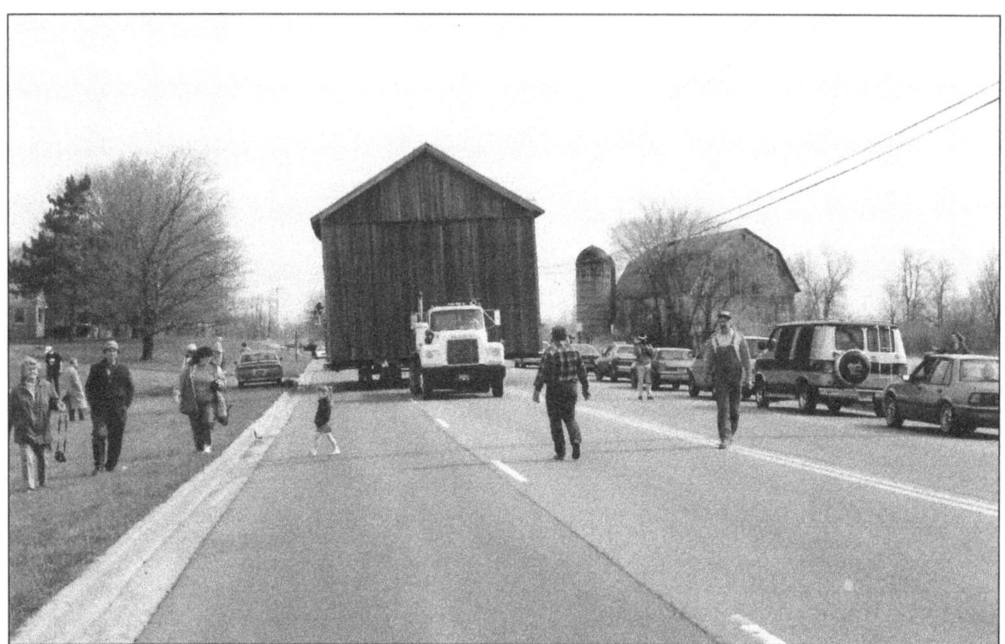

The barn was located across the road from the village on land that had been owned by the Unruh family. Because of its proximity to the village, the barn had the shortest distance to travel. Unlike the relocation of the schoolhouse, which required a significant effort to travel the distance, the barn was driven across the road, and delighted residents walked along with the building.

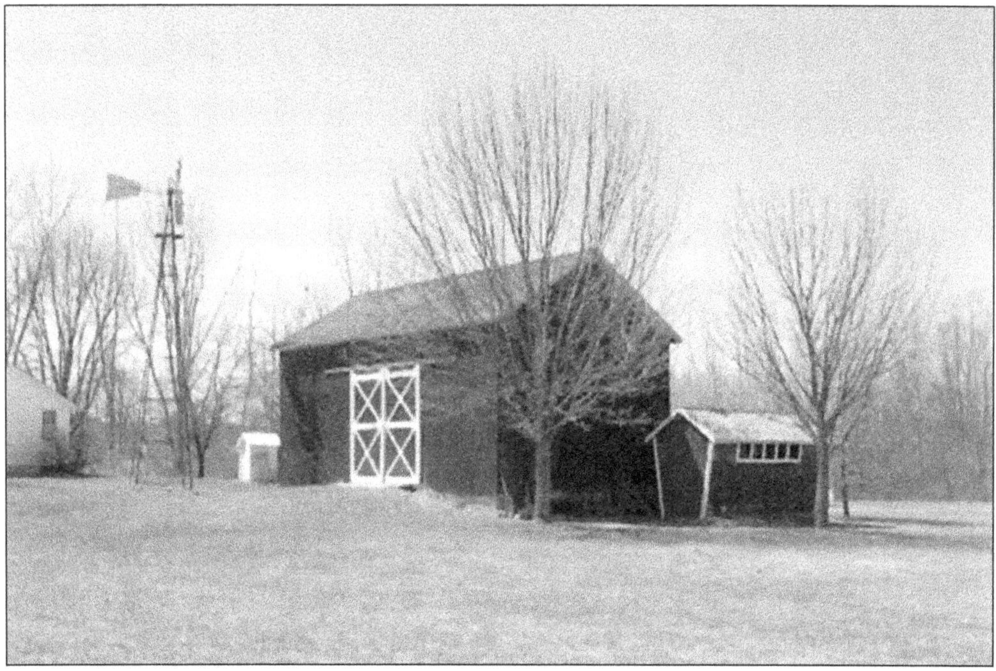

The relocation of the barn helped complete the farmstead component of the village when it joined the Grettenberger farmhouse, the windmill, and the outhouse behind. The corncrib pictured in the above photograph was donated in 2006 by Yvette Schroeder and was originally located at a farm on Dobie Road.

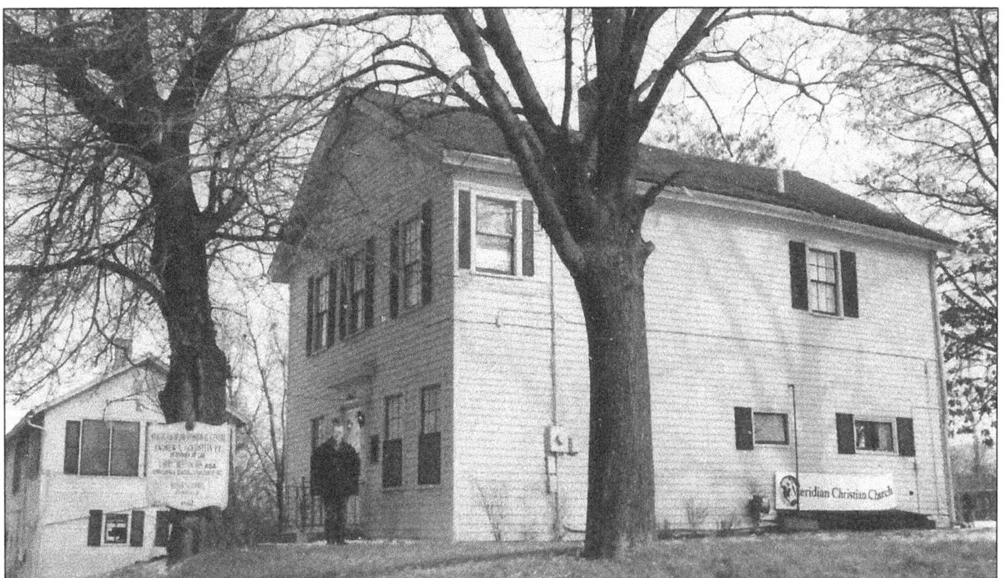

Located along Okemos Road just south of the former medical offices of Dr. Breckenfeld, the Barnes House was historically significant because it was constructed in 1849 and was the first frame building constructed in the village of Okemos. All buildings, home and commercial, prior to that time had been constructed with logs. The builder of the house was Melzor Turner, a cabinetmaker who came from New York State in the 1840s.

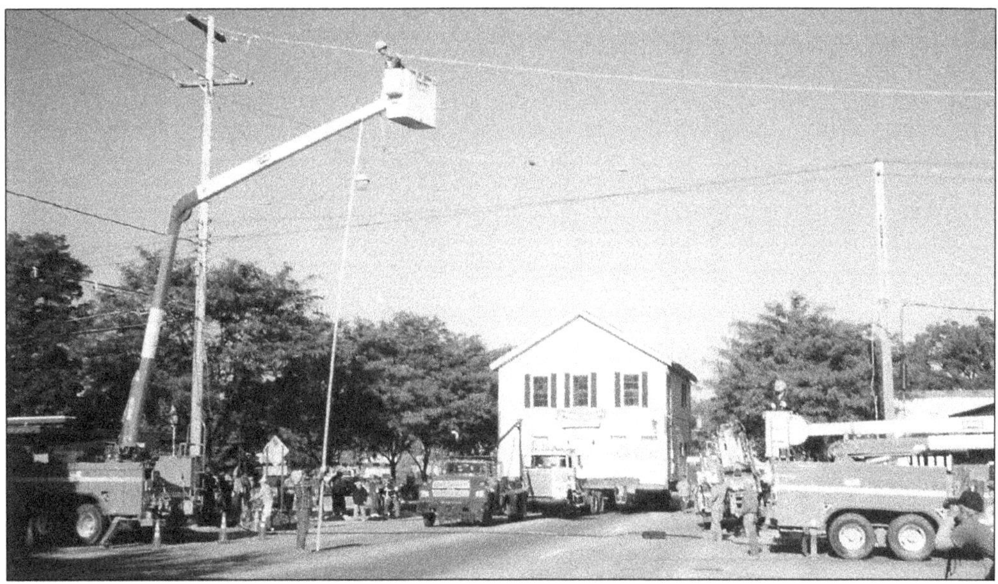

Once again, road improvements by the Ingham County Road Commission endangered the historic structure, and the commission agreed to donate the building to the Friends of Historic Meridian. Although the building was donated, the cost to move it was significant. Over the 20 years the Friends of Historic Meridian had worked to relocate historic buildings, the moving costs had escalated. Moving the building the approximately three quarters of a mile from its original site to the village now involved raising traffic signals at five different intersections. Paula Gangopadhyay worked with local businesses to raise the money. The schoolchildren at nearby Central Elementary also raised money to help with the move.

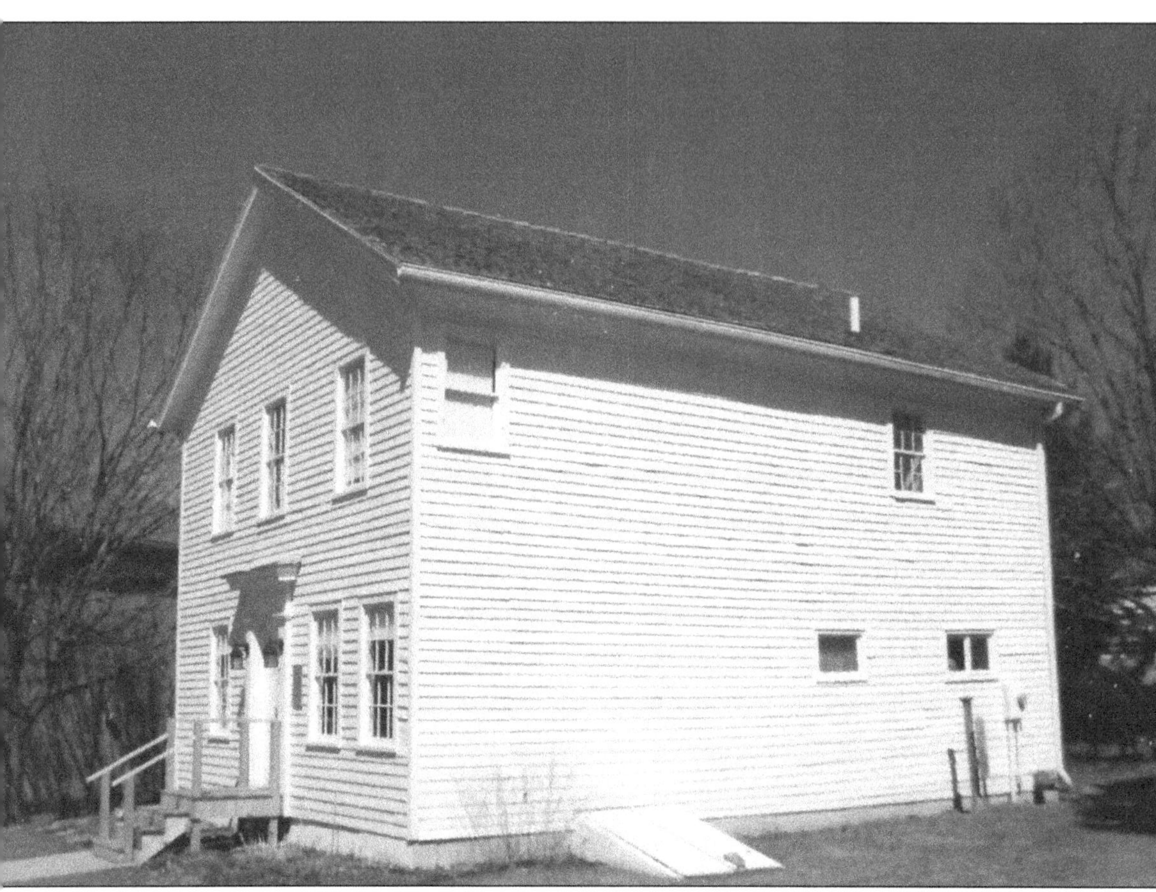

Another basement was dug for the relocated building to allow for heat, air conditioning, and plumbing for a half bath. Several rooms have been designed to show a 19th-century inn and tavern. In addition, the building houses the archives for the Friends of Historic Meridian, source for many of the photographs in this book. The building also serves as the meeting location for the board of the Friends of Historic Meridian.

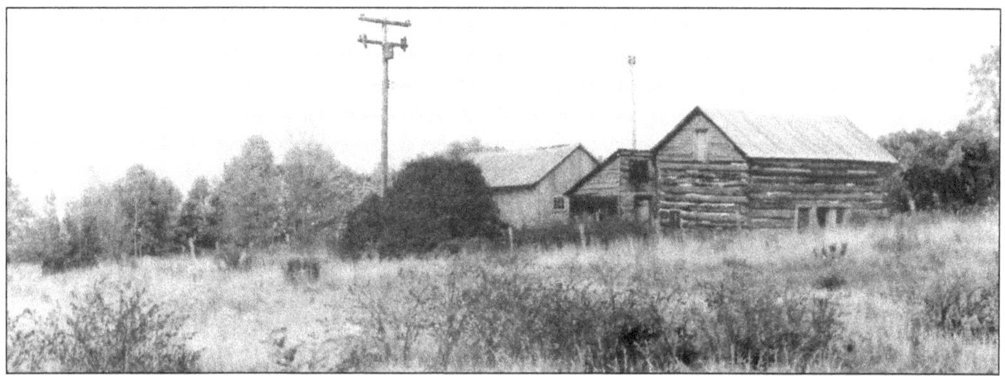

In the mid-19th century, Jim Perkins and his wife, Alice, started a farm in Williamstown Township immediately to the east of Haslett. The original structure was made from logs and added to with frame construction in later years. After the couple died, the property was purchased by Michigan State University professor Ervin VanderJadt. A modern house was already on the property, so the professor planned to destroy the old, overgrown building. Jane Taylor, Haslett Middle School teacher, heard of the plans and convinced the professor to donate the building to the school district. Jane, along with Robert Copland and Ray Koerner, developed a program to teach the middle school students about pioneer living and outdoor education.

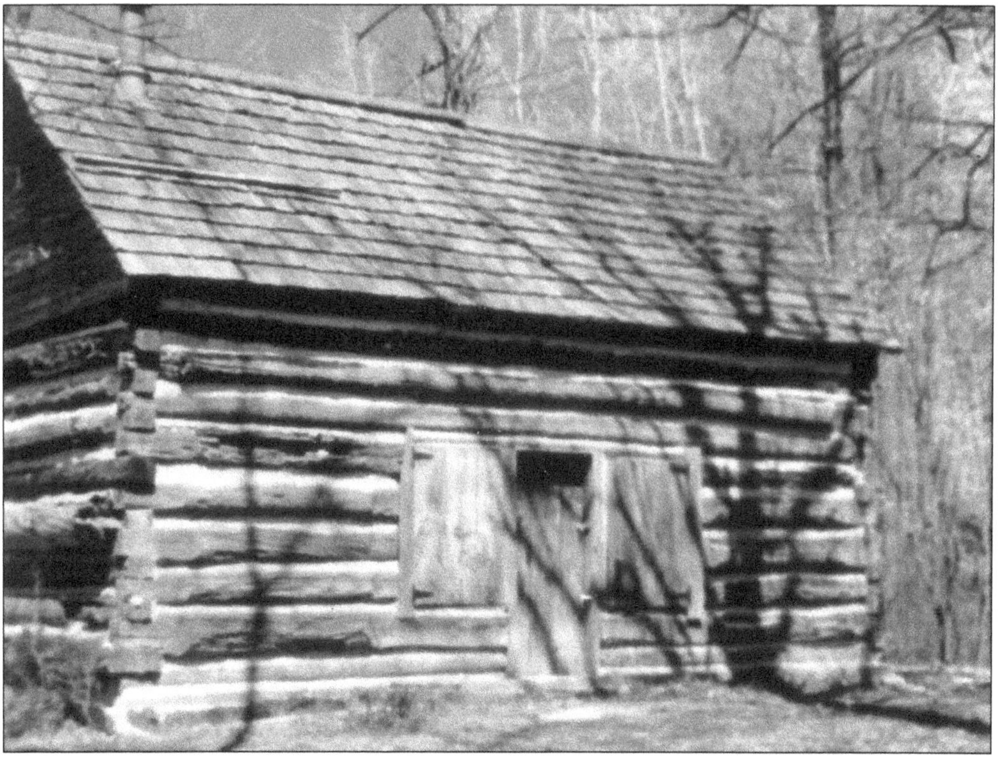

After the program was terminated, the building was closed, and it attracted vandals over the years who caused considerable damage. The Friends of Historic Meridian acquired the building from the Haslett School District in 2007 and moved it to the village. Surprisingly, even though the building was one of the smallest moved to the village, the ever-increasing costs of moving utilities prohibited it from being relocated in one piece. The cabin was taken apart, and the pieces were tagged and moved to the village.

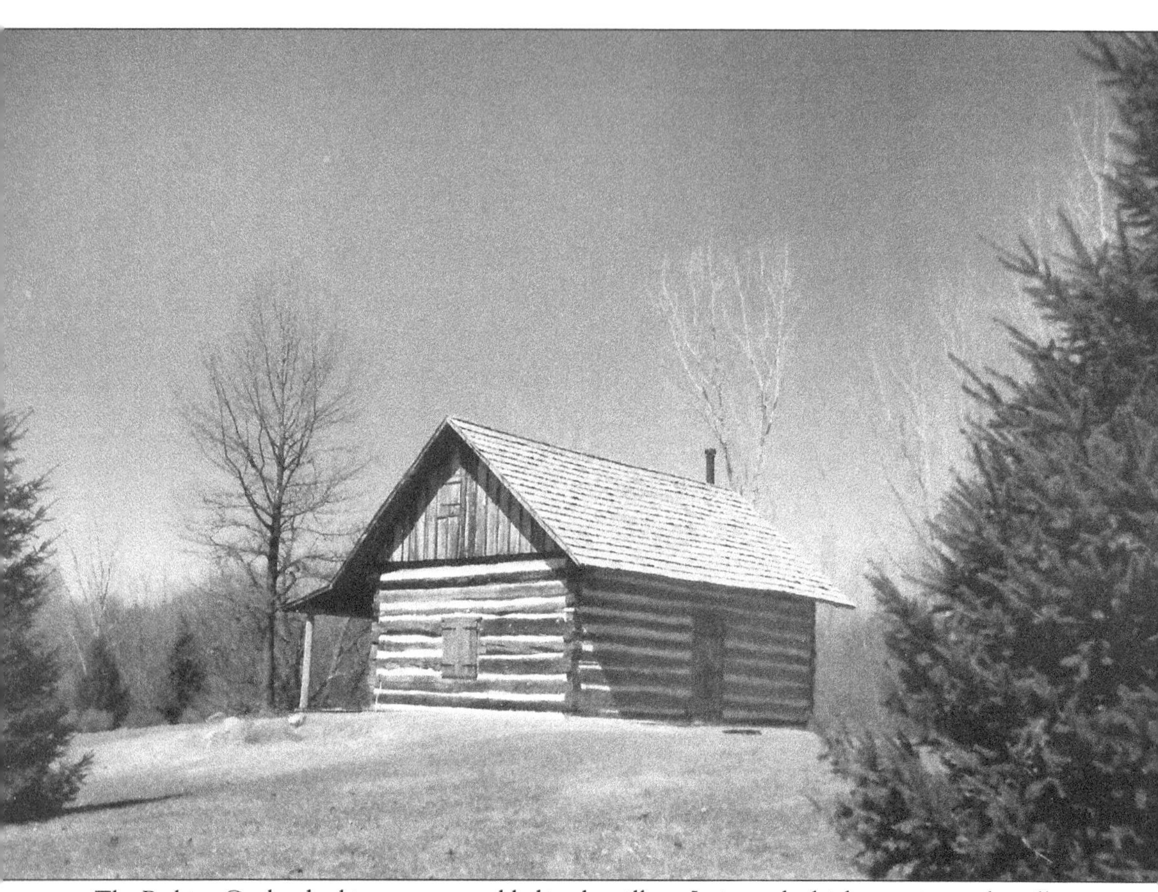

The Perkins-Copland cabin was reassembled in the village. It sits at the highest point in the village on the hill behind the brick Heathman-Herre building. A front porch was added overlooking the village pond to assist in students' participation and shield them against the weather.

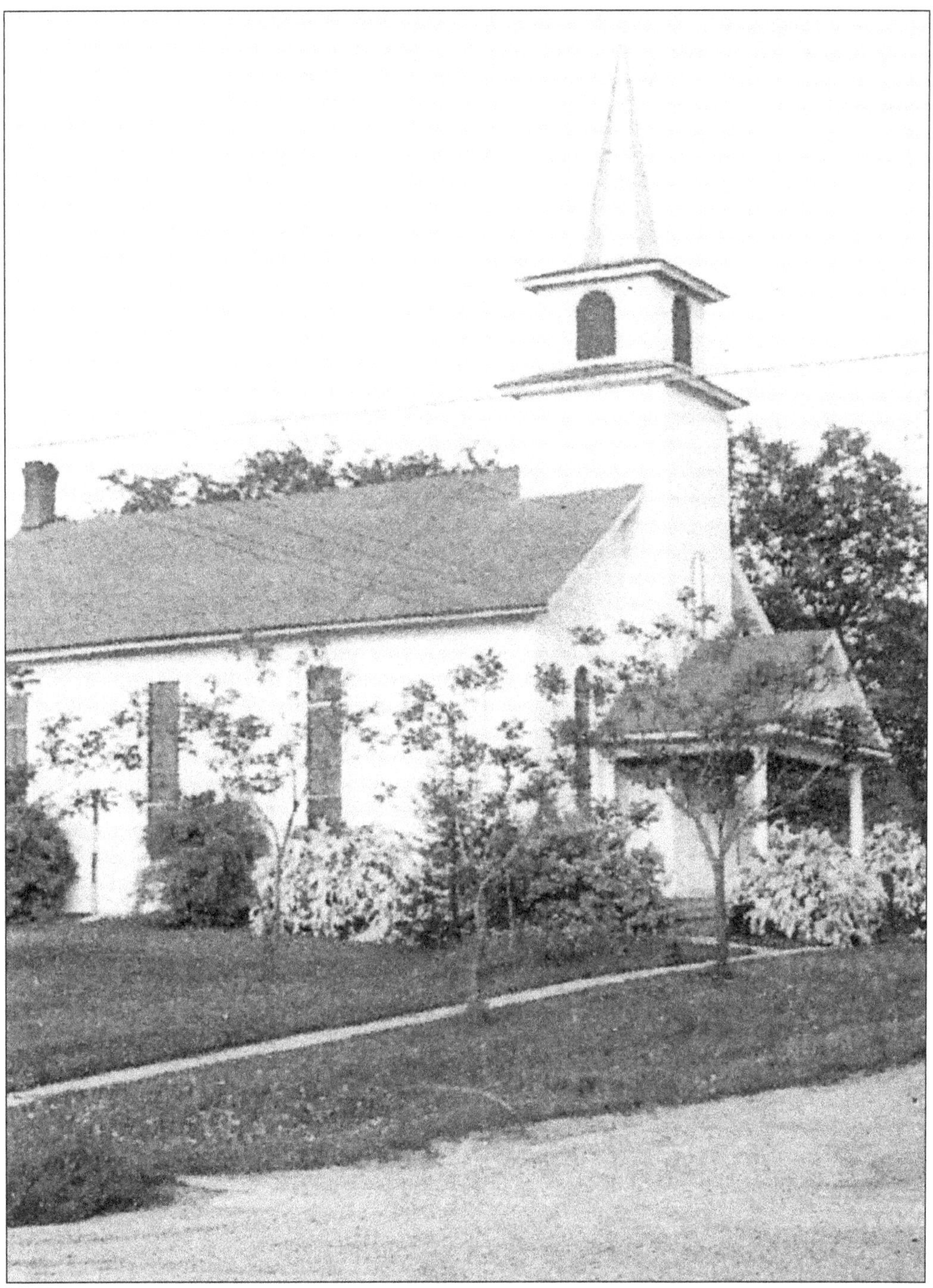

The Methodist Episcopal church of Okemos was built in 1870 at the corner of Okemos Road and Methodist Street. An expanding congregation outgrew the old building, and in 1969, the original church was torn down and a larger one was constructed. The Friends of Historic Meridian had long sought to find a church to move to the village but with no luck. The floor plan drawings were discovered in 2008, and a fundraising effort was begun to bring back the old church as a replica to the village.

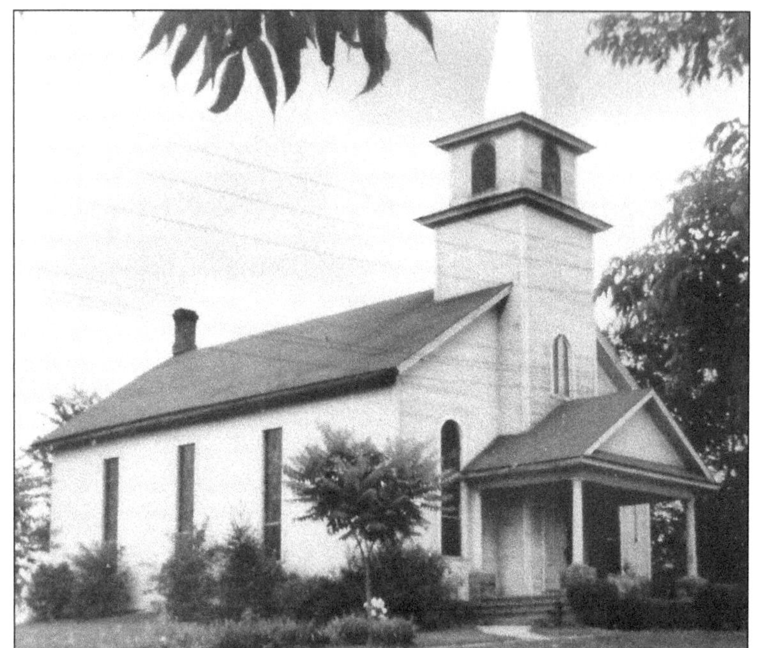

Partnering with the Charter Township of Meridian, the Friends of Historic Meridian began the construction project with a ground breaking at the Fall Heritage Festival in September 2008. Construction continued through the winter, and the first scheduled activity, a wedding, took place in the completed chapel in June 2009.

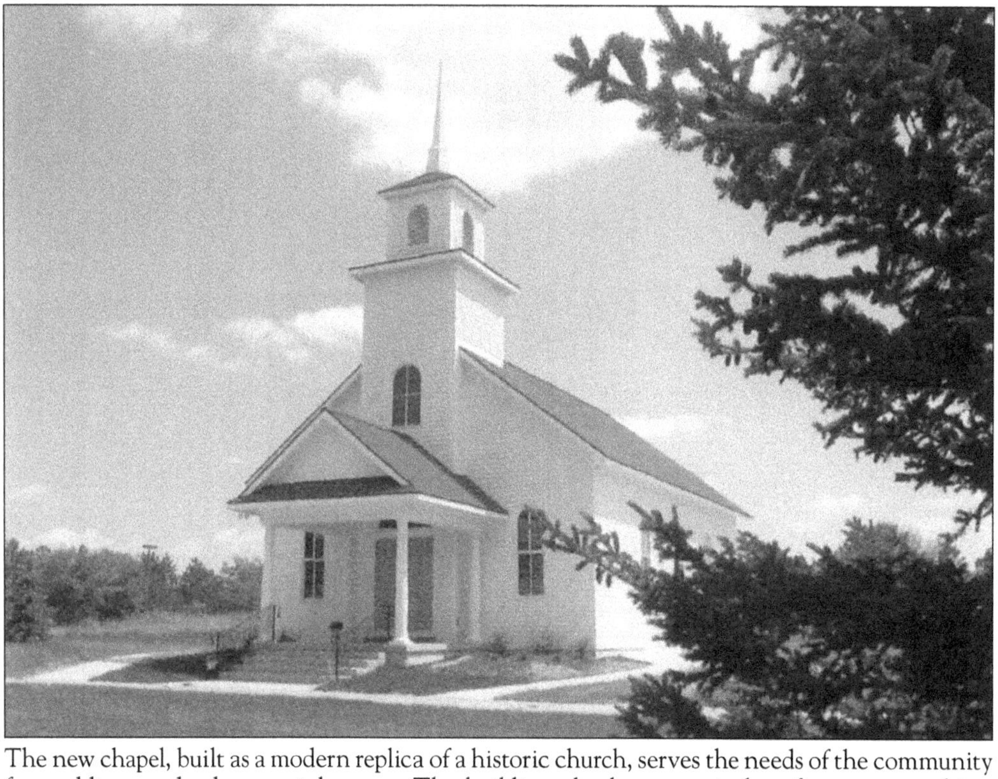

The new chapel, built as a modern replica of a historic church, serves the needs of the community for weddings and other special events. The building also hosts musical performances and is a major attraction during community events such as the Fall Heritage Festival and Christmas in the village. Modern construction permits required some modification of the original plan in order to provide handicap access and bathroom facilities.

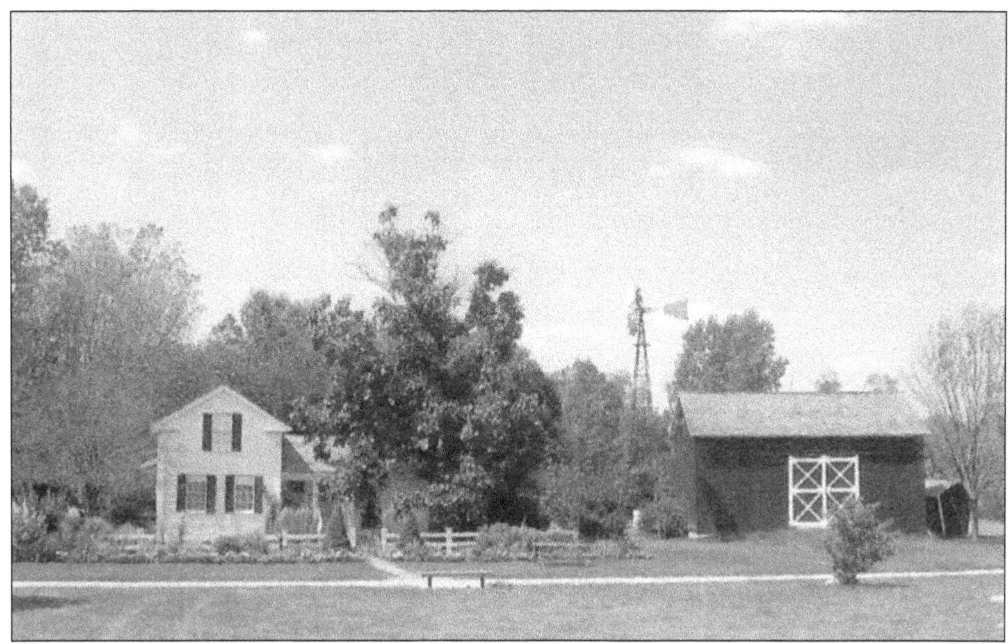

The Meridian Historical Village has grown over the past 40 years to include a farmstead used to teach area students and adults about life on a farm in the 19th century. The above photograph shows the farmstead from the farmhouse to the corncrib. The farmstead is located immediately across the green from the schoolhouse. The tollhouse (not pictured) is immediately to the left of the farmstead.

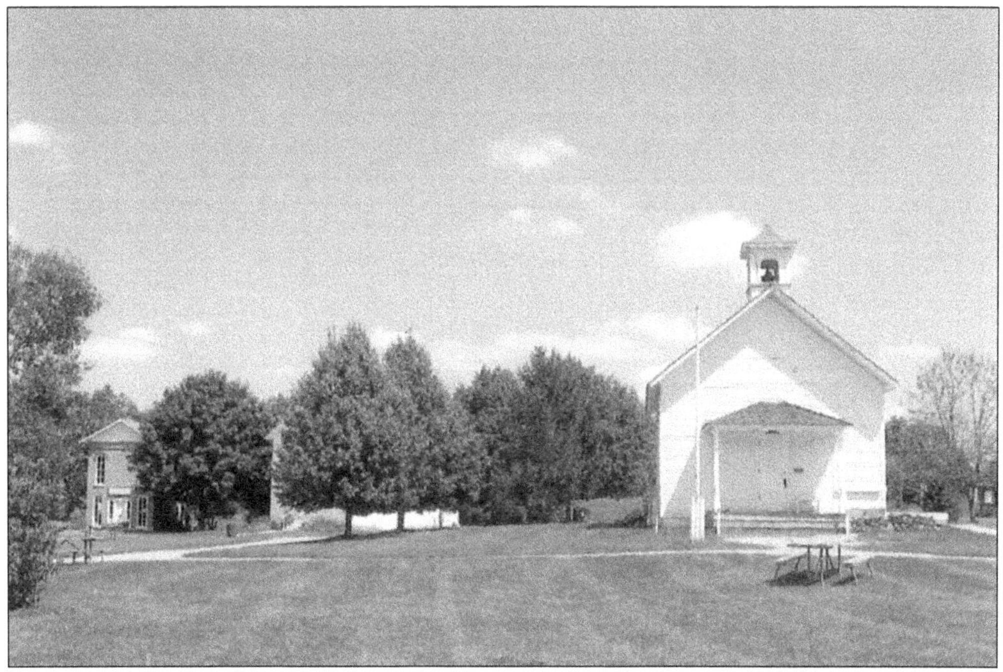

The village also includes a "town" area that features the brick Heathman-Herre building serving as the general store, the Barnes House as an inn and tavern, and the one-room rural Randall School. Behind the buildings, at the top of the hill (not pictured), is the Perkins-Copland log cabin.

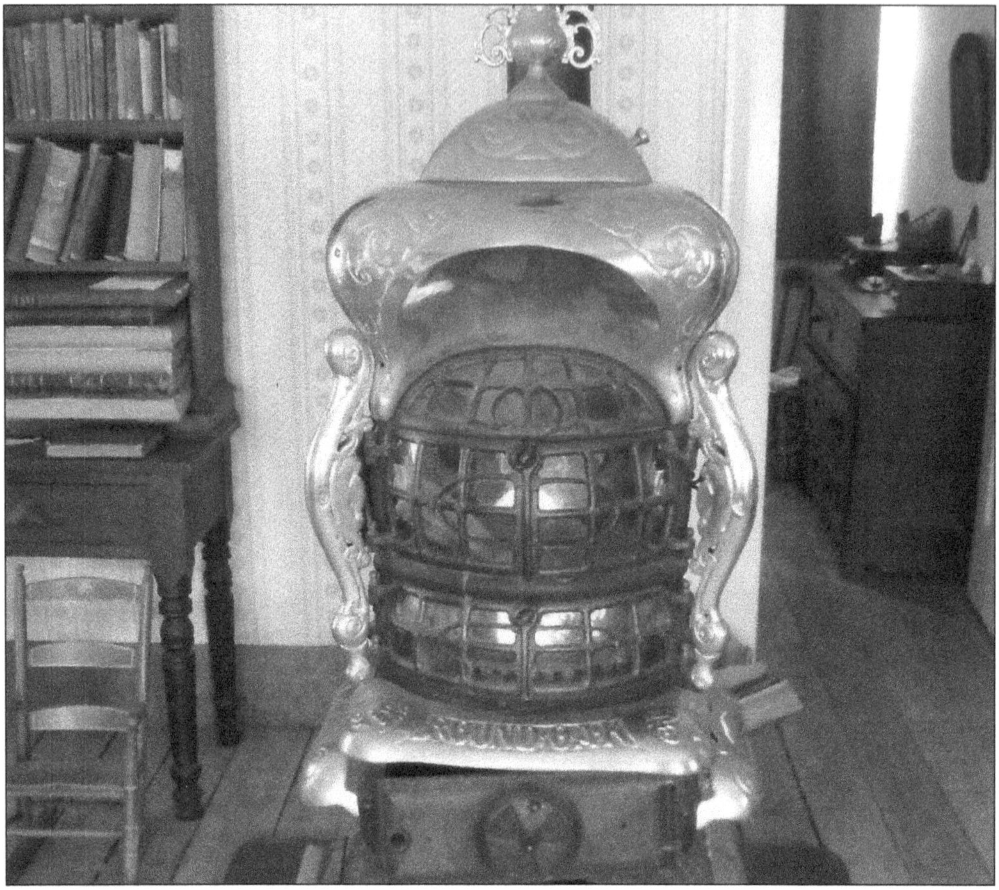

The beautiful stove in the farmhouse parlor came from the Round Oak Stove Company in Dowagiac, Michigan. The company was started by Philo D. Beckwith in 1855 and began building stoves in 1867. The advantage of the stove was its shape and draft mechanism. The upended cylindrical body drew like a chimney, and the position of the air-intake doors beneath the fire helped the draft.

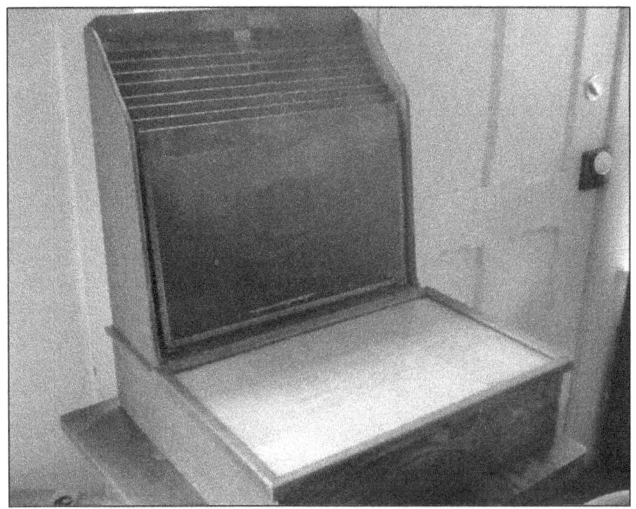

Patented in 1899, this storage box served as a cash register in the early 20th century. Families who traded with the store owner were listed in alphabetical order in pencil on paper along with their account numbers (001 and above). The upper portion of the box included metal sheets with numbered hinges. All receipts were stored under the hinges, with account numbers listed. The store owner tallied up the receipts at the end of the month to determine how much each family owed.

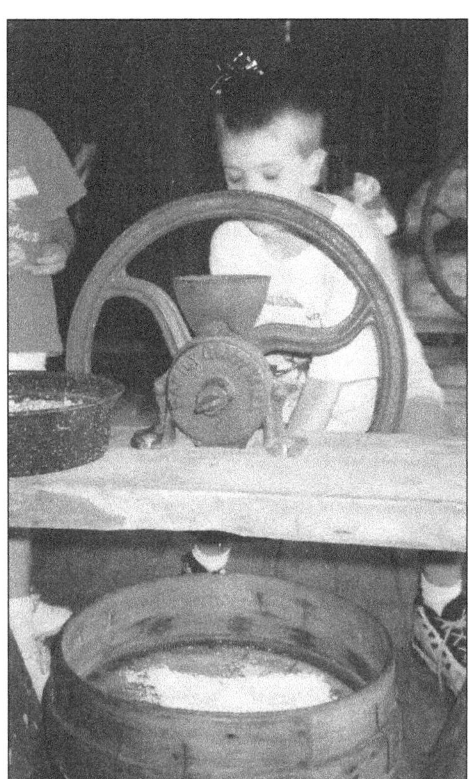

Campers attend a weeklong morning camp held each August at Meridian Historical Village. The children participate in activities each day that focus on a specific area of 19th-century living. They experiment with gardening and with tools used to harvest and bring food to the table, like the gristmill (right).

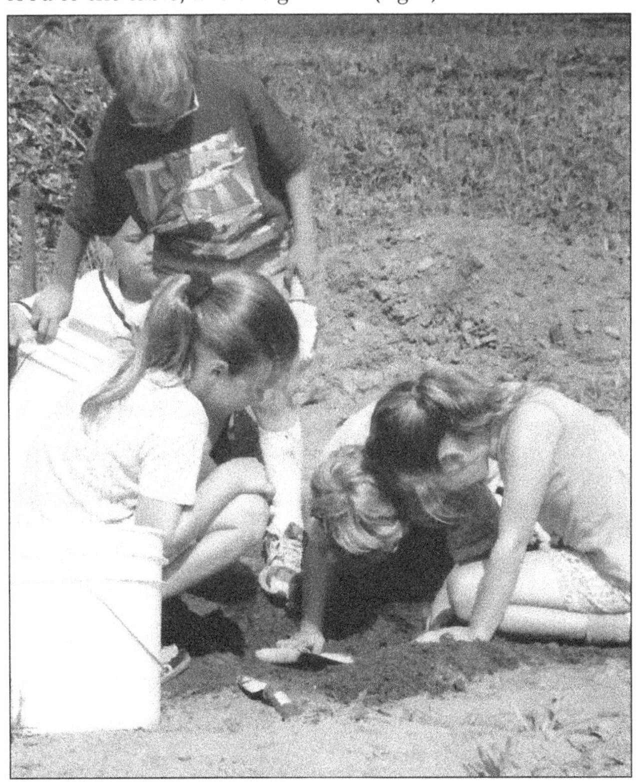

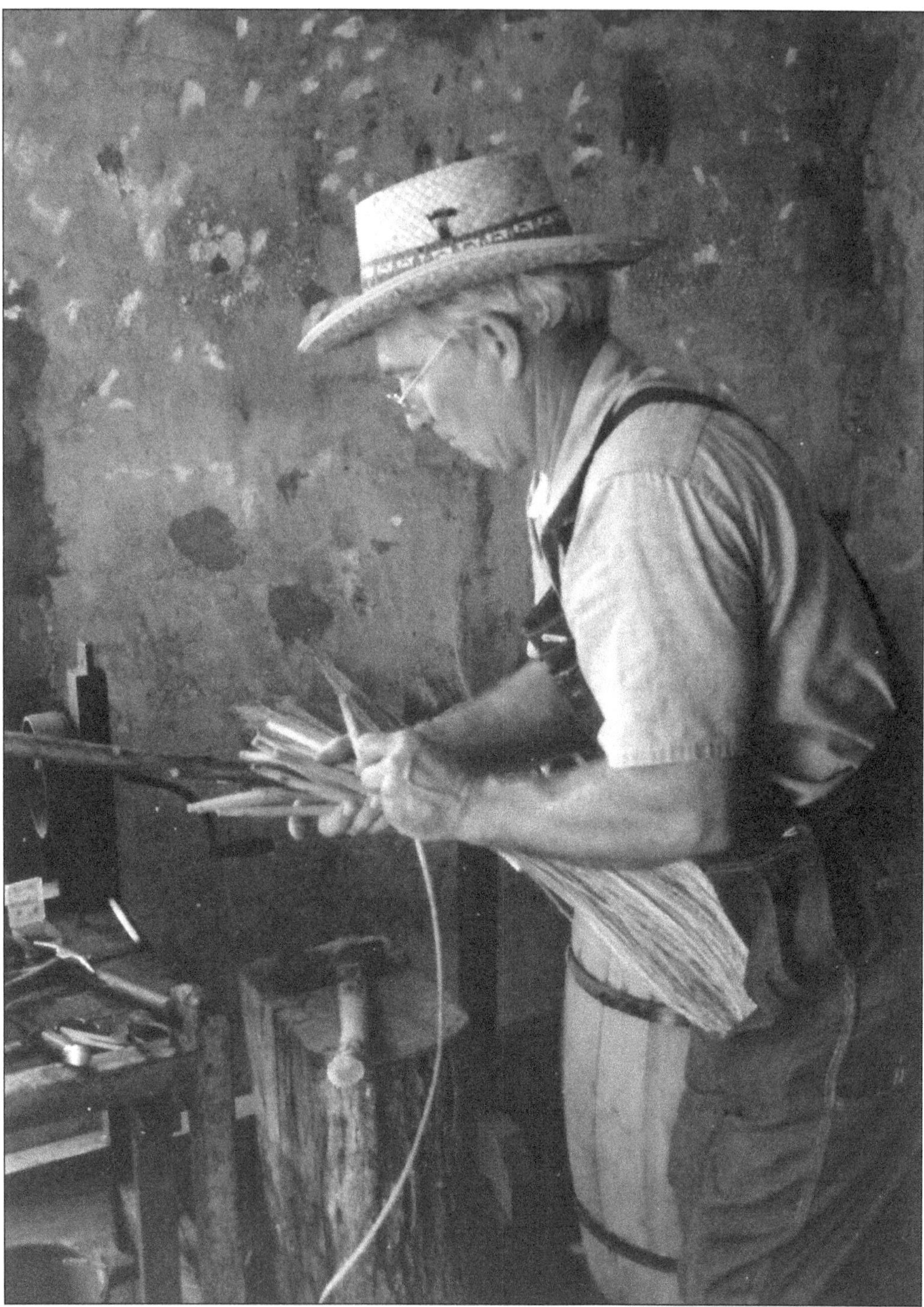

Each September, the Friends of Historic Meridian organization partners with the township Parks and Recreation Department to host a township-wide celebration of the area's rich cultural history. Reenactors participate in community events such as the Fall Heritage Festival to provide a living history environment to educate visitors. Volunteer Tom Knox demonstrates how to make a broom.

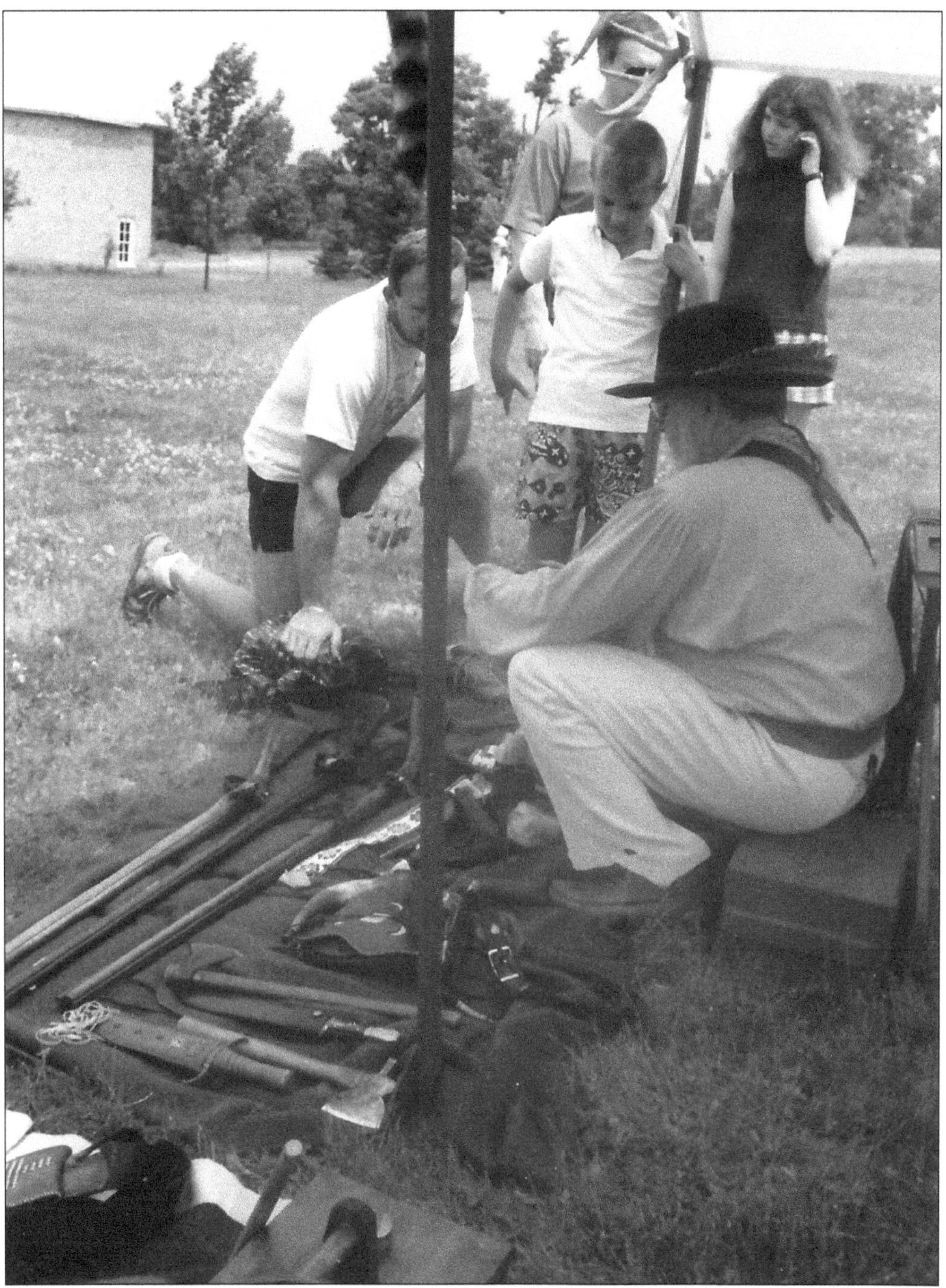

Children are able to learn both at camps and at community events such as the Fall Heritage Festival. Education has included bee keepers, llama breeders, sheep farmers, and others. This period actor displays the weapons and tools commonly used by members of the community to protect and work their land.

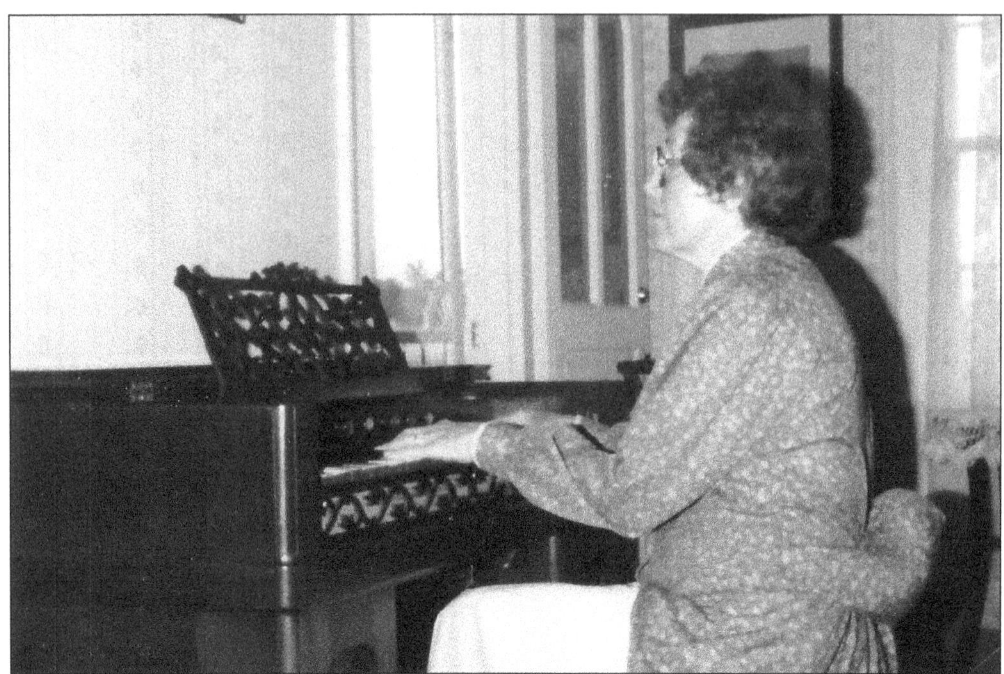

Music has always been an important part of educating the community about life in the 19th century. This image shows one of the original members of the Friends of Historic Meridian, Sally Neuman, playing the antique pump organ. The instrument cannot be operated with electricity; instead, foot pedals must be pumped in order to move air through the bellows to produce music.

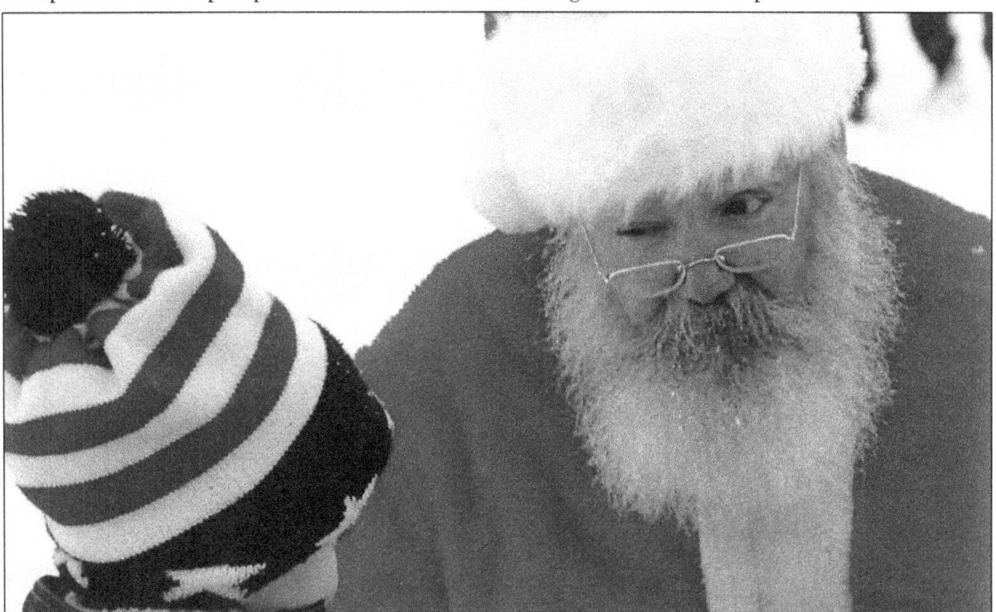

Each December, the Friends of Historic Meridian organization, with the help of the township Parks and Recreation Department, hosts an event for the community to step back in time to the slower pace of the 19th century. All the historic buildings are decorated for the holidays and are open to the public. Each year, the highlight of the event is the lighting of the community Christmas tree and a visit from Santa Claus. (Photograph by Anna Gillette.)

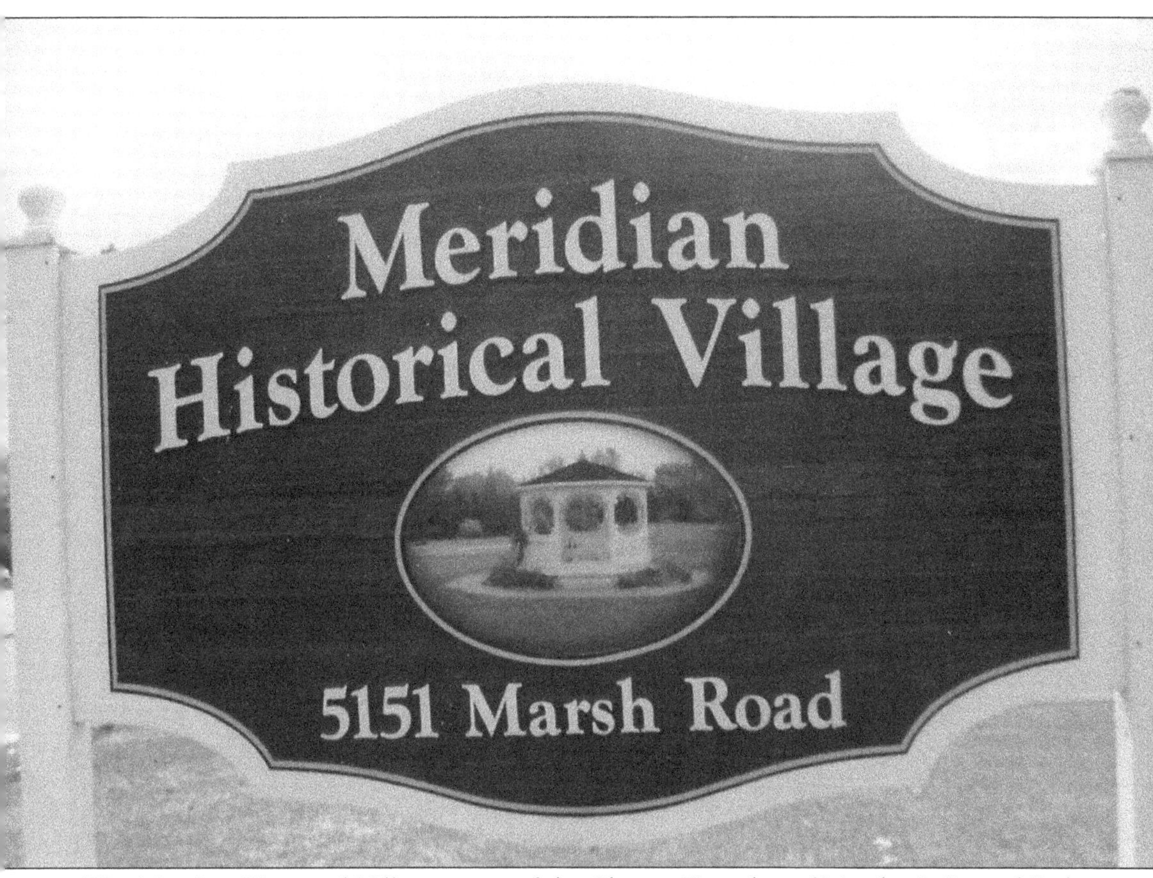

The Meridian Historical Village is part of the Charter Township of Meridian's Central Park complex. The village is operated via a partnership between the Friends of Historic Meridian, the Charter Township of Meridian, the Meridian Township Parks and Recreation Department, and the Meridian Garden Club. It serves as a community resource to educate the public about the rich history of the local community.

www.ingramcontent.com/pod-product-compliance
Lightning Source LLC
LaVergne TN
LVHW060625110826
845147LV00015B/941

* 9 7 8 1 4 6 7 1 1 4 3 9 4 *